W9-BBU-441

Ethics Through Corporate Strategy

❏ ❏ ❏

DANIEL R. GILBERT, Jr.

New York   Oxford
OXFORD UNIVERSITY PRESS
1996

Oxford University Press

Oxford New York
Athens Auckland Bangkok Bombay
Calcutta Cape Town Dar es Salaam Delhi
Florence Hong Kong Istanbul Karachi
Kuala Lumpur Madras Madrid Melbourne
Mexico City Nairobi Paris Singapore
Taipei Tokyo Toronto

and associated companies in
Berlin Ibadan

Copyright © 1996 by Oxford University Press, Inc.

Published by Oxford University Press, Inc.
198 Madison Avenue, New York, New York 10016

Oxford is a registered trademark of Oxford University Press

Library of Congress Cataloging-in-Publication Data

Gilbert, Daniel R., 1952–
  Ethics through corporate strategy / Daniel R. Gilbert, Jr.
    p. cm.—(The Ruffin series in business ethics)
    Includes bibliographical reverences and index.
    ISBN 0-19-509624-X
    1. Business ethics. 2. Strategic planning—Moral and ethical aspects. I. Title. II. Series.
HF5387.G55 1996
174′.4—dc20

9 8 7 6 5 4 3 2 1

Printed in the United States of America
on acid-free paper

I DEDICATE THIS BOOK TO THE 532 PERSONS
WHO HAVE COMPLETED MY
MANAGEMENT STRATEGY AND POLICY
COURSE AT BUCKNELL UNIVERSITY.

Ethics Through Corporate Strategy

those relationships. I wrote my doctoral dissertation, "Strategy & Justice," to defend this proposition, among others.

4. Now, it is true that the concept of corporate strategy is rarely the subject of critique for its possible meanings. I joined Ed Hartman, John Mauriel, and Ed Freeman to read critically several different corporate strategy models in *A Logic for Strategy*. We developed that critique in a customary language of business, not ethics per se.

5. Once we reinterpret many of the well-known accounts about corporate strategy as variations on a single theme about organizational processes, we can quickly come to the conclusion—through comparative ethical analysis—that that way of talking is thoroughly and ethically inadequate. Still, the idea of corporate strategy is worth rethinking as a way of talking systematically about ethics and business. This is the thesis I recently defended in *The Twilight of Corporate Strategy: A Comparative Ethical Critique*.

By traveling the foregoing line of reasoning, I have arrived at the point of intellectual departure for *Ethics Through Corporate Strategy*. I am ready to invent a new way of talking about business by inventing a new way of talking about corporate strategy. Thus, with regard to the concept of corporate strategy, I undertake in this book an act of "retrieval," as Charles Taylor elegantly portrays his own project in *The Ethics of Authenticity*.

This book is written to anyone who takes seriously how he or she talks about human interaction, and the particular subset of human interaction that we call business. From the very beginning, I deliver an ethical polemic about the customary language of the business world. That way of talking is an abomination, if we analyze ethically the way we have become accustomed to talking about business and about appropriate places for persons in the world, a subset of which is called business. I invite you to think carefully about your role in using that language.

I seek to provoke the kind of strong reaction that accompanies self-scrutiny on so personal a matter as one's accustomed way of talking, one's language. I want you to respond, at first, "He's making that up. That cannot be true." On the first count, I take full responsibility. This book is my interpretive creation. The truth of what I say, on the other hand, is not for me alone to determine. The truth of this book is something that each reader also has a hand in determining. I make that kind of self-discovery possible in three principal ways. Each is predicated on the ethical assumption that no language about human association can ever be benign. How we talk matters because we talk in a world of inevitable and intense contact with others.

One ethical truth available in this book involves personal integrity—that is, the coherence of our respective lives. How we talk about others profoundly influences how we act toward them, for better or worse. This truth holds whether we talk and act as journalists, politicians, spouses, teammates, executives, or taxi drivers. Think of all the actions that follow from distinguishing between human beings in such antithetical terms as citizen and illegal alien, daughter and illegitimate child, coach and player, fraternity member and "independent," veteran and rookie, executive and employee, major leaguer and minor leaguer, male and female. In all these cases, language matters because a particular way of talking becomes the vehicle for treating some persons as less worthy than others. If you have ever lived in the second half of any of these pairings, you know what I mean. Reading this book is an opportunity to think about the consistency between how we talk and how we act.

A second ethical truth that is available here is a rhetorical one. How we talk about others can influence how those in our audiences will talk about others and act accordingly, for better or worse. This responsibility is perhaps most obviously pertinent to what we as educators do. After all, our livelihood revolves around trying to persuade others to look at the world through our rhetoric. But my point applies as well to the languages used by parents, journalists, coaches, and executives. When journalists and executives praise "killer competitors," think about the message that is sent about acceptable behavior in the marketplace. When executives talk about eliminating the jobs of thousands of men and women as "strictly a business decision," think about the message that is sent to their proteges about acceptable managerial behavior. Reading this book is an opportunity to reflect on what we actively encourage others to do with their lives. It is an opportunity to think about a duty that follows from the way we talk about others.

A third ethical truth available in this book deals with moral courage. How we talk about others can become easily and comfortably and seductively routine, for better or worse. It is so easy and comfortable and downright seductive to talk with others who talk like we do. It is all the more comfortable and seductive to talk about other human beings—whether they are included in our circle of conversation partners or outside it in communities of their own—in ways that are confirmed by those with whom we talk. This how a "pro-choice" community persists, a "pro-life" community persists, and a "pro-Greek" (fraternity) community persists on college campuses. In each case, a language about others serves as a focal point for that community. As the members of such communities talk with one another, they each leave their fingerprints on the language that they share.

Now, some talk about other human beings is harmless enough, such as when mother and father share delight in their child's growth. And some talk about other human beings is downright justifiable, such as when one writes a letter of recommendation for a colleague. It is a different story, however, when we talk within our friendly circles—and hence gain the confidence to act—in ways that separate ourselves from other human beings. The contemporary debate about abortion is a vivid case in point. It is a different story, too, when we talk and act in ways that silence other human beings because they do not talk as we do. Any critic and any newcomer in a community knows about that kind of exclusion. In either kind of situation, we face a choice that is as plain as day. We can ignore the consequences of our talk and action, retreating to the warmth of our "home" communities, or we can resolve to change the way we talk, and hence change the very communities in which we move. Reading this book is an opportunity to take the courageous step of saying "enough" when we see our own voices, and our hands attached to those voices, separating us from others who are different from us. It is an opportunity to take voluntary steps to change the way we talk about other human beings and hence who we are. That takes moral courage.

I have used "we" quite deliberately throughout this opening commentary. Membership in the category of "we" is wide open. There are no application forms, waiting periods, background checks, or renewal notices. Executives and professors are welcome. So, too, are politicians and taxi drivers and journalists—anyone can step forward and join with me in the conversations to which I want this book to contribute around the question: *What can we accomplish as a community of men and women who take seriously a language by which ethics and business are complementary ideas?* To cteate that community is to abandon the customary language about business that has been years in the making. I write this book to show what it can mean to substitute a new language about business for the dubious business discourse that has shackled too many men and women for too long.

Lewisburg, Pa.   D. R. G., Jr.
April, 1996

ACKNOWLEDGMENTS

This book is as much a significant destination in my life as a teacher as it is a milepost in my scholarly journeys. I have been working out the argument of *Ethics Through Corporate Strategy* in the course of teaching "Management Strategy and Policy" for seven years at Bucknell University to 532 students. Every one of those students has made contributions to my journey of creative trial-and-error that now takes the form of this volume. I dedicate this book to them all.

I have many meanings in mind when I refer to my students' contributions. Some have been healthy skeptics. They have questioned, poked, and prodded me into clarifying what I mean. Some have been creative partners in my intellectual journey. They have taken rudiments of the framework that appears in this book, applied it to problems that have been puzzling them, and produced creative new interpretations of the business world and their own lives. Still others, quite frankly, have been pains in my neck. They were "free riders" counting down the days in their final undergraduate semester. Ironically, they have also been contributors. Their presence has compelled me to think about how I could tailor this framework to the context where I can connect with even the most recalcitrant senior. These particular students have challenged me, as much as anyone has, to develop a narrative that each can "try on for size" in his or her own life story. Some of my students have contributed in all three respects. I am indebted to them all. Bucknell is a special place because of them.

Still, I am proudest of those who reappear, after several months or years, to say, "You know, I never got that point until just now." For them, the liberal education ideal of lifelong, self-propelled learning has begun to blossom. When I see this happen, I gain more confidence that I can contribute to that liberal education ideal by talking about strategy and ethics in the same sentences. Bucknell is a special place also because I have the opportunity to talk in that way and to be taken seriously.

Several Bucknell colleagues have accepted my invitation to join my classes to discuss their lives as strategists. I am grateful to Richard Skelton, Louise Knight, Juliene Simpson, Sid Jamieson, and Rick Hartzell for sharing their experiences with us. Nancy Weida has been a steady counselor about making strategic reasoning intelligible to undergraduates.

Gordon Meyer, John Miller, Timothy Sweeney, Douglas Candland, Chris Zappe, and Larry Shinn have been steadfast with their encouragement and generous with their time.

This book would not have been written without the unwavering support, scholarly wisdom, and good humor of R. Edward Freeman, dating to my doctoral student days at the University of Minnesota. Herbert Addison and his colleagues at Oxford University Press have supported my work steadfastly and patiently. James Tully did a superb job of copyediting. Along the way, Kate Rogers, Diane Swanson, Craig Dunn, James Gaa, and Robbin Derry have added their distinctive forms of encouragement. They can find their names and contributions in the fine print of the chapter notes. I vividly remember the telephone call from John Rutland in 1987 that began, "I think that you are onto something when you talk about strategy and conventions." It has taken me this long, John, to shape that "something" into this book. I must also thank those who have contributed greatly to my life as a writer: Pat and Nicholas Meyer; Emma, Molly, and Benjamin Wellen Freeman; Maureen Wellen; John and Victoria Gilbert; Joan and Daniel Gilbert, Sr.; Michael, Karl, and Chris Gilbert, are all at the top of this list. I am grateful, too, for the financial support that has made this research possible. Bucknell University sabbatical-leave funding has been generous. The seeds of this research were planted during my doctoral studies at the University of Minnesota. Thus, I want to acknowledge belatedly the financial assistance that I received in those years from the University of Minnesota Graduate School, the then-unnamed School of Management, and, with John Mauriel's assistance, the Bush Foundation.

I associate writing with a convergence of persons and places in those "right" moments when an idea, a phrase, a paragraph, or an entire argument becomes crystal clear. Writing on wintry mornings at Toftrees in State College, Pennsylvania—sustained by blueberry muffins and coffee and good humor from the staff—is one such recollection. Once again, I have had the pleasure of reading and writing at a home away from home offered so generously by Peggy, Brett, and Ken Finch. For *this* book, that home is in Nebraska. And, as always there were my beloved Philadelphia Phillies, Philadelphia Flyers, and Minnesota Twins. In the course of cheering their accomplishments or booing their lapses, I put together significant portions of this book at Veterans Stadium, the Spectrum, and the Hubert H. Humphrey Metrodome, respectively. You need not read too far into this work to realize what I mean.

I also associate my writing projects with activities and places where serendipitous moments just seem to occur. When I least expected it, *Ethics Through Corporate Strategy* became a book while I was hiking in the Adirondacks and the Pine Ridge, wading in the waters of the North Carolina Outer Banks, canoeing through the Sandhills, just strolling the grounds of the University of Minnesota campus on summer evenings, and logging all those rehabilitative miles walking around the track at Christy Mathewson Stadium at Bucknell. These were the times of solitude that balanced the fury with which I want to say something different about how we can talk about business and our humanity in the same breath.

ACKNOWLEDGMENT OF PERMISSIONS

I am grateful for permissions to use the following sources:

K. Andrews, *The Concept of Corporate Strategy*, rev. ed. (Homewood, IL: Richard D. Irwin, 1980). Copyright © 1980 by Richard D. Irwin, Inc.

C. Browne, "Hagar the Horrible," *Philadelphia Inquirer*, 12 April 1991:24-D. Copyright 1991 © by King Features Syndicate Inc. Reprinted with special permission of King Features Syndicate.

F. F. Church, "A Modest Revival in Business Ethics?" *New York Times*, 22 December 1985, Section 3:3. Copyright © 1985 by The New York Times Company. Reprinted by permission.

B. Feder, "Helping Corporate America Hew to the Straight and Narrow," *New York Times*, 3 November 1991, Section 3:5. Copyright © 1991 by The New York Times Company. Reprinted by permission.

Excerpts from *Babbitt* by Sinclair Lewis, copyright 1922 by Harcourt Brace & Company and renewed 1950 by Sinclair Lewis, reprinted by permission of publisher throughout the world except for the British Empire. Permission for the British Empire has been granted by Jonathan Cape Ltd., Random House UK Limited.

Competitive Advantage: Creating and Sustaining Superior Performance by Michael E. Porter. Copyright © 1985 by Michael E. Porter. Reprinted with permission of The Free Press, an imprint of Simon & Schuster Inc.

R. Rorty, *Contingency, Irony, and Solidarity* (Cambridge: Cambridge University Press, 1989). Copyright © 1989 by Cambridge University Press. Reprinted with the permission of Cambridge University Press.

D. Sanger, "U.S. Settles Trade Dispute, Averting Billions in Tariffs on Japanese Luxury Autos," *New York Times*, 29 June 1995, A1. Copyright © by The New York Times Company. Reprinted by permission.

From *Company Man* by Brent Wade. Copyright © 1992 by Brent Wade. Reprinted by permission of Algonquin Books of Chapel Hill, a division of Workman Publishing Co., New York, NY.

CONTENTS

Ethics Through Corporate Strategy

1

A Critical Comparison

I

You have heard this monologue before, no doubt.

"Of course we want business to be more ethical. That is simply common sense. Who could possibly argue against such a position? What politician, executive, journalist, taxi driver, or professor could resist advocating such a position? Very, very few, probably. Naturally, once we endorse this position there is little doubt about what we must do. We must expose and publicize the many instances of insider trading, toxic waste dumping, toxic waste burning, deceptive advertising, shoddy product design, shoddy product testing, questionable lending, questionable campaign contributions, and avoidance of one obligation after another that occur repeatedly in the business world. What else could we do?

"The business world, after all, is full of people like those convicted in the savings-and-loan and insider-trading scandals, like those who chose to ignore problems with exploding auto gas tanks, like those accused of padding expense accounts, like those whose propensity for misbehavior helps make federal corrections a growth industry in Union County, Pennsylvania. These individuals are all around us, always trying to get away with something. They must be uncovered and called to account for their shady deeds. We must get tough with ethical violators. They must be stopped. What we need are more codes of conduct, more extensive investigative procedures, stiffer civil and criminal penalties, tougher judges, and more timely congressional action.

"Such changes only scratch the surface, however, if we want business to be more ethical. We must also alter the conditions that foster unethical business behavior in the first place. We must change the way people behave, change their incentives.[1] What we need are more codes of conduct, more enlightened executives, more sophisticated criteria for managerial compensation, more extensive ethical training programs, more experiments with organizational structures that hold people accountable, and more practical advice from business schools to assist in the training process.[2]

"Further still, the emphasis in business must be on having values. Business people used to have solid values. Too many business people these days do not have values. Let's apply some good old American integrity, determination, and managerial savvy to the problem of unethical business behaviors. Let's have business, higher education, and government join forces and declare war on unethical business practices. Let's force ethics into the world of business. Who could possibly argue against this?"

I will.

I am going to argue that this familiar rhetoric is ripe for a thorough intellectual challenge. What I have just sketched is a way of talking that emphasizes ethics as something that must be injected *into* the business world from *outside* the normal course of business activity. I call this a *logic of "ethics from the outside."*

I want to examine critically this way of talking that so many have accepted as a matter of course. Indeed, I will go so far as to argue that "ethics from the outside" is comparatively less useful than another way of talking about ethics in the business world. Clearly, then, this project is all about alternative ways of discussing ethics and business.

The project flows from one guiding critical question: *What can it mean to say "we want business to be more ethical"?* This question invites us to search for multiple responses. Just as clearly, this project is all about choosing how to talk about ethics and business. Thus, my guiding critical question becomes: *What do we want to mean when we say "we want business to be more ethical"?* With one answer to that question, which I will develop in this book, the statement "we want business to be more ethical" should be something that we never again take simply as a matter of course.

II

You have probably not heard this monologue very often when people talk about business.

"Of course, we want business to be more ethical. If we value the prospects for our lives, we should never be content with 'idling in neutral.' We must believe that it is worthwhile per se to push ourselves toward becoming new-and-improved persons over time. That conscious act of striving is crucial if we want to create the richest meanings that we can for our personhood. True, we will each face setbacks and have doubts. True, we can never be quite sure where such a road leads. But these facts of life only make the effort more interesting and fulfilling. It is liberating to commit ourselves to search for lives of possibilities, rather than bemoaning what we could have been. It is quite enough to think of our lives as always 'under construction.'[3]

"The business world could be quite a conducive place for activating this choice to lead a life of self-improvement. After all, each of us is a participant there. And, more and more people who participate with us in the business world are talking as if the commitment to strive toward better lives is a capital idea. Take the notions of excellence and total quality. What businessperson would extol sustained mediocrity? Take the practice of innovation. What business owner would celebrate less sophisticated ideas and methods? What businessperson would advocate turning back the clock on the digital information superhighway? In modern "business talk," restructuring is preferable to falling apart, reengineering is preferable to bureaucracy, and social responsibility is an advance over social irresponsibility.[4] We come then to the concept of strategy. What business owner would advocate drifting along, or perpetuating the past for old-time's sake? Very, very few, probably. Strategy, after all, is an antidote to both alternatives. In short, all this modern business talk about change and progress seems to support the commitment we can make to live a journey of self-directed improvement. Of course, we must keep in mind that the business world can never be isolated from the rest of our lives. It is challenging enough for each of us to lead *one* life!

"This is indeed a daunting agenda for any person to tackle. Actually, it is a three-way daunting commitment we must make. First, the commitment to live a search for self-improvement never goes away. Second, the commitment encompasses the whole of our lives. Third, if this is not enough, living this way is something that we can never expect to do alone. Inevitably, we are trying to put together our lives in the neighborhoods of others attempting to do the same sort of thing. What successes we enjoy and failures we endure, as we create who we are, are always realized in settings full of other human beings. These settings include family, parenthood, friendships, neighborhoods, avocations, school, and business, to name a few.

"Because this search is as complex as it is promising, we each must have a framework for plotting and replotting our courses. What we need is a road map from which to choose our routes. Three particular questions will serve as a useful map, if 'we want business to be more ethical.' Each question emphasizes an 'either/or' choice that we face in our travels.

"We can begin by asking ourselves, 'Do I set and monitor my own standards and life course, or do I mimic what others do and say?' Live autonomously, or live as a borrower?[5] Travel creatively, or travel on autopilot? This is one choice by which we can conduct a search for a better kind of existence. Every serious student knows the importance of it. Every marriage partner also has reason to make the choice. In business, entrepreneurship is an affirmative, self-directive reply to this question. So, too, is whistle-blowing.

"We can move then to ask ourselves, 'Guided by my standards, regardless of their originality, do I acknowledge that my actions can influence others' actions at the same time and place that their actions can influence mine, or do I act on my own terms and schedule?' Live interdependently, or live independently? This is another crucial choice for each man and woman bent on self-improvement. Acquaintances can deal with it as they ponder and experiment with the possibility of friendship. So, too, can teacher and student, player and coach, teammate and teammate, orchestra conductor and concertmaster, spouse and spouse, and any other pair of human beings who interact regularly.

"The business world is prime territory for this question, too. Parties to contracts, competitors, competitor and regulator, and employer and employee can acknowledge their mutual influences as they interact. Then again, many lawyers have profited handsomely sorting out the mess left behind when people interact as if their actions will not affect others, as if those who are affected will not respond. Major League Baseball often seems to operate that way.

"We then are prepared to ask ourselves a third question: 'In the course of interacting with others, however attentively, do I acknowledge my hand in shaping the outcomes of those interactions jointly with my partners, or do I chase what pleasure is available and leave others to fend for themselves?' Live by self-restraint, or live by appropriation? This is still another choice to make in a life of self-improvement.[6] We temper our actions in the presence of others, for the better, when we make room for another driver near a freeway entrance ramp. We appropriate gains for ourselves when we wash our cars during a drought emergency. Indeed, we can mark the passage from childhood to adulthood when one internalizes, and routinely acts on, a self-restraining response to this question. Business practice presents the same choice time and again. A retailer can confront it in the presence of a willing, but naive (or financially strapped) customer. Manufacturers can face it when deciding what to do with waste by-products. They face this same kind of choice when they discover that use of their products is accompanied by harmful yet avoidable consequences. Tobacco company executives know about this kind of choice.[7] A supplier has reason to reflect on this question when his new pricing plan is aimed at pushing a rival to the brink of bankruptcy.

"All in all, these questions frame our lives of self-discovery quite comprehensively, quite pointedly, and quite durably. Throughout, the emphasis is squarely on values. Standards involve values. Sensitivity to our influences on others involves values. Values are plainly evident when we voluntarily place restraints on our behavior, or choose not to do so. As we work through each choice, we are inevitably expressing, through our deeds, how we prefer to live. Values are the names we give to those preferences. And there are as many values as there are preferences and persons activating their preferences in their daily lives.[8]

"When we accept this story in the course of living a search for whom we can become, we sign our names to the petition that reads, 'We want business to be more ethical.'

"Who could possibly argue against this?"

I have just sketched a story thoroughly infused with ethical concerns. It is a story where ethics applies "already through and through" the life of each character, not outside it. This ethical story line holds quite generally, applying as readily to business practice as it does to any other kind of worldly practice that turns on human interaction. Each person in this account, by the very act of wrestling with these three questions, pursues ethics as a way of life. Anyone who has studied ethics knows the value of posing these questions. I want to make them useful, as well, to those who have not studied ethics but who are willing to reflect about the lives that one leads in the course of business and everyday life.

The first question addresses a person's effort to create, live, and revise a meaningful or "good" or "better" life. The worth of one's personhood is a central concern in the study of ethics.[9] The second question portrays relationships as conduits of influence and consequence, sometimes for better and sometimes for worse. Ethical analysis enables us to distinguish and justify the differences between "better" and "worse" in such instances as the exchange of information (honesty) and the fulfillment of commitments (promises).[10] The third question calls attention to the proposition that our progress toward a "good" life hinges on the restraints that we voluntarily apply to our actions when we influence the course of others' lives. That proposition is central to any ethical tradition in which relationships are the focal points.[11]

So, all three questions in this road map are ethical questions—i.e., dealing with matters of an ethical kind. Clearly, there is persistent debate about answers to these questions.[12] However, that intellectual exchange does not make them any less queries of a thoroughly ethical kind.

The upshot of this second monologue is that each man and woman is engaged in a pattern of interactions—business or otherwise—that also is simultaneously a pattern of acts of the ethical kind. My account follows from the assumption that ethics can be an organizing concept *central* to *every* (business) *person's* life. What results is a *logic of "ethics already through and through"* business practice and human existence more generally.

III

I write this book as a contest between the logics of "ethics from the outside" and "ethics already through and through." Both are responses to the following question: What do we want to mean when we say "we want business to be more ethical"? Moreover, I interpret each logic as the antithesis of the other. Thus, I will make my case through comparative critical argument. In so doing, I follow Richard Rorty's account of the conduct of criticism:

> Interesting philosophy is rarely an examination of the pros and cons of a thesis. Usually it is, implicitly or explicitly, a contest between an entrenched vocabulary which has become a nuisance and a half-formed new vocabulary which vaguely promises great things.[13]

"Ethics from the outside" will be the entrenched "nuisance" in my analysis. I argue that "ethics already through and through," on the other hand, "vaguely promises great things" for the way we talk about ethics and business.

Any critical intellectual showdown requires a common ground on which the competing perspectives can be distinguished and then compared.[14] For the criticism to be credible, that common ground must consist of a third perspective that is "friendly" to the two competing perspectives.[15] For the criticism to be more credible still, I must situate a decisive criterion on that common ground. With such a criterion, I will be able to argue for the relative merits of one perspective over the other perspective. A movie critic has in mind these two concerns with critical credibility when, for example, she compares two films about World War II (common ground) for their attention to the veterans' lives in the years after the war (decisive criterion).

My third perspective, which I will work out in detail in Chapter 2, is framed by the concepts of differences, centers, and margins. I sketched the logics of "ethics from the outside" and "ethics already through and through" at the outset of this chapter to show both logics dealing with multiple persons and multiple ways of living (differences) in all sorts of relationships (centers) through which those people interact to produce a world that could be "more ethical" (margins) than it was before they met. This framework of differences, centers, and margins is the setting in which I will answer my guiding critical question: What do we want to mean when we say "we want business to be more ethical"?

My decisive criterion deals with the different people who make up the "we" who are seeking a more ethical business world. I will compare the relative merits of "ethics from the outside" and "ethics already through and through" by asking: *Which logic provides a greater prospect that each human being can make a distinctive contribution to the world?* Educators appeal to some version of this criterion when they develop curricula through which their students can prepare for living as world citizens. Managers and journalists appeal to some version of this criterion whenever they talk about corporate social responsibility.[16] This criterion—which I will call *a criterion of distinctive worldly contribution,* for short—integrates a framework of differences, centers, and margins. Differences are highlighted by the place for each person's distinctive contribution. Centers are highlighted as places in which each person can contribute to a larger world. Margins are highlighted in the idea that persons can contribute something that was not previously available to the world. Contribution involves more than accepting the status quo.

With this criterion of distinctive worldly contribution, I will pronounce "ethics already through and through" a clear-cut winner and "ethics from the outside" a clear-cut loser. This plan of critical comparison is depicted in Figure 1–1.

In Chapter 2, I will discuss two kinds of justification for using a framework of differences, centers, and margins as the site for a critical showdown. First, I will show that this is a framework that we each can "try on for size" and find eminently useful as we lead our daily lives. We can deal with differences, centers, and margins as we live in such everyday settings as families and friendships and in such business settings as dealings with a trusted auto mechanic, travel agent, and hair stylist, for example. Further, in each of these associations, the differences, centers, and margins frame opportunities for us and others to make distinctive worldly contributions.

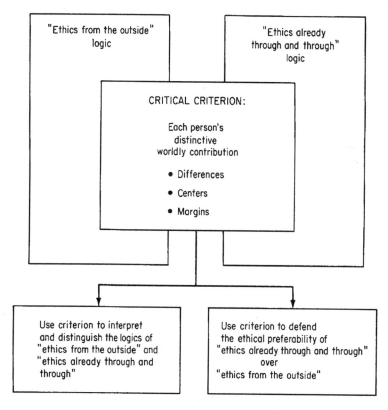

Figure 1–1. Plan of comparative critical argument

Second, this perspective—and decisive criterion—is one to which a diverse group of thoughtful writers, who have gone before me in considering the place for ethics in each person's life, could agree. In particular, those who talk about ethics from the standpoints of contractarian, liberal pragmatist, feminist connection, and communitarian ethics all have something to say about differences, centers, and margins. Across these seemingly different ways of talking, I will interpret a common concern with, and hope for, persons trying in their own ways to contribute to a better world. Each justification, I will show, is capable of mustering diverse support for the decisive criterion by which I want to evaluate two different approaches to "we want business to be more ethical."[17]

IV

"Ethics from the outside" per se in my interpretive creation. You will not find the designation in any article, book, index, or even footnotes written about business and management. You will nonetheless find the logic in widespread use. "Ethics from the outside," I maintain, has captured the fancy of many management educators, managers, and business commentators who subscribe faithfully to its assumptions and conclusions by emphasizing either an ethics of prevention or an ethics of bullying stakeholders. These two vocabularies of ethics are the particular "nuisance" applications of the logic of "ethics from the outside" that I will challenge. My case against both vocabularies hinges on my claim that "ethics from the outside" teeters on the brink of a non sequitur.

Specifically, the road paved with "we want business to be more ethical" does not automatically and commonsensically pass through the assumption that ethics is alien to most people's dispositions and experiences. That assumption is the hallmark of "ethics from the outside." Without it, an ethics of prevention, which turns on such enforcement mechanisms as stiffer penalties and expanded government regulation, deserves much less emphasis. Without it, too, an ethics of bullying stakeholders— implemented through such managerial mechanisms as codes of conduct, ethical training programs, and rewarding acquiescent competitors— loses its luster. Preventative and bullying measures are top priority if we accept this assumption about people and ethics as the truth. I want to call into question the ethical implications of this assumption.

If it is true that ethics is foreign to most people's dispositions and experiences, then we should not routinely expect to find ethics prominent in, or "inside," such human activities as business. And, if this is so, then we must look for guidance to those (few) people for whom ethics *is* intelligible.[18] These experts in ethics, acting from a position "outside" the ethics-poor world of business, are the catalysts in the "ethics from the outside" way of talking. The catalyst could be a regulator or a consultant. Most often—according to management educators, managers, and journalists alike—the catalyst will be the corporation's highest-level executives acting above—hence, "outside"—the moral deprivation that is inherent in his organization.[19] This expert's interventions are crucial if "we want to make business more ethical" from the outside. Thus, the logic of "ethics from the outside" unfolds along a separation between insider and outsider. This distance is central to the coherence of "ethics from the outside." It is also the seed of its logical undoing, against a standard of each person's distinctive worldly contribution.

Neither the insider nor the outsider can ever make much progress by "ethics from the outside." Those on the "inside" of business are doomed to remain there. They are always dependent on, and subordinate to, the expert who intervenes from the outside. After all, ethics is foreign to the lives that these insiders lead. These insiders can never graduate, by the logic of "ethics from the outside," to stand on their own as distinct persons who are sensitive to others and hence prone to contribute to others' lives. Otherwise, the outsider has lost his or her franchise.[20]

Those on the "outside" are also destined to remain where they are. As people who take ethics seriously, they have little to learn by growing closer to those who reside "inside" the ethics-starved territory that they want to change. After all, what could one who understands something about ethics learn from an inhabitant of a world where such an understanding is presumed missing? And, as lonely warriors battling on behalf of the larger world to make business "more ethical," these "outsiders" dare not jeopardize their role by dabbling in new ways of thinking about ethics and business. These experts stay the course, by the logic of "ethics from the outside," because they are our only hope.[21] Thus, positioned as they are, the "outsiders" are trapped. They can never hope to grow through their contacts with the "insiders," because they can never agree, by the logic of "ethics from the outside," to accept business "insiders" as ethical equals. To do so would amount to renouncing the franchise.

Neither the insider nor outsider can ever make much progress by the logic of "ethics from the outside," because, for that story to make sense, they cannot come together to acknowledge a common bond in a community. Indeed, a community of persons, in which each is assured the same level of opportunity to make distinctive worldly contributions as one desires, is antithetical to the logic of "ethics from the outside."[22]

Instead, "ethics from the outside" is a story of imprisonment. On this view, those on the inside of business are prisoners of their own lack of ethical sophistication. Hence, when it comes to questions of ethics, their lives must be controlled. Their "captors" are the outsiders who are capable of restoring ethical order—that is, the "more ethical" end—in the ethics-poor world of business. This separation between captors and prisoners is depicted in Figure 1–2.

Here is where the logic of "ethics from the outside" unravels. No metaphor portraying human interaction as imprisonment can ever be friendly to the idea of personal originality in making contributions to the

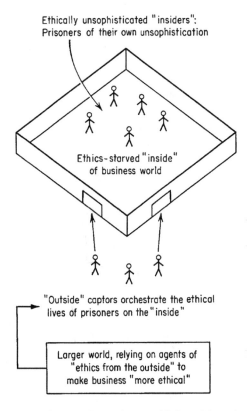

Figure 1–2. "Ethics from the outside" and imprisonment

larger world. Prisoners are not permitted to mingle with "good" citizens. They are locked away. Prisoners are not permitted to stake a bold claim of originality. They dress alike and march to a schedule made by someone else. For "ethics from the outside" to work, a sufficient population of "insiders" must always be available for expert "outsiders" to influence. What is more, the development of a human community involving insider and insider, and insider and outsider, lessens the need for outsiders who presumably can make business "more ethical." The fraternity of expert outsiders certainly will not encourage that!

Thus, "we want business to be more ethical" collapses into—indeed, is undermined by—an apology for the ethical status quo. In that status quo, there is no place for a generalized account of persons trying to make their distinctive contributions in a world of differences, centers, and margins. A *more ethical* business world simply and logically cannot result from this way of talking.[23] An ethics of prevention (Chapter 2) and an ethics of bullying stakeholders (Chapter 3) are two futile manifestations of that way of talking.

V

My project turns on the belief that we do not need to be sidetracked by the non sequitur that supports and unravels "ethics from the outside." We have options if we want to make sense of the statement "we want to make business more ethical." One such option is "ethics already through and through." This alternative way of talking offers the promise that we can move from a view of persons as prisoners to a view of persons as creators in contexts that they jointly coordinate and color as they interact.

In opposition to the entrenched vocabularies of prevention and bullying that help sustain ethics from the outside," I create a vocabulary that I call Strategy Through Convention. Informed by "ethics already through and through," Strategy Through Convention is a story about persons seeking to lead lives of self-improvement through their autonomous, interdependent, and self-restrained efforts. Strategy Through Convention provides a reconstructed, and decidedly unconventional, account of business relationships, by means of a reconstructed account of corporate strategy. I create this vocabulary to satisfy—indeed, to promise "great things" about—the decisive criterion of distinctive worldly contribution.

Strategy Through Convention draws in a novel way on the vocabularies of game theory, liberal pragmatism, a pragmatist philosophy of language, contractarian ethics, certain feminist discourses about relational growth, and communitarianism.[24] From each vocabulary, I draw support for the concept of convention as a way of talking about relationships and persons seeking to prosper by contributing to others' lives. I choose this concept because conventions are vehicles for advocating and living lives structured and enriched by differences, centers, and margins.

Conventions are social understandings sustained through the actions and preferences of distinct human beings.[25] Conventions can accommodate differences between persons, although not all conventions do so automatically. Conventions also have particular meanings for the parties to them, and thereby provide centers in their respective lives. Further still, each convention is a product of time and place and the different persons who sustain it. Hence, conventions are contingent phenomena. A given convention is perpetuated, by the parties to it, at a margin between it and another convention that the parties could initiate, at a margin between it and some past convention between the parties, at a margin between it and some new future convention, and at a margin between it and no convention at all.

Furthermore, the "marginal" acts by which conventions are sustained and changed are those of the human beings who are parties to the convention. Hence, we can always keep each party's ethical responsibilities in plain view if we talk about human interaction in terms of conventions. There is no place to hide, and no separation of insider and outsider, in this account. Whether persons flourish or wallow in the context of a convention is a matter of what they practice or do not practice, force majeure notwithstanding.

Thus, convention is a concept that keeps the spotlight on the "we" and the "ethical" in "we want business to be more ethical." With "convention," we can talk about each person's distinctive worldly contribution whereby "worldly contribution" means *contribution to others through human relationships.* We cannot talk about such a generalizable idea of contribution, on the other hand, if we talk in a language of prevention and bullying. The divide between outsider and insider in that language undermines the idea of "we."

The contest between "ethics from the outside" and "ethics already through and through"—two ways of thinking about ethics and business, two ways of talking about differences, centers, and margins—thus becomes a showdown between the two vocabularies of "ethics from the outside" and Strategy Through Convention, one particular vocabulary of "ethics already through and through."[26] I show this in Figure 1–3. Accordingly, I advocate the following thesis in this book:

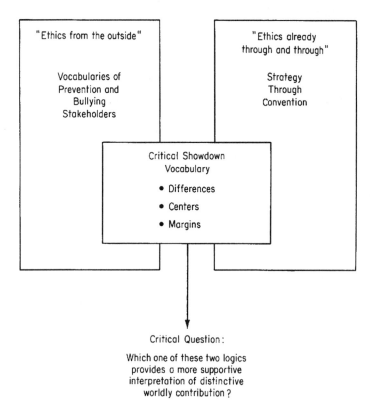

Figure 1–3. A critical showdown for Strategy Through Convention

"We want business to be more ethical" takes on a new, more sophisticated, and more promising meaning in support of distinctive human contributions to the world—relative to the best available ways of talking about business and ethics— if we retell our stories by means of the logic of "ethics already through and through," and a useful place to start is with a reconstructed, ethically infused account of corporate strategy.

This is how I arrive at the theme of this book: *Ethics Through Corporate Strategy*.

VI

"Ethics Through Corporate Strategy" is actually a shorthand reference to two principal contributions that I want this book to make. Ironically, I proceed from the same starting point as do the proponents and purveyors of "ethics from the outside." Like them, I "want business to be more ethical." However, greater prospects for that kind of progress come from talking in the "half-formed new vocabulary" of Strategy Through Convention, not the two vocabularies of prevention and bullying stakeholders to which we have become accustomed. Thus, the contributions of this book go far beyond the novelty of the Strategy Through Convention vocabulary per se. The book is organized around two new things that Strategy Through Convention "vaguely promises" us the opportunity to do.

First, I will demonstrate that an ethics that celebrates distinctive human contributions in a world of relationships can be located at the very heart of a reinterpreted conception of corporate strategy. Hence, I create a place for an *ethics* of distinctive worldly contribution *through*(out) a discourse about *corporate strategy*. This is one interpretation of the book's theme.[27] With Strategy Through Convention, you cannot avoid dealing with distinctive persons and what they hope to do through their ties to one another. Men and women use conventions to conduct their associations. To talk about conventions then is to talk about persons, their ties, and what can come of those ties. Every sentence, every guiding question, and every concept of my Strategy Through Convention account steers you in this direction. *By this new vocabulary, every sentence about corporate strategy is also a statement about an ethics of distinctive worldly contribution in human relationships.* I devote Chapters 4 and 5 to the task of working out this meaning of "ethics through corporate strategy."

Second, I will demonstrate that an ethics that celebrates distinctive human contributions through human relationships can infiltrate and give us reason to question other familiar areas of business discourse. These areas have traditionally been separated from the discourse of corporate strategy.[28] Thus, I create a way to spread an *ethics* of distinctive worldly contribution *through* (by means of) my new vocabulary for *corpo-*

rate strategy. In particular, I will show how Strategy Through Convention can not only render obsolete the traditional discourse that distinguishes business function (e.g., marketing) from business function (e.g., finance), but also give us both a way and an ethical justification for no longer talking about business functions at all. I address this opportunity in Chapter 5.[29]

VII

It is important, too, for me to be clear about where I do not intend to tread with this book. I do not intend to challenge "ethics from the outside" in an empirical showdown. Whether or not this view of ethics and business contributes to more or fewer ethical violations in business, relative to any alternative view, is not my concern here. That is not an issue of the critical, ethical kind.[30]

Still, what I have to say will probably have implications for the types of enforcement and prevention mechanisms that I have described as contemporary practices of "ethics from the outside." However, these implications will be by-products of my argument, far from the main theme. If my challenge is plausible, then others will have a cue for writing a new kind of story about ethics and business. In that kind of story, enforcement and prevention are not the first things that come to mind, because "ethics from the outside" will not be the guiding logic.

Nor do I intend to deliver advice about how businesspersons can make more money by incorporating ethics into their strategic deliberations. That kind of advice, it seems to me, is one more manifestation of "ethics from the outside" thinking. Moreover, for my argument to contribute to debates about the very ways we talk about business, I must act as a literary and ethical critic, not as an apologist for business-discourse-as-usual. What I have to say here is very practical, because thinking about how we talk and act on that talk is about as practical as one can get.[31] This book will not be very "practical" for those who are looking for soothing advice about how to perpetuate the familiar discourse about business. After all, I write this book to reject that way of talking in a showdown with "ethics already through and through."

VIII

Let me conclude this introductory statement where I began. Of course, we want business to be more ethical. That is simply common sense. But wait just a minute! There is more than one meaning that we can give to "we want business to be more ethical." Once we reflect on, and critically compare, two competing meanings for that claim, we can learn that the way we are accustomed to talking about ethics and business has less "common sense" than we have led ourselves to believe. Indeed, that accustomed language is an ethical nuisance. Hence, it is an impractical way for us as human beings to talk about business.

I write this book to give reasons for no longer talking in terms of "ethics from the outside." I want to render "ethics from the outside"— which so many have accepted for so long as a matter of course— irrelevant for business discourse. En route to a new kind of story about corporate strategy, I offer a new way of talking about ethics and business. That new story is told in a language that I call "ethics already through and through." With that new story, I provide one means for ensuring that concerns of the ethical kind and concerns of the business kind can converge on the prospects for human community and hence can coexist in every sentence of every story that you and I create. Who could possibly argue against this?

2

A Pragmatist Ethics of Differences, Centers, and Margins

I

You and I can learn more about making business more ethical from the creative efforts by Bill Watterson ("Calvin & Hobbes"), the late Jay Ward ("Rocky & Bullwinkle"), Dean Young and Stan Drake ("Blondie"), W.P. Kinsella (*Box Socials*), Gish Jen (*Typical American*), and Douglas Coupland (*Generation X*) than from reading about all the white-collar criminals ever convicted. I have come to this conclusion long after the day when, in my first month at Bucknell University, a student—I will call him "Senior"—entered my office with a proposal for heightening his classmates' awareness about ethics.[1] I threw cold water on Senior's idea. And I would do so again. My only regret is that I did not have a better reason at the time for dousing the idea. The water in my bucket was relatively tepid then. I have Watterson, Ward, Young, Drake, Kinsella, Jen, and Coupland to thank for helping me now fill the bucket with an icy concoction, a better intellectual reason for dousing Senior's idea.[2]

Senior wanted me to help him sponsor a guest speaker who would talk about the sinister side of business. Senior wanted me to help him arrange for a speaker to travel the twenty miles to Bucknell from another Central Pennsylvania institution: the Allenwood federal minimum-security prison where white-collar criminals received room and board. Senior's naivete about making such arrangements was considerable. He thought that I could call Allenwood officials and ask the equivalent of "Can Bobby come out and play this evening?" Still, what concerned me more was the implication in the proposal that business and ethics were linked by and through law enforcement institutions.

I was a new kid on the block at Bucknell when Senior came to me. I learned quickly that I had moved into a departmental neighborhood where a law-and-order approach to business and ethics lingered from the past. The message in the air was, "Here is the law. Do not break the law. Be an ethical businessperson." My alternative approach was to emphasize certain logical connections between ethics and business institutions.[3] That approach did not turn on counting who was being naughty in the business world. For that reason, Senior's proposal was a hurdle.

Thus, I started filling my bucket by saying to Senior, "Think about the stakeholder implications here, and let's talk again in a day or two." I wanted Senior to practice some self-criticism and to abandon the idea voluntarily. I knew that he already knew something about the stakeholder concept. Apparently he did not want to tackle my assignment. Several days later, word got back to me that "Gilbert threw cold water on the idea."

The proposal never resurfaced. But years later in my search for justifiable ways to link ethics and business, Senior and his idea came to mind. Long dormant in my memory, Senior's proposal now seems to be a very useful way to compare two meanings that we can give to "Of course we want business to be more ethical" and to demonstrate the relative merits of one meaning over the other. That comparison is the subject of this chapter.

II

"Of course we want business to be more ethical" is a loaded statement about our day and age. It does not emerge out of thin air. It is not a truth of Nature. I have created this statement, and I have done the loading.[4] I load "Of course we want business to be more ethical" with three ideas in particular.

First, the "we" in the statement is broadly inclusive.[5] I put no qualifiers on who can belong to the "we" whose members want something. This unqualified "we" leaves plenty of room for human beings who want to be known on their own terms. Second, the something sought by the members of "we" is a transformation of some kind. "To be more ethical" is not a trivial matter, because "to *be* more" points to changes in the very constitution of something. Third, the something that is ripe for possible transformation is business, an institution that affects the lives of everyone included in "we."[6] "We want business to be more ethical" points to the prospects for institutional change in the "local" settings of business in which members of a particular "we" participate as employers, employees, customers, kibitzers, regulators, and so on.

These three ideas converge on what we might call a politics of inclusion and institutional transformation.[7] A politics of inclusion deals with those who can belong to a particular "we" on their own terms. A politics of institutional transformation deals with the enduring arrangements by which those persons get along in their particular "we" and join new neighbors in the process. This politics should look familiar, even if the designation might not.

Inclusion and institutional transformation frame a perspective with which we can understand many public and private initiatives that have sparked debate in our democratic society. These initiatives include national health care, public education reform, the so-called digital information superhighway, affirmative action, disposal of toxic and nuclear wastes, abortion, and immigration. In each instance, the breadth of membership in a particular "we" is at issue. In some of those instances, belonging to a "we" in the first place is at issue. Immigration and affirmative action are cases in point. In each instance, significant changes loom in the lives of those who belong to a "we." In each instance, competing proposals for transforming an institution—such as health care in the United States—are central features of the debate.

In each of these contemporary cases, members of a particular "we" seek ways to protect what is important to them, and they frame the prospects for particular kinds of institutional change in such terms. The opportunity to retain the services of a family physician in any new national health care system is a case in point about a politics of inclusion tied up in a politics of institutional change. Another case in point is the content of a public school district curriculum, as the members of many local "we's" are learning.[8] Still another case in point is the information superhighway in rural America. As the "hype" builds for this infrastructure, members of a "we" are asking whether the information superhighway will, like the interstate highway system, bypass their lives and communities altogether.[9]

I introduce a politics of inclusion and institutional transformation as a point of departure from which I will defend the following claim in this chapter: A framework of differences, centers, and margins—and a derivative criterion of distinctive worldly contribution—is a comparatively more useful way to activate the statement "Of course we want business to be more ethical" than is a very common approach to business and ethics, an approach implied in Senior's proposal.[10] By the end of this chapter, I will have justified a Pragmatist Ethics of Differences, Centers, and Margins as a basis for the critical comparison between "ethics from the outside" and "ethics already through and through" that I will conduct in Chapters 3 and 4. The purpose of this chapter, then, is to show from where a Pragmatist Ethics of Differences, Centers, and Margins comes, as a prelude to using this framework as a critical device. I sketch the political place and importance of this framework in Figure 2–1. Along the way, I will demonstrate the relative uselessness of one version of "ethics from the outside," a version about prevention of unethical action. The comic characters Calvin and Hobbes, Rocky and Bullwinkle, Blondie and Dagwood Bumstead, and the protagonists in the novels *Box Socials*, *Typical American*, and *Generation X* will "assist" me with the demonstration.

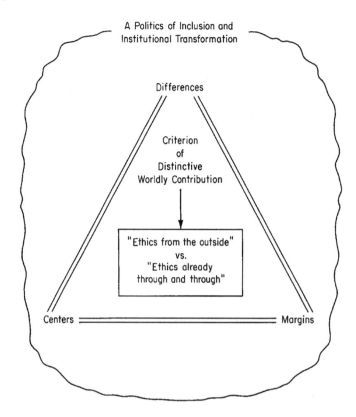

Figure 2–1. The place and usefulness of a Pragmatist Ethics of Differences, Centers, and Margins

III

Mention business ethics to people who have thought at all about the business world and you will probably hear one, or more, of four kinds of responses. First, some will tick off the names and misdeeds of well-known businessmen who have ended up in prison.[11] Second, some will bemoan absences of honesty, belief in the common good, loyalty, and integrity in the business world. Third, some will name the *Exxon Valdez* oil spill, Three Mile Island, the *Challenger* explosion, chemical deterioration of the ozone layer, or the latest catastrophes that come to mind. Fourth, some will bemoan the general state of moral decline in modern society. They will point an accusing finger at business for contributing to that decline through video games, water pollution, network television programming, and cigarettes.

These four responses make up what I call an Ethics of Deadbeats, Dullards, and Derelicts' Disasters Driving the World Into Moral Decline.[12] This ethic is one possible initiative in the search for a "more ethical" business world. It is an ethical basis for the proposal that Senior brought to me.

This Ethics of Deadbeats, Dullards, and Derelicts' Disasters Driving the World Into Moral Decline is an ethics of prevention. Advocates of this view emphasize what can, and probably will, go wrong in and around the business world. This is a view of the ethical kind in two respects. First, it turns on a vision of conduct that is Right, which must be continued, and conduct that is Wrong, which must be stopped. Second, this view is a blueprint by which some people (those in the Right) should intervene in other people's lives (those in the Wrong).[13] With this emphasis on trouble and the prevention of trouble, an Ethics of Deadbeats, Dullards, and Derelicts' Disasters Driving the World Into Moral Decline is a vehicle for "ethics from the outside" (Chapter 1). The preventers operate from a position "outside" the trouble-ridden world "inside" business.

Deadbeats, according to this view, are people who impose costs on the business world for their own personal gain.[14] Dullards, according to this perspective, are people who lack such honorable virtues as compassion, courage, obligation, and imagination when they conduct business. Derelicts, on this view, are people whose ignorance and negligence contribute greatly to disasters in the course of business. These people are derelicts in their duty to sustain management's control over organizations, markets, resources, and the natural world.[15] Disasters are disruptions in that flow of control. Decline, on this view, is our collective slippage from those halcyon days when, in meteorological terms, the barometer of moral values was high and steady.[16] This Ethics of Deadbeats, Dullards, and Derelicts' Disasters Driving the World Into Moral Decline enjoys enormous popularity in the business media and in the academic world.

IV

Members of both the business and general media have conferred celebrity status on certain business "deadbeats." Garry Trudeau has done this in his "Doonesbury" comic strip. In one story line, Trudeau provides a satire of a business-school course offered by a well-known financier convicted on violations of securities laws.[17] In another story line, Trudeau labels a group of tobacco executives the "Carcinogen Seven."[18]

Others in the business media have joined Trudeau in creating the business deadbeat as a kind of antihero.[19] The publishers of *Business Ethics* magazine announce in an advertisement that theirs is "the only business magazine for the *good guys.*"[20] The First Annual American Business Ethics Awards are designed to recognize "The Rewards of Doing It Right."[21] Programs such as these recognize consistently proper behavior in the daily course of business, the antithesis of the deadbeat's track record. If you can more confidently name certain business "deadbeats" than you can name the members of the Bush and Clinton cabinets, you have been touched by the media campaign to sustain this ethic. Senior certainly was. He wanted me to help him arrange for the visit of a "deadbeat" to Bucknell.

In the academic world, textbooks and journals are crammed with cases about deadbeat behavior. In his book *Business Environment and Public Policy*, Rogene Buchholz introduces chapters with one case of business misdeed, or suspected misdeed, after another. Buchholz includes among the legacies of the business deadbeat: Manville asbestos compensation; Beech-Nut apple juice; EDB pesticide contamination; the Standard Oil Trust; the costs of smoking borne by the nonsmoking public; alleged price-fixing by certain university officials; Wedtech; sex discrimination at Price Waterhouse in Washington, D.C.; worker exposure to benzene; the *Exxon Valdez* oil spill; and the Firestone 500 radial tire.[22]

Across the past decade, numerous papers about the behavior of business deadbeats have appeared in the *Academy of Management Journal*. These analyses include:

1. "Board Composition and the Commission of Illegal Acts: An Investigation of *Fortune* 500 Companies."[23]
2. "The Impact of Announcements of Corporate Illegalities on Shareholder Returns."[24]
3. "Peer Reporting of Unethical Behavior: A Social Context Perspective."[25]
4. "Can Illegal Corporate Behavior Be Predicted? An Event History Analysis."[26]

The "deadbeat" has made regular appearances in the *Journal of Business Ethics*. A classic study about the prevention of deadbeat behavior is "A Behavioral Model of Ethical and Unethical Decision Making."[27] In a recent volume of the *Journal of Business Ethics*, the business deadbeat is the focus of four papers:

1. "Ethical Statements as Smokescreens for Sectional Interests: The Case of the U.K. Accountancy Profession"[28];
2. "Unethical Practices in Competitive Analysis: Patterns, Causes and Effects"[29];
3. "The Influence of Role Conflict and Self-Interest on Lying in Organizations"[30]; and
4. "Softlifting: A Model of Motivating Factors."[31]

Deadbeats are prominent in these very titles.[32]

In the campaign against business deadbeats, corporate codes of ethics have captured widespread attention. "Ethics Codes Spread Despite Skepticism," according to 1988 *Wall Street Journal* article.[33] In a 1991 *New York Times* story, we can read how corporate ethics officers are

"Helping Corporate America Hew to the Straight and Narrow."[34] According to a 1992 *Business Week* story, "The Best Laid Ethics Program . . . Couldn't Stop a Nightmare at Dow Corning. What Happened?"[35] There is now even a publication called *Corporate Conduct Quarterly*.[36]

V

The campaign against business dullards is waged vigorously by those at the Harvard Business School who have argued for years that the legitimacy of business depends on the business leader's moral fiber.[37] In their book, *Can Ethics Be Taught?*, Thomas Piper, Mary Gentile, and Sharon Daloz Parks depict the dullard as another species of business antihero whose moral makeup can be altered through the M.B.A. curriculum.[38] Piper, Gentile, and Parks describe how their Harvard colleagues went looking for this antihero tendency in incoming M.B.A. students. Piper notes:

> For many, there is an absence of worthy myths and dreams, leaving them vulnerable to unconsidered and inadequate goals.[39]

Some on the Harvard Business School faculty—Piper, Gentile, and Parks report—prefer that business leaders possess a very different set of moral characteristics:

> What is needed, within and across our institutions—public and private, corporate and educational—is a rediscovery of purpose and principle, of responsibility and worth, and of accountability in terms appropriate to the twenty-first century.[40]

To plug the gap between the dullard and the moral business leader, according to Piper, Gentile, and Parks, the Leadership, Ethics, and Corporate Responsibility program was launched.[41]

Long before the Harvard initiative was underway, Kenneth Andrews at Harvard was creating a prominent place for managerial values in three editions, spanning more than two decades, of *The Concept of Corporate Strategy*. Andrews writes about a "prototype" who is definitely not a dullard:

> The prototype of the chief executive that we are developing is, in short, the able victory-seeking organizational leader who is making sure in what is done and the changes pioneered in purpose and practice that the game is worth playing, the victory worth seeking, and life and career worth living.[42]

Andrews has declared "open season" on the business dullard in the company of such other commentators as Suresh Srivastva, Clarence Walton, Robert Golembiewski, and Kenneth Goodpaster.[43]

Members of the business media expose and shame the business dullard by singing the praises of businesspersons who make social contributions of their own choosing. When the editors of *Business Week* honored the "Best of 1993," they included executives who defied the "dullard" antihero. These executives did such honorable things as: (a) "involve employees"; (b) "emphasized leanness and focus"; (c) "remade a stodgy Bell corporate culture," showing that "It takes strength and vision" to do so; and (d) "knows the values of patience."[44] These persons are the antitheses of the business dullard.

Another prominent part of the anti-dullard campaign in recent years is media attention to business support for, even intervention in, the nation's public schools.[45] The executives who have pioneered such initiatives are people of vision, and benevolence, the argument goes. They, too, are antitheses of the business dullard. Business journalists today are making manufacturers Ben & Jerry's and Tom's of Maine exemplars in the campaign against business dullards, just as they sang the praises of William Norris at Control Data several decades ago.[46]

VI

Dereliction of business duty and the disasters that can ensue have entered the business news and academic research under the rubric "crisis management." Crisis management is a prevention campaign. Paul Shrivastava makes this clear in the first article of the first edition of *Industrial Crisis Quarterly*.[47] Crisis management is a prevention campaign led by experts who assume that derelicts could slip through crisis-prevention systems. Journalists and researchers needed to create the derelict antihero to tell their story about crises.[48] "Human error" is the derelict's fingerprint in the crisis-management story.

Forecasting where and when the unnamed derelict might show up next is a key part of crisis-management research and practice.[49] So, too, are detailed narratives about crises, such as the Tenerife air disaster.[50] Indeed, crisis management is so important—argue Ian Mitroff, Chris Pearson, and Thierry Pauchant—that it "needs to be integrated into the field of Strategic Management."[51] So important is this prevention campaign that entire issues of *Journal of Management Studies* and *Journal of Business Administration* have been devoted to crisis management.[52]

VII

Decline in a collective measure called "moral values" is a favorite theme in the media. A *Time* magazine cover story in 1987 posed the question: "What Ever Happened to Ethics?"[53] A 1987 Touche Ross & Co. survey reported that corporate executives were concerned with "decay in cultural and social institutions."[54] More recently, a *Newsweek* cover story announced, "The Politics of Virtue: The Crusade Against America's Moral Decline."[55]

Business journalists compete cleverly to pronounce the collective guilt of businesses for contributing to this societal condition. Business ethics, according to this view, is a subset of collective moral values and is an index akin to, and as volatile as, the Dow Jones Industrial Index, consumer confidence index, and the meteorologist's wind-chill factor.[56] Business ethics is an index that usually is in decline, if we are to believe in "The Decline & Fall of Business Ethics," as announced in a 1986 *Fortune* story, and "The New Crisis in Business Ethics" announced six years later in *Fortune*.[57]

So deep runs this belief in moral decline that apparent reversals in this trend make headlines:

1. A 1985 "View from the Pulpit" in the *New York Times* reports "A Modest Revival in Business Ethics?"[58]
2. A 1989 *Chicago Tribune* columnist announces "Ethics Comeback Can't Be Ignored."[59]
3. "Businesses Are Signing Up for Ethics 101," according to a 1988 *Business Week* article.[60]
4. A 1991 *Business Week* commentator reports "What's Behind Business' Sudden Fervor for Ethics."[61]

Academic commentators have helped drive this bandwagon. Articles titled "The Management Ethics 'Crisis': An Organizational Perspective" and "The Crisis of American Business" appeared more than a decade ago.[62] A 1989 issue of *Business Insights* bears the vivid title, "Crisis in Ethics."[63] Kenneth Goodpaster predicates a model of leadership on "the moral malaise" of our times.[64] The systematic tendency toward moral decline has a prominent place in crisis-management research. Danny Miller proposes that there are "some very common types of pathological organizations."[65] Pauchant and Mitroff call such organizations "crisis prone" and trace such difficulties to a collective moral climate called corporate culture.[66]

VIII

This Ethics of Deadbeats, Dullards, and Derelicts' Disasters Driving the World Into Moral Decline, as popular and coherent as it is, is a relatively unhelpful approach if we want business to be more ethical. There are two reasons for this. Each reason points to how this particular ethics is antithetical, even hostile, to a politics of inclusion and institutional transformation. These reasons are part of what I wish I could have discussed with Senior when he brought me his proposal.

First, an Ethics of Deadbeats, Dullards, and Derelicts' Disasters Driving the World Into Moral Decline is an ethics of exclusion, not inclusion. The prevention emphasis is a dead giveaway on this point. On this view, it is someone's obligation to keep deadbeats, dullards, and derelicts, whose sloppy work precipitates disasters, away from impressionable good employees.[67] On this view, there are Bad persons and there are Good persons. Nothing in this split is friendly to the idea of inclusion—a broadly defined "we" made up of some eccentric characters—when we talk about business.[68] Instead, this ethics proceeds straightaway from a basic categorization that excludes certain persons. If you are a dullard inside the business world, for example, there is not much room for you—as you want to be known—as a contributing participant in this ethic. In this view of the business world, your status as a "dullard" is determined by those nondullards who think you should be a different person, regardless of what you think about your own life.

This exclusionary emphasis becomes entrenched when the advocates of this view nominate a certain class of people in the business world—i.e., senior executives—to head this prevention campaign.[69] These executives are automatically agents of the Right, on this view, against the forces of deadbeats, dullards, and those who are derelict in their duties. A generalized "we" involved in the effort to make business "more ethical" is not friendly to an Ethics of Deadbeats, Dullards, and Derelicts' Disasters Driving the World Into Moral Decline.[70] This is quite clear in the crisis-management story where only experts are permitted entry into the process.[71] Clearly, then, this is an account of "ethics from the outside."

Second, an Ethics of Deadbeats, Dullards, and Derelicts' Disasters Driving the World Into Moral Decline is one of the status quo, not transformation. The prevention emphasis is a giveaway here, too. On this view, business can become "more ethical" if only people did *not* misbehave, did *not* underachieve and compromise the trust placed in them, did *not* make catastrophic mistakes, and did *not* yield collectively to the temptations of a lesser moral life. At best, this ethics defers, until the work of prevention is done, the progress that persons can make through transformed institutions. At worst, this ethics systematically stymies human striving, deferring it indefinitely until things are "cleaned up" in the business world. We can do better if "of course, we want business to be more ethical" is to be meaningful in the democratic context of inclusion and institutional transformation in which I have placed it.

IX

In the years since Senior's short-lived proposal, I have become convinced that an ethics of prevention—such as an Ethics of Deadbeats, Dullards, and Derelicts' Disasters Driving the World Into Moral Decline—is optional. Another option for making business "more ethical" makes more sense to me, against a backdrop of a politics of inclusion and institutional transformation. I began to envision this option at an unlikely intellectual intersection. On some occasions, I was pondering the world through my customary dosage of contemporary novels and newspaper comics and "Rocky & Bullwinkle" videos. At times, I was pondering the world as I read about liberal pragmatist literary criticism, contractarian ethics, communitarian ethics, a feminist ethics of connection, and the politics of liberal education. Over time, those two paths of contemplation began to converge on the same intellectual space.[72]

I decided that my excursion into fiction and satire and my readings in ethics and politics converged on the same kind of story. In that story, identifiable human beings are trying to create more meaningful lives for themselves by participating in each other's lives. These men and women are pragmatists, in both a commonplace and formal meaning of the term. They are pragmatists because they are experimenting in ways of living, weighing and testing alternatives that they make up as they go.

Here is an account of inclusion, I thought. Here is an account of persons transforming their institutions in their own "local" settings. Here is a story about human beings creating new ways of getting along, using their minds, day in and day out. Here is a different ethics in the making. Here is an intellectual space where prevention does not need to be the driving issue. I call this account a Pragmatist Ethics of Differences, Centers, and Margins, which is another framework for talking about a "more ethical" business world. It is a framework drawing on some of the best in contemporary political and ethical scholarship, some of the most poignant and thought-provoking contemporary novels, and some of the most hilarious and ironic contemporary cartoons.[73]

X

Differences is a perspective available to anyone who believes in the distinctiveness of a person's chosen pursuits, in the distinctiveness of that person's reasons for those pursuits, and in the distinctiveness of that person's life history. *Distinctiveness* is a person's claim to be taken on his or her own terms. We begin to take differences seriously when we are able to listen to others' own voices and, over time, develop a more and more sophisticated interpretation of each voice.[74]

W.P. Kinsella makes this point accessible with his portrayal of the life of young Jamie O'Day in *Box Socials*. Jamie's mother likes to say, "We're hillbillies, though we won't always be that way, unlike some we know."[75] She calls those others "white trash." No small part of Jamie's pre-teenage years is bound up in getting to know voices of the "white trash" citizens who live in the vicinity of Fark, Alberta. Hopfstadt teaches Jamie about loyalty and driving a tractor. Bertha Sigurdson teaches Jamie something about love, charity, and poverty. Velvet Bozniak teaches Jamie about pride and self-deception. Truckbox Al McClintock teaches Jamie something about stardom and failure. All in all, Jamie O'Day understands distinctiveness long before he reaches adulthood.

Courage is necessary if one is to adopt this perspective on the world. Once you open the door on differences, you have crossed into new intellectual territory forever. There is no turning back to the simple pleasures of taxonomies and typologies about who human beings are.[76] In this new territory, a "differences" perspective gives meaning to a politics of inclusion and institutional transformation in two regards.[77]

First, a "differences" perspective eases us into taking inclusion seriously, because distinctiveness is something we can appreciate in those people with whom we are most closely associated. With differences right under our noses, we have a touchstone of understanding from which we can move "outward" to encounter an increasingly diverse array of human beings and include them in our worldview. In this way, a "differences" perspective can become a self-perpetuating practice of taking inclusion seriously.

The idea that a healthy appreciation of differences can begin at home is vividly portrayed by Bill Watterson in the comic strip "Calvin & Hobbes." Calvin and his long-suffering parents are so different that his father once suggested that Calvin came into the family through a "blue light special" at a well-known discount store.[78] Calvin's parents have their eyes opened to a different approach to life through their son's daily antics. Whether Calvin is creating a horde of unconventional snow figures or trying to avoid the after-school mauling by his tiger Hobbes or wandering in and out of his fantasy worlds as Stupendous Man and Spaceman Spiff, Watterson provides a sympathetic portrait of two parents trying gamely to see the world as a place that includes some eccentric characters, starting right in their home.[79]

Jay Ward and his collaborators on the video "Rocky & Bullwinkle" cleverly locate differences—and lives that include a place for others—in the social and political climate of the 1950s. The "home" in "Rocky & Bullwinkle" is the recurring interaction between the heroic duo of Rocky the Flying Squirrel and Bullwinkle J. Moose and the "fiendish" spies Boris Badenov and Natasha Fatale. "Our heroes," as narrator William Conrad calls them, are a picure of a particular set of American values.[80] Rocky and Bullwinkle lead lives in which alcohol, tobacco, profanity, gambling, gluttony, and sexuality (much less sexual promiscuity) have no place. They are polite, resilient in the face of adversity, and trusting toward the U.S. government, despite numerous experiences that might test that fidelity. Boris and Natasha, on the other hand, are distinctive masters of disguise, deception, evil, and ironic profanity ("goodness," "purity," Boris spits). In the lives led by Rocky and Bullwinkle, we are reminded that we each move in a "home" territory in which we cannot avoid including other distinct characters in our worldview. Rocky and Bullwinkle would have nothing to do, if they did not take the presence of Boris and Natasha seriously.

Second, "differences" is a perspective from which we can each draw inspiration about making changes in how we live in association with others. If we include in our view of the world the distinctiveness of others' lives, we can find hope—and we can resolve—that we could live differently. Differences is thus an impetus to take steps to bring about changes in how we associate with others in our institutional arrangements.

Kinsella helps us make a connection between differences and the impetus to transform our ties to others. In a culminating episode in *Box Socials,* Jamie O'Day begins to fathom the grinding poverty in which Bertha Sigurdson lived and died. On an excursion to find Bertha's grave, Jamie resolves not to eat the lunch that his mother packs, musing, "Perhaps by the time I got home, I thought, I might have some idea of what it was like to be really hungry."[81] The ever-so-brief opportunity to include Bertha in his life stuns Jamie:

> I decided as I turned away, my fingers tracing the nettle welts on my cheek, that this was my story, that I'd lived it, and someday I'd tell it, but not too soon, for right now it would hurt too much.[82]

Through Kinsella's narrative, we can imagine that Jamie might someday be inspired to act on the difference between his family's modest comforts and the Sigurdsons' poverty.

In *Typical American,* Gish Jen provides a moving portrayal of people changing their lives together as they include new voices in their circle of friends and associates. In America, Ralph and Helen Chang meet and fall in with such "typical Americans" as Grover Ding, a self-made millionaire. As they open their lives together to new characters. Ralph and Helen experience opportunities for personal freedom that they never knew in their native China as Yifeng and Hailan, respectively. They use that opportunity in America to open a fried chicken restaurant. Sadly, the Changs, along with Ralph's sister Theresa, use their newfound freedoms to transform their family into nothing like the family traditions that they knew as children. "Typical American" is a private joke to them at first.[83] Later, the label becomes a cruel reminder of what they have done to each other and what version of family they have created for their daughters.

A differences perspective is useful, but only to a point. If we want to advance a politics of inclusion and institutional transformation, we cannot rely solely on the idea of differences. For one thing, there is no guarantee that, if we wanted to join with others to live through transformed institutions, we could muster the support necessary to make that change. The O'Day family and their neighbors in the Six Towns area lacked the institutional means, such as a functioning church and school, to escape the isolation and poverty that lingered in rural Alberta after the Great Depression.

Moreover, certain persons can make it their distinctive aims to interfere with others' distinctive pursuits. In "Rocky & Bullwinkle," Boris and

Natasha make the demise of "moose and squirrel" their distinctive life work.[84] Dagwood's boss, Mr. Dithers, is a tyrant who specializes in "micromanagement." Calvin's teacher, Miss Wormwood, has a distinctive approach to education, in which there is no room for imagination. Grover Ding's distinctive, acquisitive way of life includes a penchant for adultery. These three distinctive approaches frustrate the particular projects of Dagwood, Calvin, and Helen, respectively. Differences can use a boost, if we want to take inclusion and institutional transformation seriously. This is where centers and margins can usefully enter the story.

XI

"Centers" is a perspective accessible to anyone who believes that distinctive human beings live in and through distinctive relationships, each of which can be governed by some specific understanding that the parties share about their relationship. This relationship is central in their respective lives, and their shared understanding is at the center of that relationship. The parties look to that shared understanding as they conduct their relationship.

"Centers" is a perspective bearing an incessant reminder that we can each live distinctively in the course of living *in* relationships with other distinctive people.[85] Centers, like differences, are there is you go looking for them. Centers, like differences, play a key role in a politics of inclusion and institutional transformation.

Dean Young and Stan Drake narrate the life of Blondie Bumstead as a vivid case in point about inclusion and a centers perspective.[86] Blondie is rarely more than one frame from the company of others, and she is never out of voice range. When conducting her catering business, she is talking with clients or with her partner, Tootsie, or with her husband, Dagwood, discouraging him from sampling the food. When reading, Blondie is always in the same room with Dagwood, talking with him. Her leisure time always involves conversations and exchanges with somebody else.[87]

It is through centers shared with others that Blondie lives a life that includes those who are different from her. She and Cora Dithers, the boss's wife, share a "center" in which they talk over lunch every so often. Cora is a pompous complainer. Blondie is not. Still, they sustain their center. The idea of centers thus adds to the argument for a politics of inclusion. If there is a center that "holds" between us and another person, then we each have some room to be our distinctive selves. Without such a center, two distinctive persons can, at best, move in parallel and miss an opportunity that comes from closer ties. Calvin's parents ("Calvin & Hobbes") learn this again and again. Exasperating as he can be, Calvin is, after all, their little boy. Raising him is a center in their marriage, and they talk about their marriage in the course of reacting to Calvin's escapades.

Shared understandings at centers of relationships with others can be, in turn, springboards for our efforts to change the ways we live with others and to change the institutional contexts in which we interact. An institution is a particular center of shared understanding and is a particular vehicle by which a particular group of distinctive persons go about their relationships. Moreover, by a centers perspective, each person lives a distinctive life at the intersection of numerous, particular institutional centers, such as his or her family, business, school, and church. Two transformative implications follow from this.

First, a center of shared understanding is a focal point for the parties to a relationship to ask, "Does this institutional center work well for us?" Douglas Coupland enables us to grasp this point in *Generation X*. His protagonists Dag, Claire, and Andy have left their "McJobs" because they found themselves in work settings where no one could answer this question affirmatively.[88] Coming together in Palm Springs, California, Dag, Claire, and Andy search jointly for a sense of "home" as a center in their lives. Ironically, they talk often and candidly about their parents and siblings, long after their respective families have ceased to function meaningfully as centers for anyone.[89]

Second, living through multiple centers can provide each distinct person with an introduction to alternative institutional arrangements. Not only are there individual differences in living, but there are also different kinds of centers. Calvin's beleaguered parents muse on this when, after another of Calvin's antics, they wonder whether other families go through such surprises. Transformation requires a vision of "where to next?," and a centers perspective makes it possible to address that question. In the absence of a viable alternative center, Young and Drake show us, Dagwood's resignation from Mr. Dither's company is short-lived. Dagwood and Blondie struggle to define a new center in their working lives, but they know no shared understanding about work and home other than the one in which Dagwood is at the office. Not surprisingly, Dagwood returns to Mr. Dither's employ.[90]

A centers perspective does contain a place for prevention. This should be welcome news for those who are addicted to the idea that ethics is synonymous with prevention of Wrong. Jay Ward and his collaborators ("Rocky & Bullwinkle") provide a vivid, and satirical, case in point. There is a center of understanding among the Pottsylvanian spies—Boris, Natasha, Fearless Leader, and Mr. Big—about the definition and consequences of wrongdoing. Fearless Leader reminds Boris and Natasha after every one of their bungled projects that Mr. Big could choose to end their careers. Mr. Big is the epitome of prevention. He is very seldom seen, but his name is invoked to drive fear into Boris and Natasha. Mr. Big is a very small man who casts a large shadow, thanks to a well-placed desk lamp. Boris and Natasha know the rules. They get their second chances with the strings of punishment attached.

As useful as a centers perspective can be for sustaining a politics of inclusion and transformation, there are three important limits to this way of talking. First, a particular center can trap parties in an enduring cycle in which they fail to grow.[91] Boris and Natasha in "Rocky & Bullwinkle" never learn from their goofs. Their center is not conducive to self-criticism. In Gish Jen's book *Typical American*, Ralph and Helen were trapped, as Helen muses, in their fried chicken business and the lure of "money worship" in which

> it did seem a brand of alchemy that turned those metal trays of mottled chicken, with those loose flaps of pimply skin, into a happy household.[92]

In Kinsella's *Box Socials*, Edytha Rasmussen Bozniak, her mother, and her daughter, Velvet, trapped themselves in a center of fiction about Velvet's parentage. Edytha's pregnancy outside the center of marriage is never discussed in the center shared by the residents of Fark, Alberta.[93]

Second, a particular center can pollute other centers around and through which distinctive persons want to live. Mr. Dithers and Dagwood collaborate to create such a roller coaster work environment that Dagwood contemplates quitting. This, in turn, unsettles the particular long-standing center that Dagwood and Blondie and their children had shaped as their home life.

Third, a particular center can be so useful to the distinctive persons who share it that they are lulled into believing that "it has always been this way." Thus, they can be wholly unprepared for changes in the world around their center. Douglas Coupland's protagonists in *Generation X* talk a great deal about their respective parents in this light. Moreover, Coupland leaves it for us to ponder whether Dag, Claire, and Andy leave themselves open to being unprepared, in view of the particular center that they shape in Palm Springs.

Jay Ward and his collaborators satirize the U.S. government, and the military in particular, on this point about complacency. Led by such smugly self-confident characters as "General Consternation," the military never succeeds in foiling the Pottsylvanian spies. It takes two resilient private citizens, Rocky and Bullwinkle, to save the day each and every time.

It is at these three logical limitations that a margins perspective enters the picture.

XII

"Margins" is a perspective available to anyone who believes that whatever happens in human relationships—when distinctive human beings interact around distinctive centers of meaning—occurs over time at the intersections of those persons' pursuits, at the margins they create by trying to live distinctively. There is nothing predetermined, on this view, about the destination of human interaction. No collective mind or collective action or invisible hand governs the course of human interaction. What happens will happen as a joint result, on this view. What happens is a phenomenon that is contingent on what particular human beings do when they meet on the many particular margins, or boundaries, of their lives. In short, what happens is the joint responsibility of the parties involved.[94]

This conception of margins is brilliantly portrayed by Ward in "Rocky & Bullwinkle." Each episode of this video begins with "our heroes" pursuing some commonplace project, such as Bullwinkle collecting cereal boxtops.[95] Boris and Natasha then appear and try to exploit that project for their own ends and to hasten the demise of Rocky and Bullwinkle. In each episode, the story is contingent on what the heroes and the villains jointly create. Every time, Boris and Natasha fail. On a margins perspective, we can account for the spies' incompetence along a margin between what they do *and* what Rocky and Bullwinkle do.

A margins perspective obligates us to take a broad view of inclusion in our lives. Margins is a perspective about mutually contingent actions. On this view, we must be on the lookout for not only the parties with whom we interact closely and voluntarily, but also third parties "out there" whose actions can affect a relationship of ours closer to home. Captain Peter ("Wrong Way") Peachfuzz periodically appears in "Rocky & Bullwinkle" as a third party and, as his name suggests, complicates the margins for everyone every time.

In Kinsella's *Box Socials*, personal privacy among the residents of the Six Towns area is something created in this marginal and inclusive way. Every one of Kinsella's characters—from the mysterious Flop Skalrud to Edytha Rasmussen Bozniak—has a secret. And, everyone knows that everyone else has a secret. Olivia O'Day tells her son, Jamie, "Good gravy, Jamie, folks are *allowed*."[96] Yet, on a margins view that Kinsella enables us to use, those secrets remain secrets because these people operate on some version of what Jamie heard his mother tell his father:

"John Martin Duffy O'Day," said my mama, "everyone knows that a lifetime of smirking behind your hand is a lot better than a few seconds of triumph."[97]

Flop Skalrud's secret is safe, in short, thanks to the particular ways his neighbors live on the margins of their relationships in the Six Towns area.

A margins perspective enables us to think about changes in our lives of relationships, because everything is open to redefinition along the margins of human interaction. A margins perspective offers a constant reminder that relationships—and the patterns of relationships that we call institutions—are always subject to transformation at the hands of the parties to them.[98] In this way, a margins perspective ensures a place for transformation in a politics of inclusion and institutional transformation. Moreover, thinking in terms of margins ushers in an historical dimension into a politics of inclusion and institutional transformation.

On a margins perspective, each relationship sits on an edge between what it has been and what it could become for the parties involved. This means that any margin shared by two persons is in transition from a past to a future in which the relationship endures or fails. On this view, the parties to a relationship—along with third parties who influence or are influenced by that relationship—literally construct the relationship ("make it up") as they go along. In *Generation X*, Dag, Claire, and Andy do this quite self-consciously. In *Typical American*, Helen Chang muses prophetically, "How dangerous a place this country! A wilderness of freedom."[99] Ralph and Helen Chang make it up as they go, hopefully, at first, as new Americans, and then make it up, tragically, as "typical Americans." On a margins view, each person's hand in transforming a social institution—such as a family—is always in plain view. No one actor's actions determine what happens in a particular relationship over time.

XIII

Differences, centers, and margins form an ethical framework, a way to see human beings, such as ourselves, seeking some conception of a good life and some conception of enduring ties to one another.[100] Differences, centers, and margins also form a pragmatist framework, by a commonplace meaning of "pragmatist." It is a way to see human beings, such as ourselves, striving to make something meaningful of their lives *in* their relationships *in* their own corners of the world. With a pragmatist framework of differences, centers, and margins, we can think of our lives as narratives that we write. Claire puts the point this way in *Generation X:* "Either our lives become stories, or there's just no way to get through them."[101] On both an ethical count and a commonplace pragmatist count, Calvin and his parents; Rocky and Bullwinkle and Boris and Natasha; Blondie and Dagwood; the O'Days and their neighbors; Dag, Claire, and Andy; and the Changs all blaze a trail for us. In their worldly lives, we can grasp the meaning of what I call a Pragmatist Ethics of Differences, Centers, and Margins.

This framework of differences, centers, and margins is also a pragmatist account in a more formal sense of "pragmatist." It sits at an intersection between what, on one hand, I have interpreted from the creative work of Watterson, Ward, Young and Drake, Kinsella, Jen, and Coupland and what, on the other hand, a number of contemporary liberal pragmatist critics have said about inclusion and institutional transformation.[102] The liberal pragmatist believes that our worldly lives are valuable per se. The liberal pragmatist also believes that our worldly lives are always subject to change.[103] On a liberal pragmatist account, a worthy life is a life of experimentation—hence, "pragmatist"—with better and better ways to define ourselves and better and better ways to get along with one another. I draw inspiration from these beliefs as I create and apply my Pragmatist Ethics of Differences, Centers, and Margins. Several brief passages of liberal pragmatist "support" for that framework follow. I will call on this support throughout the book.

XIV

Charles Taylor writes about the appeal of authenticity in our day and age. Authenticity is one way to think about living distinctively. Taylor links authenticity with originality: "Authenticity involves originality, it demands a revolt against convention."[104] Taylor argues that, as authenticity has come to occupy a more a prominent place in our modern culture, we have lost sight of a sense of center, of common purpose, in our institutions. He traces this loss to "the dark side of individualism" and to the appeal of what he calls "instrumental reason."[105] Instrumental reason is an expedient, self-centered decision process. As such, it is an antithesis of a margins perspective, as I have developed that idea. Taylor is by no means a foe of authenticity. Rather, he wants us to "retrieve" authenticity by reinventing it as a way to live jointly in what he calls the situations of "ordinary life."[106]

Richard Rorty proposes that we think of our lives in modern liberal democracies as searches in two spheres, neither of which is collapsible into the other.[107] One is a private life devoted to what Rorty calls self-creation. The self-creator drives herself to be distinctive. She lives in fear that she will one day decide that hers is a replica of someone else's life.[108] The other sphere is a public exchange about justice. The point of that exchange, Rorty argues—and Taylor concurs—is to create an ever-widening sense of centers in which we should "keep trying to expand our sense of 'us' as far as we can."[109] Both spheres are lived on margins with other human beings. As Rorty has long argued, when it comes to the institutions of modern democracies, it is "just us."[110] Rorty has no use for the proposition that

> finite, mortal, contingently existing human beings might derive the meanings of their lives from anything except other finite, mortal, contingently existing human beings.[111]

According to both Rorty and Taylor, then, many interesting things in life "happen" inasmuch as we live our lives along the margins where we meet others.

Stanley Fish argues that contemporary debates about such ethical values as fairness and free speech—which are centers to which we can appeal—are inevitably and naturally political matters.[112] He rejects the idea that fairness and free speech, for example, can be defined and applied from some position outside the daily workings of particular communities. Fish predicates his pragmatist argument on a strong conception of differences among human beings:

> [I]f everyone were the same—believed the same things, envisioned the same future as a realization of the same hopes brought to fruition by the same agreed-upon means—there would be no problem because there would be no politics (politics after all is unthinkable apart from difference and faction), and the question of fairness would never arise.[113]

As a pragmatist, Fish wants us to accept that we give meaning to the centers that we hold dear. We do so at the margins where our lives meet, "right there in the middle of the fray," where a center such as free speech is "an object of contest" among contending interpreters.[114]

Judith Jordan, Alexandra Kaplan, Jean Baker Miller, Irene Stiver, and Janet Surrey argue that women, unlike men, develop a distinctive sense of self that is inextricably linked to others. They call this a "self-in-relation" conception of human development.[115] Surrey observes:

> Our conception of the self-in-relation involves the recognition that, for women, the primary experience of self is relational, that is, the self is organized and developed in the context of important relationships.[116]

Those relationships are centers in women's lives. Jordan and her collaborators thus locate women's psychological development on the margins between parties to those relationships.

Cornel West takes us on a new tour of the centers in American life through the lens of race. West argues that many black Americans live under a "nihilistic threat" that makes a mockery of their hopes to live distinctively.[117] West argues that the modern institutions of liberalism and conservatism are centers ill-suited to contribute anything to the restoration of black American communities. He goes further to argue that the modern corporation and the marketplace are institutions that have undermined the traditions that once provided centers of hope to black Americans:

> These traditions consist primarily of black religious and civic institutions that sustained familial and communal networks of support.[118]

To rejuvenate the centers through which the tide of nihilism in black America can be stemmed, West proposes a "politics of conversion."[119] This politics would be practiced at local margins, "on the ground among the toiling everyday people, ushering forth humble freedom fighters."[120]

The upshot is that a framework of differences, centers, and margins could muster the support of thoughtful liberal critics who are concerned with inclusion and institutional transformation in our world.[121] From this circle of support, I am now ready to answer the question: What can we do with a Pragmatist Ethics of Differences, Centers, and Margins? I will conclude this chapter by giving two answers to this question.[122]

First, I will use this framework to place and justify "distinctive worldly contribution" (see Chapter 1) as a criterion with which I will critique "Of course we want business to be more ethical" in Chapters 3 and 4. Second, I will argue why we should abandon an Ethics of Deadbeats, Dullards, and Derelicts' Disasters Driving the World Into Moral Decline. If a politics of inclusion and institutional transformation is a useful way to make sense of our world, and if business is one corner of that world, then this view about deadbeats, dullards, derelicts, and declines is comparatively inferior.

XV

The contrast is a sharp one, set against a backdrop of a politics of inclusion and institutional transformation, between an Ethics of Deadbeats, Dullards, and Derelicts' Disasters Driving the World Into Moral Decline and a Pragmatist Ethics of Differences, Centers, and Margins. Three particular contrasts are instructive. Each contrast gives meaning to the criterion of distinctive worldly contribution with which I will conduct my critical analysis in Chapters 3 and 4.

First, with a plurality of differences, centers, and margins, we can create room for a fascinating cast of characters as we look at our world. An emphasis on deadbeats, dullards, and those who are derelict in their duties, on the other hand, turns on a single fundamental difference between Good, about which we need not say much, and Bad, three personifications of which must be prevented: deadbeats, dullards, and derelicts. In an ethics that honors plurality of differences, centers, and margins, there is ample room for persons making *distinctive* contributions to the world. That is not true in an ethics predicated on the importance of prevention. On that view, the prevention task is assigned to a few guardians of the Good. Furthermore, "distinctive prevention" makes little sense.[123] When prevention is the order of the day, imaginative forays by people like Calvin ("Calvin & Hobbes") do not count for very much.

Second, with a plurality of differences, centers, and margins, we can envision a world of institutions that are always in flux, always under revision. This view opens the door to the possibility that we can each make distinctive *contributions* to the ebb and flow in the histories of our institutions. An emphasis on deadbeats, dullards, and derelicts' disasters, on the other hand, discourages us from believing that we can make a difference in the future course of our institutions. On this view, we either toe the line of Good or we do not. We are expected, on this view, to "not become part of the problem." That is a view hostile to the idea of distinctive worldly contribution.

Third, with a plurality of differences, centers, and margins, we can envision a future, framed by our institutions, that is distinctly different from, while still connected to, a particular past marked by particular institutions. In this temporal view, we can see the effects of our having contributed along the margins of our relationships with others. We can see our fingerprints, for better or worse, in our own times. And we can imagine our fingerprints, for better or worse, on the lives of those who follow us in the future. Accordingly, we can commit ourselves to living a life that is "good" in terms of the contributions we make.

An Ethics of Deadbeats, Dullards, and Derelicts' Disasters Driving the World Into Moral Decline, on the other hand, turns on a timeless Good that transcends our time and our marks on our world. This leaves very little room for leaving our own mark on the relationships that frame our lives, except to prevent Bad behavior and to isolate people who are prone to behaving badly. This version of "ethics from the outside" offers an impoverished conception of human beings' distinctive worldly contributions.

XVI

In sum, a Pragmatist Ethics of Differences, Centers, and Margins is an ethics about possibility. The heroes in that account are experimenters; they never stop experimenting in how they live in and through relationships. They experiment, moreover, in conversations and interactions with other experimenters in their neighborhoods. Both Calvin and Blondie are quintessential experimenters in this way. A Pragmatist Ethics of Differences, Centers, and Margins is a view in which human beings aspire and make adjustments in a world of inclusion and transformative possibilities.[124]

An Ethics of Deadbeats, Dullards, and Derelicts' Disasters Driving the World Into Moral Decline, by contrast, is an ethics about preserving some way of life against the threats posed by human beings who seek to experiment with their lives together. The heroes in this ethics are tyrants and the accomplices whom they employ as prison guards.[125] They never stop looking for ways to catch, incarcerate, and shame the deadbeats, dullards, and derelicts among us who are driving the world into moral decline. They relish the opportunity to deter the "experimenter" tendency in each of us, and to imprison us if we succumb to that urge. This is an ethics that trivializes human aspiration generally and, accordingly, trivializes any politics of inclusion. This is also an ethics that trivializes human adjustment and, accordingly, trivializes a politics of inclusion and institutional transformation.

A sharp metaphorical comparison wraps up the comparative case that I have been making for a Pragmatist Ethics of Differences, Centers, and Margins. By an ethics emphasizing deadbeats, dullards, derelicts, and decline, you have done well if you have found some method for controlling the number of mice running around your residence. By an ethics emphasizing differences, centers, and margins, you have done well if, from time to time, you and your contemporaries reexamine the practice of catching mice and then move from there together to face new questions about coexistence among human beings.[126]

XVII

I believe that now, years later, I have a better response to Senior about his proposal. That response goes something like this:

"I'll agree to work with you to arrange a guest speaker's appearance, on several conditions. First, let us agree that this speaker must say something that is accessible to everyone in the audience. This includes your classmates and my colleagues. I assume that business misdeeds and subsequent prison life do not pass this test of accessibility.

"Second, let us agree that this speaker must have something to say about ethics as a vehicle for creating something new in some corner of the world for the persons who occupy that corner. Someday, if penitent, the prisoner whom you have in mind might be able to do that. But let's find someone who right now lives a life that is both accessible to us *and* that is transforming others' lives in some way.

"I know that these conditions might, at first, seem to limit considerably our pool of candidates for guest speaker, but there is no reason to be discouraged. There are men and women in this town right now who are leaving their mark on their corners of the world. They do so by accommodating the many ways in which human beings live differently. They do so by acknowledging and helping amend the understandings they share with others. They do so by taking seriously their contributions to growing or failing relationships. In the process, they are making their marks on the business institutions in which they move.

"These persons practice what I call a Pragmatist Ethics of Differences, Centers, and Margins. For starters, here are the names and addresses of several persons who can share with us some thoughts about making business 'more ethical' in this contributory sense of the term 'ethical.' These are persons who lead lives that can open our minds to matters of inclusion and transformation—two political ideals long a part of our democratic processes. What do you say about this, Senior?"

I have probably lost my opportunity forever to persuade Senior with this perspective. As some alumni do, he has cut his ties with me, but I now realize that he has left a significant impression on me. "Of course we want business to be more ethical" is a more complicated matter than the "of course" might suggest.

From that conclusion, I now move to consider one more compelling reason why a Pragmatist Ethics of Differences, Centers, and Margins— justified with Senior's "assistance"—is a useful perspective on business institutions. That reason takes me to the customary way management educators talk about persons' distinctive contributions in business relationships (Chapter 3). In Chapter 2, I have shown the relative uselessness of an Ethics of Deadbeats, Dullards, and Derelicts' Disasters Driving the World Into Moral Decline as a preventative application of the logic of "ethics from the outside." In the next chapter, I reach the same conclusion about a manifestation of "ethics from the outside" in which bullying stakeholders is a popular sport.

3

The Stakeholder Containment Imperative

Corporate America has the Baldridge Award. The motion picture industry has the Oscar. Members of the recording industries in the United States and Canada confer the Grammy and Juno awards, respectively. College football players can be honored either with the Heisman Trophy or the Outland Award. Professional ice hockey has the Stanley Cup. Professional athletes can be honored with Most Valuable Player and Comeback Player awards. The world community has the Nobel Peace Prize. Each year, the University of Minnesota and the University of Iowa football teams play for the Floyd of Rosedale trophy.[1]

A comparable opportunity for public recognition has not been available to those people who are intrigued by ideas such as organizational design, leadership, motivation, human resources, and strategy. These people are students of management practice. Something can be done about the lack of public recognition for their accomplishments. In this chapter, I propose, defend, and nominate the inaugural winners of the Original Orthodoxy on Property (OOP-1) and Ordinary Ode on Privilege (OOP-2) awards for those who advance the study of management practice.[2]

II

The Original Orthodoxy on Property award honors groups of management students who create daring ("original") variations on the time-honored proposition that private property ("orthodoxy on property") enables business to serve society legitimately.[3] Qualifying for this award requires considerable agility. On one hand, nominees must

42

range far from the familiar cliches about the legitimacy of modern capitalism. Otherwise, they can do nothing original. On the other hand, nominees must march alongside their peers in their loyalty to the institution of private property.[4] The inscription on the award acknowledges such agility. It reads: "Got out of step, but not out of line."

The winners of the Original Orthodoxy on Property (OOP-1) award emulate two of Gary Larson's "Far Side" cartoon characters. One is the cow who pauses from grazing to issue, in amazement, an original proclamation, "Hey, wait a minute! This is grass! We've been eating grass!"[5] She then resumes grazing.[6] The other role model for OOP-1 is the dog Rex. In the middle of a high-wire circus act, Rex wrestles with "one nagging thought": "He was an old dog and this was a new trick."[7] Rex continues with the act. Like these two self-critical animals, winners of the Original Orthodoxy on Property award are honored both for taking a risky perspective on what has long been familiar and for doing so to confirm that familiar belief.

The Ordinary Ode on Privilege (OOP-2) award honors groups of management students for their reliance, with no particular special effort ("ordinary"), on tried-and-true defenses ("ordinary ode") of managerial prerogative ("ode on privilege") in an era when many of their peers are working furiously to create new justifications for managerial privilege.[8] Winners of this award must likewise display considerable agility.[9] On one hand, they must be conversant about the emerging odes to managerial privilege, so that they can distance their ordinary efforts from such revisionism. On the other hand, these self-styled "ordinary" defenders of managerial privilege must welcome changes in management practices. Such changes represent opportunities for these nominees to confirm their ordinary defense of managerial privilege. "Standing still is hard work" is the inscription on this award.

Winners of the Ordinary Ode on Privilege (OOP-2) award emulate the protagonists in two well-known, contemporary cartoon strips. One is the fictitious Hagar the Horrible, drawn now by Chris Browne. Hagar is a fictitious Viking and the epitome of managerial privilege. As he departs on yet another mission to plunder in Europe, he proclaims with little intellectual effort, "I'm off to make the world a better place in which to live." His wife, Helga, responds, "But only if you're a Viking."[10] In so doing, Helga reminds Hagar that he is speaking only from his privileged perch in the medieval world. The other character is, once again, Bill Watterson's Calvin ("Calvin & Hobbes"). Calvin sets up a sidewalk stand to sell one privileged view of the world. His product is "A Swift Kick in the Butt," which retails for one dollar.[11] Sales are nonexistent. When his pet tiger Hobbes asks why, Calvin sighs with the frustration of an "ordinary" defender of privilege, "Everybody I know needs what I'm selling."[12]

III

The OOPs awards might seem to honor very different deeds. Winners of the Original Orthodoxy on Property award stick out their necks. Winners of the Ordinary Ode on Privilege turn back the clock on management thought. Nonetheless, compelling evidence shows that members of *the same group* of management researchers deserve to win both the inaugural OOP-1 and OOP-2 awards.

These winners are the creators and proponents of four different approaches to research about corporate strategy: (1) competitor selection, (2) strategic groups, (3) collective strategy, and (4) game theory for managers.

These researchers win the inaugural OOP-1 award because they interpret corporate strategy in ways that highlight differences, centers, and margins. They take us to the doorstep of a novel proposition: Corporate strategy could be justified according to a Pragmatist Ethics of Differences, Centers, and Margins whereby each person's opportunity to make a distinctive worldly contribution is honored (see Chapter 2).[13] These award winners highlight differences between distinct strategists who have aims of their own choosing.[14] According to these award winners, strategy is a practice of continual interaction among strategists who have some degree of influence over each other. The marketplace is a center where these strategists act, respond, and respond anew. Consequently, the margin where progress is made, or not, by each strategist is located squarely in the relationships that they share with each other. Throughout this kind of account, corporate strategists are trying to make wise use of the corporate property that is entrusted to them.

This is an original approach for justifying corporate strategy as the use of private property. Customarily, researchers defend corporate strategy either on economic grounds as the search for economic rents, or on biological grounds as the struggle for organizational survival under Darwinian conditions.[15] These management students deserve OOP-1 because they advance, in their own novel ways, the proposition that a mainstream concept like corporate strategy can serve us well, "if we want business to be more ethical."

These same students of management win the inaugural OOP-2 award because they predicate their accounts on a corporate strategist's fear of other human beings. To people who claim privileged positions for themselves, the fear of losing such privilege is a constant companion.[16] In each of these four accounts about corporate strategy, corporate strategists are vulnerable creatures because other strategists are different and, hence by this logic, are suspicious people. They are also vulnerable because relationships with people who are different can be an uncertain phenomena, and because some unusual things can happen along the margins of human interactions. All these vulnerabilities are masked in these award-winning accounts by a recurring theme: A corporate strategist's pursuits should automatically take priority over another (different) strategist's pursuits.[17]

This defense of managerial privilege is about as ordinary as it gets, predicated as it is on the corporate strategist's fear of the influences of other people. One could read this modern-day defense of managerial privilege alongside the defenses of managerial privilege that Alfred Sloan and Andrew Carnegie provide in their autobiographies and come to the conclusion that time has stood still on the subject of managerial prerogative.[18] But these award-winning researchers do something that makes theirs even more ordinary odes to privilege.

These researchers depict corporate strategists who are busy building defenses around their positions of corporate privilege. This is a story of corporate strategists going beyond merely staking a claim to a privileged place for their aims. It is in fact a story about corporate strategists erecting tangible and unmistakable reminders to others about that privilege. For this twofold ordinary defense of managerial prerogative, the researchers who tell this story about corporate strategy earn the OOP-2 award.

My destination in this chapter is this conclusion:

> By winning the OOP-2 award, as ordinary defenders of managerial privilege, these students of management extinguish the encouragement that we can take from their winning the OOP-1 award as commentators who provide an original kind of argument for the use of private property.

This is a disappointing conclusion about corporate strategy, as we have come to know the idea. It is disappointing because these four award-winning accounts are the best that corporate strategy can offer, if "we want business to be more ethical" in a way that celebrates the democratic criterion of each person's distinctive worldly contribution (see Chapter 2). By contrast, the well-known rent-seeking and Darwinian justifications for corporate strategy do not take this kind of contribution seriously.[19] If these awards-winning accounts fail us in the campaign to make business "more ethical," then we have reason to ask why we should keep talking about corporate strategy at all. That reason is the platform on which I will make my argument in Chapter 4.

I move toward my destination for this chapter in four steps.

First, I will name this awards-winning genre about corporate strategy the "Stakeholder Containment Imperative." Accordingly, I will identify the awards-winning researchers as members of what I call the Containment Crew.

Second, I will interpret the Stakeholder Containment Imperative as one logical application of a Pragmatist Ethics of Differences, Centers, and Margins. It is this impeccable logic that earns the Containment Crew members the OOPs awards and, at the same time, disqualifies them from leading the "Of course we want business to be more ethical" campaign. I will call on the support of two recent literary figures to create this interpretation.

Third, I will link the Stakeholder Containment Imperative to a notorious institution of modern capitalism: the company town. The company town is the antithesis of a world in which each person's distinctive worldly contribution can count. In the company town, the corporate strategist earns an unflattering name. I will derive that name from an everyday human practice that is an ever-present threat to a world in which each person has room to make a distinctive worldly contribution.

Finally, I will show how competitor selection, strategic groups, collective strategy, and game theory for managers are all case examples of the Stakeholder Containment Imperative and are all case examples of the familiar Prisoner's Dilemma story. This link to the Prisoner's Dilemma is the undoing of the Stakeholder Containment Imperative, "if we want business to be more ethical."

IV

There are two reasons why I give the name "Stakeholder Containment Imperative" to the account that these awards winners tell and the name "Containment Crew" to the winners.

First, the Containment Crew members hold in common a keen interest in what the corporate strategist at one organization wants to know about the aims and capabilities of strategists at other organizations. These other strategists are the corporate strategist's *stakeholders*. This interest is a new twist on the familiar story of corporate strategy as the search for a lasting place for the corporation in the marketplace.[20] For paying attention so well to the stakeholders that a given strategist—who is entrusted with shareholders' property interests—expects to encounter, the Containment Crew wins the first Original Orthodoxy on Property award with an imperative about stakeholders.[21]

Second, these same researchers also hold in common a keen interest in the means by which any one strategist can lessen the influence of his or her stakeholders, the human beings with whom one necessarily interacts. This is a familiar theme sung by people of privilege everywhere. For paying attention so well to *containment of stakeholder influences,* in the name of preserving the corporate strategist's privileged position, the Containment Crew also wins the first Ordianry Ode on Privilege award.

V

The Stakeholder Containment Imperative is a story about corporate strategists who strive to turn the marketplace into the equivalent of a company town. That effort is based on a single powerful conception of differences: strength versus weakness.[22] The Containment Crew members tell a story in which the corporate strategist hungers for a position of strength, dreads positions of weakness, and applies his or her intellectual talents to satisfy that hunger and to quell that fear.

In the Stakeholder Containment Imperative story, a few shrewd corporate strategists can satisfy this hunger and quell this fear in a particular industry, if their many stakeholders remain relatively weak. Hence, the Stakeholder Containment Imperative deals with differences in terms of two caricatures of human beings. The strong (few) are recognizable for the purity of their aims. Those aims are pure simply because the strong corporate strategists believe in those aims. The weak (many) are recognizable for the relative poverty in their aims.[23] These are the corporate strategists' many stakeholders.

We can encounter these caricatures of differences in novels by Jan Kubicki and Brent Wade.[24] In *Breaker Boys,* Kubicki takes us to the coalfields of Pennsylvania in 1900. John Markham is the fictitious coal baron in the town of Jeddoh, Pennsylvania.[25] Markham invokes a "strong versus weak" worldview in this exchange with Mother Jones, the labor organizer:

> "The rights and interests of the working man," he replied calmly, "will not be protected by the likes of you, Mrs. Jones, but by good Christian men like myself to whom God, in his infinite wisdom, has given control of the property interests of this country."[26]

To Markham's claim of purity, Mother Jones responds with an expletive.

In *Company Man,* Brent Wade narrates the rise and fall of William ("Bill") Covington, a high-ranking executive at the fictitious Veratec Corporation. John Haviland is Veratec's CEO. He is also Covington's benefactor. Haviland invokes the caricatures of strength and weakness when he orders Covington to investigate labor unrest in a Veratec factory:

> "I want to squelch this whole thing as quickly as possible, and I need you to do it. I need you on the inside. It's time to take off your social worker's hat and put on your executive's hat. As far as I can see your responsibility is with the company, Bill."[27]

The executive's hat is a symbol of strength, in Haviland's mind. Social workers are weak, by implication, because they try to heal human schisms. Schisms run deep at Veratec, where Covington is the only high-ranking executive who shares an African-American heritage with the unhappy crew in the factory. "Strong versus weak" describes racial divisions at Veratec.

In *Breaker Boys,* Markham runs a company town in the fictitious village of Jeddoh.[28] Haviland, in *Company Man,* runs the equivalent at Veratec, a kind of plantation on which dark skin color invites suspicion.[29] Markham defends the purity of his aims as a "good Christian" property owner. Haviland defends the purity of his aims as a professional manager looking after other's property interests:

> "Look, Bill; this isn't a civil rights problem. I thought we'd discussed that [once before]. It's about doing business."[30]

Markham and Haviland are strong men, and they remain strong by treating the coal miners of Jeddoh and their families, and William Covington and the Veratec factory employees, respectively, as weak persons of impoverished aims. In sum, Markham and Haviland follow this imperative about differences: Keep your aims pure and keep others' aims in relative poverty. Kubicki and Wade thus help open our eyes to the part that differences play in the Stakeholder Containment Imperative.[31]

VI

The Containment Crew members build on the presumed difference between the strong (few) and weak (many) to locate the Stakeholder Containment Imperative in a colony run by the strong (few) corporate strategists. Colonies are centers in the Stakeholder Containment Imperative. They are places where corporate strategists can write and direct a script in which they, the strong people of pure aims, dominate their stakeholders, the many weak people of impoverished aims.

Two principal colonial activities take place in the Stakeholder Containment Imperative. First, the corporate strategist makes and enforces policies that govern interaction in the colony between himself and his stakeholders. Second, the corporate strategist takes steps to predict what his weak stakeholders could do to confound those policies. Through these policy-making and prediction activities, the corporate strategist seeks to preserve his company town. Once again, Kubicki and Ward create characters who can teach us a great deal about these colonial activities and about colonies as centers in the Stakeholder Containment Imperative.

The influence of John Markham's policies over life in Jeddoh is the subject of this exchange between Mother Jones and a lifelong resident of Jeddoh:

> "It appears that your John Markham has not only mined his coal but his miners as well," Mother said ruefully. "There is no hope in this town, no . . . no *life* left."
>
> "Even so, but without John Markham, there would be no Jeddoh now, would there? John Markham is Jeddoh."
>
> "I cannot deny that," Mother said with veiled sarcasm.[32]

Markham reinforces his policies by conducting surveillance on his townspeople. His agents in the campaign to predict what the miners will do next are the Coal and Iron Policemen, Sheriff William Frostbutter, and Ned the Splicer, his trusted foreman.

John Haviland maintains a similar grip on Veratec. Bill Covington wrote this about Haviland, the policymaker who craved control:

> He really was a remarkable businessman. But he made no attempt to address the legitimacy of the complaint, no attempt to understand how or why things had come to the point of combustion. It was a business problem to him. Truth didn't matter, responsibility was risk, understanding was in the way. He just wanted the whole thing to disappear, preferably on his terms.[33]

To get "the whole thing to disappear," Haviland enlists Covington in a campaign to predict what disgruntled plant workers will do next:

> "Let me be blunt, Bill; the guy I saw was black. So I have to believe what's going on involves blacks. I'd like you to ask around, see what you can find out."[34]

Trapped in this company town, Covington obeys.

Markham and Haviland are characters who understand centers. They prosper by presiding over a colony. They believe that they can continue to run their respective colonies as long as they follow this imperative about centers: Make policy and make predictions about the movements of people who could threaten that policy.[35]

VII

The Stakeholder Containment Imperative culminates in the corporate strategist's efforts, as a strong person of pure aims, to consolidate control over the segment of the marketplace that he or she seeks to colonize. Consolidation of control is the dependent variable in the Stakeholder Containment Imperative equation. The margin between strategic success and failure, according to the Containment Crew members, is the strategist's ability to consolidate gains through interaction with his (her) many weak stakeholders. The difference between a thriving company town and an unstable company town, on this view, is how well the corporate strategist accomplishes two consolidating activities.

First, the strategist who follows the Stakeholder Containment Imperative must placate his stakeholders. Colonizers know that they need compliant colonized peoples.[36] Otherwise, there is no colony over which they can consolidate control. Thus, they play along, as colonizers living alongside those whom they colonize. Second, the corporate strategist must be prepared to punish any stakeholders who get out of line. By the Stakeholder Containment Imperative, this threat of punishment must be a credible means for the strategist to maintain control over his company town. The strategist's ability to placate stakeholders and to punish stakeholders marks the margin on which the Stakeholder Containment Imperative succeeds or fails for the strategist. Kubicki and Ward tell stories about self-styled strong men who operate along this margin.

Markham and his family live in his company town of Jeddoh. Markham sends his daughters to the public school, where they mingle with the miners' sons and daughters. Indeed, the school has a first-rate blackboard shipped in from Philadelphia.[37] Markham also provides the miners and their families with churches and medical services. He pays for funerals of workers who die keeping his mines operating. He moves among his workers, telling them: "If you have a grievance . . . I have always taken time to listen."[38] Markham's friendship with Ned the Splicer, a man respected among the miners, is a public one.

Markham also stands ready to punish his stakeholders. Union organizers are evicted from their homes unceremoniously. Mysterious deductions from pay vouchers are weekly occurrences. Markham's Coal and Iron Policemen are thugs. When the miners' rebellion nears a climax at the coal breaker, Markham announces for all to hear:

> "As long as no man or boy brings harm to my property or anyone on it, . . . he need fear no retribution, and you have my word on that."[39]

Clearly, Markham styles himself as a man of the community who treats his stakeholders with a measure of benevolence, and as one who threatens to punish stakeholders in the name of his property rights.

Bill Covington was quite aware of John Haviland's skill at placating his stakeholders. Musing on how his career was tied to Haviland's benevolence, Covington writes to a friend:

> I'm certain his intention was to be a groundbreaker—the first executive to have a black on his staff. It was important for him to appear contemporary without seeming to threaten the infrastructure. He also knew that my loyalty was perhaps more assured than most, since his offer was the only one I was likely to receive. He knew I would have no real options.[40]

Those who were disloyal to Haviland were subject first to the subtle kind of punishment that co-worker Carl Rice describes to Covington:

> "And if you have the temerity to mention how racist it all is, they look at you and say, 'Racism? Where, I don't see any? Prove it.' And of course you can never prove it because they control the information! There's always enough of them to form a consensus on anything they want to disbelieve, regardless of fact."[41]

When pushed to the edge, Haviland followed up with a second kind of punishment. Rice is fired. Covington's career hits a dead end.

Markham and Haviland know full well that, as tyrants running their respective colonies, they are walking along the edge. Hence, they operate according to this imperative about the margin between success and failure: Placate your stakeholders even as you stand ready to punish them. Theirs is the story that the Containment Crew members have honed as a blueprint for corporate strategy.

VIII

The Stakeholder Containment Imperative is an ethics of bullying stakeholders. Indeed, the Stakeholder Containment Imperative honors strategic bullies. Bullies are human beings who deliberately try to deter other human beings from making distinctive worldly contributions. Thus, an ethical argument against the bully is also an ethical argument against the Stakeholder Containment Imperative.

Bullies presume that their projects are superior, precisely *because* these are their projects.[42] Bullies advance their projects by appropriating "support" from others. Bullies appropriate that support with an incessant intimidation campaign aimed at their victims. Sometimes that intimidation is physical. Most often, it is psychological. Bullies are shrewd. They know that their prosperity continues only if they have victims to intimidate. Hence, bullies must offer their victims sufficient inducement to stick around and be bullied.[43] Calvin's bully Moe ("Calvin & Hobbes") is a master at this. As Moe extorts Calvin's toy truck, he defends his bullying: "I'm not taking it. You're *giving* it to me because we'll both be so much happier that way."[44] Calvin can only sigh, "How touching." Moe and Calvin have settled into a tacit understanding—a convention, more precisely—through which Moe bullies Calvin over and over again.

Substitute "strategist" for "bully" and "stakeholder" for "victim" and you begin to get the basic idea of the Stakeholder Containment Imperative.[45] The Stakeholder Containment Imperative, as a prescription for strategic bullying, must be rejected on two counts, if "we want business to be more ethical."

First, this imperative is a cynical rejection of the relevance of "each person's distinctive worldly contribution." Bullies are not interested in contributing to the world. Their project is to prevent others from contributing to the world.[46] This rejection of contribution to the world looms large in each of the corporate strategy accounts that I will critique in the next section.

Second, the Stakeholder Containment Imperative turns on a kind of deception practiced by the strategic bully toward his stakeholders. The bully is smart enough to realize that others do not share his cynicism about contributing to the world. Hence, he finds ways to steer others' efforts to feed his own projects. By the Stakeholder Containment Imperative, stakeholders make their distinctive worldly contributions only insofar as they help the bully maintain his position of strength and refine his skill at bullying.[47] This hierarchical interpretation of "each person's distinctive worldly contributions" is the convention by which the corporate strategist works to sustain the Stakeholder Containment Imperative. And it is a convention that unites all four accounts of corporate strategy into the Stakeholder Containment Imperative. It is a convention that skews the meaning of "each person's distinctive worldly contribution" in such a way that all four accounts are disqualified as useful ways to promote the cause of "of course, we want business to be more ethical."

What follows is a case-by-case argument for that disqualification.

IX

The quintessential account of the Stakeholder Containment Imperative is the concept of competitor selection proposed by Michael Porter in his book *Competitive Advantage*. Competitor selection is predicated on the original idea that corporate strategists have good reason, as stewards of corporate property, to welcome certain strategists into their corner of the market.

Porter writes, "Competitors are both a blessing and a curse."[48] For articulating this blessed possibility, Porter and other proponents of competitor selection qualify for the OOP-1 award. At the same time, the caricatures, the colony, and the consolidation efforts that give meaning to the Stakeholder Containment Imperative are central to the logic of competitor selection. For perpetuating this ordinary celebration of managerial privilege, Porter and other proponents of competitor selection also win the OOP-2 award.

The caricatures of strength and weakness are central to the competitor selection account. Competitor selection is a story about a corporate strategist, so-called good competitors and so-called bad competitors.[49] Porter writes to one corporate strategist. He advises this strategist on the finer points of selecting good competitors in a world in which there is always some population of bad competitors.

There is never any question in the competitor selection story about whose pursuits are pure and whose pursuits are impoverished. The corporate strategist's endeavors are pure. The good competitor is "good" only insofar as she serves the interests of the corporate strategist. Porter observes:

> A good competitor is one that can perform the beneficial functions described above without representing too severe a long-term threat.[50]

Thus, the goodness of this competitor's pursuits is clearly a derivative matter.[51] Hers are good pursuits when she acts as a subordinate—in a position of relative weakness, that is—to the corporate strategist. Her pursuits have no legitimacy, however, outside that role of servitude. Evidently, hers are impoverished aims.

The bad competitor is just plain bad.[52] The corporate strategist cannot count on her to take the role of a subordinate. Hence, competitor selection is played out in a corner of the marketplace in which the corporate strategist seeks positions of relative strength at the expense of the relatively weak good competitors and bad competitors.

Competitor selection is a colonial act. It is a decision by a colonial governor to surround oneself with willing subjects. Competitors, both good and bad, are the colonized peoples. According to Kathryn Ruide Harrigan, in this setting, competitor selection is a key policy decision that a corporate strategist must make.[53] Good competitors and bad competitors do not simply fall into the strategist's lap.

The corporate strategist must decide who are his good competitors and who are his bad competitors in the specific industry circumstances in which he competes. A key part of this policy-making process is the strategist's skill at predicting what his competitors are doing. Prediction is a vital practice because competitors, both good and bad, are not standing still.[54]

Competitor selection policies contain provisions by which the corporate strategist seeks to consolidate his control over the competitors in his colony. He can consolidate control, according to Porter, by placating good competitors, turning bad competitors into good competitors, and attacking bad competitors who could not become good competitors.[55] The corporate strategist who governs this colony is no fool when it comes to dealing with good competitors. According to Porter, the effective corporate strategist "must allow good competitors enough successes to lead them to perpetuate their strategies. . . ."[56] This allowance is a central feature of the strategic convention by which the strategist and his good competitors get along. The upshot is that the difference between successful and unsuccessful competitor selection is the strategist's ability to placate and to punish his colonial subjects, and to know when the time is right to practice one act or the other.

Competitor selection is an anthem to bullying and to the heroism that the bully ascribes to himself. The corporate strategist who practices competitor selection looks his stakeholders squarely in their eyes. That much is an original orthodoxy on property. He then tries to bully those stakeholders into profitable submission that endures as a convention. That is an ordinary ode on privilege.

X

The concept of *strategic groups* is predicated on the original idea that corporate strategists, as stewards of corporate property, should welcome other stragegists who might travel with them in the same pack. Strategic groups are collections of strategists who, despite their own chosen aims, do enough things similarly that they form semipermanent social circles in the marketplace.[57] This is an original angle on the commonplace proposition that competitors are independent entities who act on profound disinterest in anything but their own operations. For articulating this new angle, proponents of strategic groups qualify for the OOP-1 award. At the same time, the caricatures, the colony and the consolidation efforts that give meaning to the Stakeholder Containment Imperative are central to the logic of strategic groups. For perpetuating this ordinary defense of managerial privilege, proponents of strategic groups also win the OOP-2 award.

The difference between strength and weakness is as plain as day in the strategic groups story. Corporate strategists who belong to a strategic group occupy positions of strength. Their aims are pure. The strategic groups story is written to, for, and about them.[58] The strategist's stakeholders within the strategic group occupy a position of weakness, relative to the strategist. All we know about them is that, for some moment in the sands of time, their pursuits suit the corporate strategist just fine.

On the other hand, the strategic groups story is not written to, for, or about the corporate strategist's stakeholders. Theirs is an impoverished existence in the marketplace. As for anyone else, such as the strategist's suppliers, who might participate in this corner of the marketplace, she might as well be doing business on another planet. There is nothing said about her aims, which are evidently too impoverished to warrant any space in the strategic groups story.[59]

Strategic group membership is a choice available to the corporate strategist. This choice is crucial because, as Karel Cool and Dan Schendel argue, strategic group membership can have profound implications for the performance of a corporation.[60] Run with the wrong crowd, the argument goes, and you could pay dearly for it.

Corporate strategists believe that they can prosper from membership in a strategic group, but they also believe that there is some stakeholder in that group who hungers for their place.[61] Thus, each corporate strategist must devise ways of monitoring and predicting stakeholder movements. Sharon Oster proposes a perspective for this typical colonial process:

> In the equilibrium analysis of strategic directions, firms will want to focus most heavily on members of their strategic groups and less on further-flung rivals.[62]

The colonial governor can never rest, because he can never forget that he is running a colony.[63]

The corporate strategist is no fool about the stakeholders who reside in the strategic group that he wants to govern. There are economic rents to be garnered by all who travel in a pack of competitors.[64] These rents are available precisely because the corporate strategist is surrounded by compliant neighbors.

The corporate strategist wants these compliant neighbors to stay put, and wants them to honor a convention through which he can continue to reap rents. He values stability within the strategic group almost as much as he values the rents that can be reaped. This is why strategic group policies must go hand in hand with an unambiguous corporate strategy. It is crucial that the corporate strategist placate these neighbors by playing an unmistakable hand consistently.[65]

Meanwhile, the corporate strategist must stand ready to deter unwelcome stakeholders from moving into the neighborhood. The entry of new competitors is the corporate strategist's nightmare.[66] Deterrents to that entry are the corporate strategist's "best friends." In the strategic group colony, the deterrents of choice are called *mobility barriers, entry barriers,* and *exit barriers.* Briance Mascarenhas and David Aaker prescribe this colonial defense system:

> The challenge for strategists is to create entry barriers into one's group while reducing exit barriers, and to recognize that different barriers may be needed to keep out potential competitors from differently positioned groups.[67]

This is a blueprint with which the corporate strategist seeks to consolidate his control over the colony. It is his plan for punishing pretenders to his colonial throne.

"Strategic groups" is an anthem to bullying and to the heroism that the bully ascribes to himself. The corporate strategist who practices according to strategic groups looks his stakeholders squarely in their eyes. That much is an original orthodoxy on property.[68] He then tries to bully these stakeholders into profitable submission that endures as a convention. That is an ordinary ode on privilege.

XI

Collective strategy is predicated on the original idea that a corporate strategist, as a steward of corporate property, should think of some of his competitors as potential soulmates with whom he can more safely travel the marketplace. This is another departure from the commonplace belief that competitors are, to apply the words of Elizabeth Wolgast, "social atoms."[69] For articulating this view on relations among strategists, proponents of collective strategy qualify for the OOP-1 award. At the same time, the caricatures, the colony, and the consolidation efforts that give meaning to the Stakeholder Containment Imperative are central to the logic of collective strategy. Therefore, proponents of collective strategy also qualify for the OOP-2 award. Theirs is one more ordinary rendition on the theme of managerial prerogative.

The corporate strategist who practices collective strategy craves a position of strength. Marc Dollinger observes: "Collective strategy attempts to overcome strategic weakness through interorganizational and collective activity."[70] Graham Astley urges that we look at these people as "statesmen."[71] A statesman is, of course, interested in the strength of his state. On the other hand, we only know that, as Astley put it, the strategist's stakeholders in the collective are "specific others."[72] Evidently, their aims are impoverished in relation to what the strategist is trying to accomplish as a statesman. That weakness makes them useful, of course, to the strategist who wants to be the statesman for the collective, and there is certainly no place in the collective strategy story for anyone who is not part of the collective. Their lives are presumably so impoverished that they are irrelevant to the strategist-who-would-be-a-statesman.

Collective strategy is a colonial act; it is a convention shared by members of some group of strategists whereby they can keep their colonized brethren at bay. In this vein, Dollinger notes:

> It represents a search for predictability and stability, an attempt to control the environment, and an attempt to negotiate order among organizations.[73]

A colonial governor also does this. Couple his thirst for control with the corporate strategist's unflagging belief in the rightness of his ways and you have the profile of a colonial governor. To consolidate their control over the colony, colonial governors must practice what Rudi Bresser and Johannes Harl describe as an ongoing act of agility:

> What is relevant is the ability to react to instabilities by switching from more collective forms of strategizing to more competitive ones, and vice versa.[74]

The corporate strategist who seeks to dominate the collective must be prepared to placate stakeholders in and beyond the collective, to punish these stakeholders, and to know when each act is appropriate for continuing his colonial power. Strategists placate by means of collective forms of "strategizing"; they punish by acting as competitors.

Collective strategy is an anthem to bullying and to the heroism that the bully ascribes to himself. Corporate strategists who practice collective strategy look their stakeholders squarely in the eye. That much is original orthodoxy on property. Then they try to bully these stakeholders into profitable submission that endures as a convention. That is an ordinary ode on privilege.

XII

Game theory for managers is predicated on the original idea that corporate strategists, as stewards of corporate property, should welcome the fact that other strategists are watching their every move and preparing responses accordingly. This is a welcome fact, ironically, because it opens up other strategists to being "picked clean" by corporate strategists who practice game theory for managers. For articulating this original idea, proponents of game theory for managers qualify for the OOP-1 award. At the same time, the caricatures, the colony, and the consolidation efforts that give meaning to the Stakeholder Containment Imperative are central to the logic of game theory for managers. For this perpetuation of managerial privilege, proponents of game theory for managers also qualify for the OOP-2 award.

The protagonist in the story of game theory for managers is the corporate strategist who can master the ins and outs of dominant strategies, equilibria, mixed strategies, game payoffs, first-mover advantages, credible commitments, and so on.[75] He is in a position of strength for mastery of these means to an end. The game theory for managers story is told to, for, and about this strategist.

On the other hand, the strategist's stakeholder in any given game is a bit player. We know that this stakeholder has strategic options, receives payoffs, values those payoffs in some hierarchy, and is sufficiently "streetwise" that she bases her moves on what the corporate strategist does. We know that this stakeholder always "rationally" prefers more of something to less of something. However, her aims are always subservient to the needs and desires of the corporate strategist.[76] Nowhere in the "game theory for managers story" is the slightest hint that this person's stakes are worthy per se.

Proponents of "game theory for managers" are so cavalier about the game stakeholder that their attempts to identify this person are self-defeating. Avinash Dixit and Barry Nalebuff caution corporate strategists that they might do things that will not win them the "love" of stakeholders.[77] The advice has no credibility. There is nothing in the "game theory for managers story" to suggest that the "other" game player has the slightest capability for love, or for that matter any other trace of humanity, other than the preference for more over less.

Game theory for managers is about the policies that the corporate strategist can pursue to derive rents for oneself. Sharon Oster reminds the strategist that economic rents are good things that happen to be fleeting.[78] They are fleeting because the "other" game player has sufficient capability, despite the impoverished nature of her aims, to encroach on the corporate strategist's territory and eventually reap some of those rents in the process.[79] For this reason, prediction of the other player's moves is a key task in the corporate strategist's policy-making process.

It is very important to the game-playing corporate strategist that the colony endure. In the game theory for managers story, strategists can hone their predictive skills if they are able to play the same kind of game repeatedly with their inferior stakeholders. This proposition about strategic prediction has been elevated to almost mythical status after Robert Axelrod observed certain "winning" patterns in experiments with the game called the Prisoner's Dilemma.[80] The corporate strategist likes repeated games, for they are breeding grounds for conventions. Those games, and the conventions that define them, enable corporate strategists to learn about their stakeholders' weaknesses and to prey on these weaknesses.

Proponents of game theory for managers know full well that they are advocating strategic bullying. And they know that bullies must have people around whom they can bully. Hence, some of these proponents feel compelled to remind corporate strategists that they must not chase away their colonial subjects. Game theory for managers can, in other words, contain a place for efforts to placate the strategist's stakeholders.

In this spirit, Keith Murnighan advises corporate strategists that trustworthy behavior, if practiced under circumstances favorable to the strategist, can pay dividends.[81] Robert Frank argues that passionate strategic behavior can win trust for the strategist.[82] Michael Porter advises strategists that the pursuit of maximum market share is not always a good thing for the strategist to do.[83] Murnighan, Frank, and Porter all advise corporate strategists to value strategic conventions by which strategists can keep playing games that are useful to them.[84]

Game theory for managers is not complete, however, without the corporate strategist's threat to punish the game stakeholder who does not know her place. In the game theory for managers story, game stakeholders always wear a *C* on their business suits. The *C* stands for cheater.[85] The game stakeholder is always presumed susceptible to temptations to cheat on the colonial arrangement that the corporate strategist oversees. This proclivity to cheat is one more manifestation of the inferiority of the stakeholder.[86] For this reason, the strategist's consolidation efforts are driven by a vocabulary of retaliation, deterrence, and other reminders of the strategist's power to punish colonized people who get out of line.[87]

Game theory for managers is an anthem to bullying and to the heroism that the bully ascribes to himself. Corporate strategists who practice game theory for managers look stakeholders right in the eye. That much is an original orthodoxy on property. Strategists then try to bully stakeholders into profitable submission that endures as a convention. That is an ordinary ode on privilege.

XIII

In the end, what is disappointing about the Stakeholder Containment Imperative is that it is the best that students of orthodox corporate strategy can offer to the "of course we want business to be more ethical" campaign. The promise of inclusion and the promise of institutional transformation are the twin building blocks of that campaign (see Chapter 1). For a fleeting moment, on the occasion of the inaugural Original Orthodoxy on Property award, it appeared that the Containment Crew members took seriously those building blocks. For a fleeting moment, one could believe that these students of management had broken free from the cynical orthodoxy of the familiar accounts of corporate strategy.

The Containment Crew members place relatively greater emphasis on inclusion of stakeholders than do the students of management who continue to tell stories about corporate strategy in the long-standing tradition of business policy. In the Stakeholder Containment Imperative, we see strategist and stakeholder looking each other in the eye. (Of course, the strategist is trying to intimidate the stakeholder.) By contrast, in such stories as dominant logic, resource-based strategy, and strategic management process, there is no pair of eyes into which the corporate strategist might look. You cannot include someone in a story about corporate strategy if you are not looking for that person in the first place. You cannot hold out hope that each person might make a distinctive worldly contribution if you do not first create a worldly place for him and her.

The Containment Crew members also place relatively greater emphasis on institutional transformation than do their counterparts who prefer the legacy of business policy. In the Stakeholder Containment Imperative, we see strategist and stakeholder sharing common ground in the marketplace and changing the face of that marketplace as they interact. (That common ground is, of course, a colony.) By contrast, dominant logic, resource-based strategy, and strategic management process are stories about strategists trying to transform only their own corporation.

It is for these two accomplishments, relative to their peers, that the Containment Crew members qualify for the inaugural Original Orthodoxy on Property award.

We can locate our greatest disappointment in the fact that the Containment Crew members also win the Ordinary Ode on Privilege award. That honor douses whatever spark of hope that we might take from the fact that these students of management won the Original Orthodoxy on Property award. Our hopes are dashed because the Containment Crew members are unable to break free from the temptation to place the corporate strategist in one of the most privileged roles that we can imagine.

You see, the corporate strategist in the Stakeholder Containment Imperative is the district attorney, the unseen jailer, in the Prisoner's Dilemma story. And that jailer has no interest whatsoever in the prospect that each person has a distinctive worldly contribution to make if given the latitude to do so.[88] Any generalized notion of distinctive worldly contribution has no place in a jailer's vocabulary.

The jailer in the Prisoner's Dilemma story knows all about differences. He thrives on the caricatures of strength and weakness. He operates from a position of strength. His aims are pure. He is, after all, the agent for the police power of the state. His prisoners are in a position of weakness. They are prisoners. They are suspected of criminal activity. Therefore the jailer must assume that the aims of his prisoners are impoverished. Otherwise, he could not practice as a jailer.

The jailer in the Prisoner's Dilemma also knows something about running a colony.[89] In the interrogation room, he is colonial governor. The jailer creates a policy that he believes will result in a confession from one of the two prisoners. In pursuit of a confession, he makes predictions about what kind of payoff the prisoners will find tempting.

The jailer in the Prisoner's Dilemma also knows something about consolidating control over a colony. He placates each prisoner with a seductive offer. "Confess, and you will get off lightly," he says to each prisoner. At the same time, he stands ready to punish the prisoner who will not talk. "Keep your mouth closed, and I'll throw the book at you," he says to each prisoner.

The Prisoner's Dilemma is not a story that is friendly to each person's distinctive worldly contribution. It serves precisely the opposite purpose.[90] The Stakeholder Containment Imperative is the Prisoner's Dilemma in disguise. The Stakeholder Containment Imperative is wholly unsuited to serve as our intellectual impetus if we want "of course, we want business to be more ethical" to advance the democratic ideals of inclusion and institutional transformation. The Prisoner's Dilemma is a blueprint for practicing coercion and tyranny in prison cells. The Stakeholder Containment Imperative serves the same function for the corporate strategist in the marketplace.

XIV

I conclude that the Stakeholder Containment Imperative deserves to be tossed onto the same compost pile of ideas where I tossed an Ethics of Deadbeats, Dullards, and Derelicts' Disasters Driving the World Into Moral Decline in Chapter 2. In so doing, I have given one more reason why the logic of "ethics from the outside" is a relatively useless rendition of "of course we want business to be more ethical." In two respects, the Stakeholder Containment Imperative is one more unfortunate example of the appeal of "ethics from the outside."

First, the Containment Crew members imply that a corporate strategist's pursuits are worthy simply because of that strategist's determination to participate intelligently in the marketplace. That is, the justification for the strategist's actions comes from a position *outside* the world of business in which he acts.[91] That "outside" position is the strategist's own resolve to be a better person. Moreover, the Containment Crew members want us to believe that the strategist's stakeholders are incapable of acting with a comparable degree of determination. That is why we learn little in the Stakeholder Containment Imperative about each stakeholder as a human being. Indeed, the Stakeholder Containment Imperative is an interplay between a select few corporate strategists, who are deemed moral agents, and many stakeholders, who are deemed something else.

On this view, nothing about the corporate strategist's interactions with stakeholders matters when it comes to justifying the strategist's efforts. On this view, he need not defend his actions "inside" the world of business relationships in which he operates. By the Stakeholder Containment Imperative, the strategists who select competitors, who decide on who their strategic "groupies" are, who decide who is in the collective and who is not, and who meet the anonymous other game player are all *automatically* justified in their pursuits. What they actually do in relation to these other strategists, such as impose irreversible costs, has no relevance to the ethical defense of their strategic pursuits, according to the Stakeholder Containment Imperative. These strategists are above and "outside" all that, by the logic of "ethics from the outside."

Second, because the stakeholders who are contained in the Stakeholder Containment Imperative are presumably second-class moral beings, there is no reason for the corporate strategist to mingle with them any more than is necessary. After all, a colonial governor dare not apear too intimate with his subjects. Thus, the Containment Crew members set most of their stories inside the colonial mansion, "outside" of the world in which the strategist meets stakeholders. True, the Stakeholder Containment Imperative is a tale about conventions by which corporate strategists interact with their stakeholders. But, as in any colony, those conventions are not open to question, much less justification in worldly terms.

This story line is one more reason why we know next to nothing about the competitors who are selected, who do not belong to the strategic group and the collective, and who are the other game players. They are there; that's all. Hence, strategists and stakeholders are strangers in the story told by the Containment Crew members. This distancing of the corporate strategist from the world of human interaction—along with the assumption that stakeholders are second-class citizens—is a telltale sign of "ethics from the outside."

XV

The way is now cleared for me to create a new story about corporate strategy. That story will turn on the logic of "ethics already through and through" (see Chapter 1). This is the subject of Chapters 4 and 5.

The accomplishments of the Containment Crew members are, ironically, a justification for starting all over in our thinking about corporate strategy. By winning the OOP-1 and OOP-2 awards, these students of management have unwittingly given us reason to question their original orthodox accounts, their ordinary orthodox accounts, and, by virtue of their accomplishments, all of orthodox corporate strategy. If we want "we want business to be more ethical" to mean something other than managerial privilege and the Prisoner's Dilemma in disguise, then we must move past the Stakeholder Containment Imperative. Both winners and losers alike in the OOPs competition have dropped the ball. OOPs, indeed.

4

Ethics and a Retrieval of Corporate Strategy

The conversation in class that morning was getting tedious. The subject was affirmative action. More than a few of my students were resisting the question that I had posed for our discussion: "Why is affirmative action so controversial in these times?" These students eagerly wanted instead to answer some version of their own question: "How can we express our unhappiness with affirmative action?" They filled the air with a familiar rhetoric: "Affirmative action undermines merit. White males are becoming victims. Employees should be evaluated on objective standards, just like we are graded. People should wait their turn; there are plenty of opportunities. White males were here first. Racial and gender preferences are not necessary any more in America." You get the idea. I admit that I was frustrated for the entire ninety-minute session. Afterward, on an afternoon walk around campus, I asked myself, "Do I really want to keep teaching a case about affirmative action in this course?" It was then that I replayed in my head her comments in class.

I will call her Searcher.[1] She came from privilege. The business world had been good to her family. The business world had also driven a deep chasm in that family. She was bitter about that. She styled herself as a Young Republican, yet she was uneasy with the cliches that many of her peers were glibly delivering that day.

Merit appealed to Searcher. She made that point quite emphatically. At the same time, she was quick to acknowledge that many persons lacked opportunities to play with her on the level playing field where she thought merit applied. Objective standards of merit appealed to Searcher. She very much wanted to emphasize that, too, yet she knew from her family's business experiences, and from working as a teaching assistant for a professor whom she trusted, that objective merit was a fiction. Searcher was busy that semester calling on family connections as she sought corporate employment in a major East Coast city. She felt no guilt in doing that, she said. Yet she empathized with friends who were members of minority groups. She knew that such corporate connections were beyond the reach of many of those classmates owing to historical reasons that they had inherited.

Searcher was trying to reconcile aloud these conflicting thoughts. In class that day, the restlessness was palpable among her Young Republican peers. They did not want to venture where she was headed. What she was trying to do, and was unable to do that day, was retrieve merit as an idea that could be useful then in the late 1980s, rather than worship merit as an idea that we inherited from the 1880s or 1950s. The possibility that Searcher is not alone in her intellectual struggle is one good reason why I keep teaching a case about affirmative action each year.

II

This chapter is an exercise in intellectual retrieval. The idea that I want to retrieve is "of course we want business to be more ethical." I am now ready to retrieve this idea from the clutches of those who advocate an Ethics of Deadbeats, Dullards, and Derelicts' Disasters Driving the World Into Moral Decline—a particular ethics of prevention—and from those who advocate the Stakeholder Containment Imperative—a particular ethics of bullying stakeholders—as ways to make business "more ethical." I cleared the way for this retrieval effort in Chapters 2 and 3, arguing there that we should toss an ethics of prevention and an ethics of bullying stakeholders onto the compost pile of ideas that do not help us link business and ethics. "Of course we want business to be more ethical" is an idea waiting for a useful meaning, awaiting intellectual retrieval.

I develop my retrieval project here under the influence of Charles Taylor, who set these parameters on the retrieval that he attempts in a recent book:

> The picture that I am offering is rather that of an ideal that has degraded but that is very worthwhile in itself, and indeed, I would like to say, unrepudiable by moderns. So what we need is neither root-and-branch condemnation nor uncritical praise; and not a carefully balanced trade-off. What we need is a work of retrieval, through which the ideal can help us restore our practice.[2]

Retrieval is the hard intellectual work of ensuring that a valued idea remains resilient. It is hard intellectual work in two respects. First, to set out to retrieve an idea is to admit that there is something problematic—"degraded," in Taylor's terms—about the place for that idea in the vocabulary used by the members of some community. Second, to retrieve an idea is to move from this self-critical admission to create some new meaning that is an improvement over the problematic meaning, all the while holding a place for the idea in the vocabulary of that community.[3] For Taylor, authenticity is the "worthwhile" idea. For Searcher, the worthwhile idea was merit. For me in this book, a worthwhile and retrievable idea is "of course we want business to be more ethical."

Retrieval is testimony to our belief in the power of ideas. This means that retrieval differs greatly from reiteration.[4] Reiteration is the comparatively easier attempt to cling to relics of ideas. Searcher was traveling the road of retrieval. Reiteration was the project of her classmates, who were merely repeating their beliefs that affirmative action should be equated with assaults on merit and white males. Searcher was already sold on the futility of exercises in reiteration.

III

The distinction between retrieval and reiteration is a useful way to watch what happens next at two well-known American corporations: Denny's Restaurants and Wal-Mart. The Denny's name has been associated recently with institutionalized racism, and hefty fines and settlements were paid for alleged racist acts at certain Denny's locations.[5] It is difficult to imagine how some prior "ideal" about the Denny's business could ever be reiterated. It will be instructive to watch whether Denny's management pursues reiteration, or pursues some retrieval course to continue with the Denny's business, *given* the facts that Denny's was not always associated with racism *and* that Denny's has now been associated with it.[6]

Similarly, Wal-Mart executives have entered a crossroads between reiteration and retrieval. More often than not these days, when the Wal-Mart name appears in the media, it is associated with campaigns to halt the opening of another Wal-Mart in some corner of Small Town America.[7] It is difficult to imagine how this perspective about Wal-Mart will fade any time soon. Whether Wal-Mart executives seek to reiterate the Sam Walton icon, or practice retrieval by adapting Walton's heralded service philosophy to the 1990s, is an interesting question to follow. Now that the "Wal-Mart way" has been questioned so publicly, and now that others can offer comparably enthusiastic service on such a large scale of retailing, there is room for some kind of retrieval effort.[8]

In both cases, there is prima facie reason to maintain a valued way of talking about the world, such as the Wal-Mart way of retailing. In both cases, too, there is good reason for those who share a vocabulary about the world to revise the meaning of a valued idea. In that way, the idea can better serve them under revised circumstances. This kind of juncture is where we are torn between our past and our future ways of talking. This kind of juncture is where we can test our intellectual mettle.

IV

My aim from the very first page of this book has been to create a vocabulary for talking about business and ethics that is accessible to those who speak in many different vocabularies. In Chapter 1, I named politicians, executives, journalists, taxi drivers, and professors as members of a diverse audience, as users of many different vocabularies whom I want to persuade with my vocabulary. That listing was no mere rhetorical flourish. We are all touched by what happens in the business world. We all have an interest in talking about business and ethics.[9]

Now, as I set out to retrieve "of course we want business to be more ethical," it might appear that I have set myself up for difficulty in reaching those human beings who use one vocabulary in particular. I refer to the executives, journalists, and professors—and, more and more these days, health care professionals, major league baseball players, public school educators, politicians, and coaches—who converse in the vocabulary that I like to call "business talk." In Chapters 2 and 3, I made it my project to discredit thoroughly a wide swath of business talk as a useful way to make business "more ethical."

A prime target in that critique was the idea of "corporate strategy." Corporate strategy is a central part of modern business talk. Corporate strategy has become the wellspring of guidance about how to run a business through marketing, manufacturing, human resources, and financing activities. Because corporate strategy is such a significant idea in the way many people talk about business, it might appear that I have turned my back on them and the vocabulary that they prefer to use. However, I am not going to let that happen. Instead, I plan to give special attention, as I work to retrieve "of course we want business to be more ethical," to the very people who have long been accustomed to talking about business in terms of corporate strategy.[10]

Hence, I am about to take a most ironic step. For the rest of this chapter, I will dig into the very compost heap of ideas on which I piled, in Chapters 2 and 3, an Ethics of Deadbeats, Dullards, and Derelicts' Disasters Driving the World Into Moral Decline and the Stakeholder Containment Imperative. Standing knee-deep in that compost pile, I will proceed not only to dig out corporate strategy, but I will make corporate strategy the *centerpiece* for my retrieval of "of course, we want business to be more ethical."

This means that I will retrieve "of course, we want business to be more ethical" by retrieving corporate strategy from the clutches of the logic of "ethics from the outside." Along the way, I will retrieve two ideas that are associated with corporate strategy: the idea of "game" and the idea of "strategic convention." Like corporate strategy, game and strategic convention were primary targets of my critique in Chapter 3 of the Stakeholder Containment Imperative. Retrieved meanings of game and strategic convention occupy central places in my retrieval of corporate strategy.

V

My plan of retrieval is to tell a story about corporate strategy, games, and strategic conventions with a logic of "ethics already through and through." I sketched this logic in Chapter 1 as a rival to a logic of "ethics from the outside." My claim is that "ethics already through and through," as one variation of a Pragmatist Ethics of Differences, Centers, and Margins, enables us to do what we cannot do with "ethics from the outside."[11] With my retrieved story about corporate strategy, which I call Strategy Through Convention, each person's distinctive worldly contribution will not only be plain to see but will be a celebrated possibility. As I have argued, "ethics from the outside" fails us if we want to celebrate that possibility. In short, Strategy Through Convention is a way to replace a logic of "ethics from the outside" in our accounts about business and ethics.

I conduct my project to retrieve corporate strategy with Strategy Through Convention in three parts. In each, I introduce a new idea with which I activate a logic of "ethics already through and through:"

1. *Accomplishments, one's autonomy stakes,* is an idea about differences.
2. *Common grounds, contingent memberships,* is an idea about centers.
3. *Conducive connections, self-restrained accomplishments,* is an idea about margins.

I will develop these ideas by linking Strategy Through Convention to corporate strategy, even as I separate Strategy Through Convention from corporate strategy as we know it. Therein is my project of retrieval.

Part of each of these three ideas can be friendly, I argue, to the way in which students of management are accustomed to talking about corporate strategy. Accomplishments, common grounds, and conducive connections are present, in spirit if not verbatim, in the everyday vocabulary of corporate strategy. The second part of each new idea, on the other hand, will look menacing to students of management practice. One's autonomy stakes, contingent memberships, and self-restrained accomplishments are unwelcome in the vocabulary of corporate strategy as we know it. These unwelcome ideas are the active ingredients with which we can place "ethics already through and through" each strategist's life and thereby celebrate each person's distinctive worldly contribution. In short, these three new ideas are the active ingredients in my retrieval vocabulary for corporate strategy.

This plan for an ethical retrieval of corporate strategy is outlined in Figure 4–1.

STRATEGY THROUGH CONVENTION

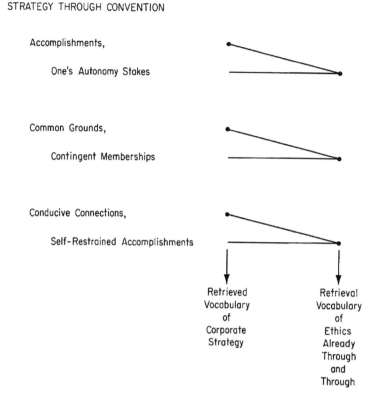

Figure 4–1. Strategy Through Convention as a retrieval of corporate strategy

In each part of the retrieval effort, I will introduce a new idea in the form of a proposition about what a vocabulary for corporate strategy should include, if "we want business to be more ethical" in a way that celebrates each person's distinctive worldly contribution. Then I translate each proposition into an ethical question for which distinctive human beings can seek answers as they practice corporate strategy. These inquisitive human beings are the central figures in the story of Strategy Through Convention. The result will be a three-part logical framework for Strategy Through Convention. In Chapter 5, I will add one more layer of meaning to that framework.

I will go to great lengths to make this new vocabulary understandable for those persons who are accustomed to talking about corporate strategy, games, and strategic conventions, and business more generally. My "partners" in this retrieval effort include a number of contemporary writers who pay special attention to accomplishments, common grounds, and conducive connections. My "partners" also include two well-known literary characters. One is Ray Kinsella, the fictitious hero of W.P. Kinsella's novel *Shoeless Joe,* and "Field of Dreams," the movie based on this novel.[12] The other is George Babbitt, protagonist in Sinclair Lewis's novel *Babbitt*.[13] We can get to know Ray Kinsella and George Babbitt as characters who live their lives by means of the three ideas with which I will pursue a retrieval of corporate strategy and, hence, a retrieval of "of course, we want business to be more ethical."[14] Ray Kinsella and George Babbitt might seem like an unlikely duo. They are, in fact, charter members of the Strategy Through Convention story.

VI

The first proposition of Strategy Through Convention is:

> If we want to take seriously, through our accounts about business and ethics, each person's distinctive worldly contribution, then it stands to reason that we must create a lasting place in those stories for each person's distinctive life, and we can do this by creating a lasting place in our stories for each person's accomplishments, by which each stakes a claim to a distinctive life.

I call the central idea in this proposition, *accomplishments, one's autonomy stakes*, which is one building block of my Strategy Through Convention story. With the idea of accomplishments, one's autonomy stakes, I create a lasting place for differences in my particular story about business and ethics.

Autonomy is a claim to think and act differently from anyone else.[15] A lifetime of efforts at accomplishment is a prime avenue for staking this claim to a distinctive life. What I try to accomplish through this proposition is a story about business and ethics that contains a fascinating array of distinctive lives unfolding over time. With this idea, an idea that advances a Pragmatist Ethics of Differences, Centers, and Margins, I can begin to tell a new story about business and ethics.[16]

Strategy Through Convention is a story in which each human being activates the idea of accomplishments, one's autonomy stakes, by living in search of answers to this question:

> What do I/you/she/he seek to accomplish and why is that the mark that I/you/she/he want(s) to leave on the world?

I call this an Autonomy Through and Through Question. No matter which way the characters of Strategy Through Convention turn, they deal unavoidably with this question and, hence, they live with the ethical matter of differences clearly in mind. That is, this particular ethical concern—a concern with charting a course for accomplishments that are one's own—already runs "through and through" their worldly existences. It already runs through and through the lives of Ray Kinsella and George Babbitt.

The fictitious Kinsella wrestles with self-doubts about his accomplishments—past and prospective—as a farmer, a husband, and a father. Ray Kinsella sets out to answer in earnest what I call an Autonomy Through and Through Question when he transforms a cornfield into a baseball field. Once he accomplishes that, he is drawn closer to the lives of a reclusive writer, a small-town doctor, a lonely storyteller, his wife, Annie, and a man shunned long ago by the baseball establishment. In their own distinctive ways, these characters hold in common a belief in the magic of the game of baseball. Like Ray Kinsella, they each seek to accomplish something through that belief in baseball, accomplishments that leave distinct marks on the world. Along the way, Ray Kinsella runs headlong into two men who are not touched by the magic of baseball: his wandering twin brother and a bullying brother-in-law. Without this belief, the brother and the brother-in-law fail to live lives of accomplishment and autonomy. They leave no mark on their world.[17]

Babbitt, the novel, concludes with Babbitt, the man, admitting to his son, Ted:

> "Now, for heaven's sake, don't repeat this to your mother, or she'd remove what little hair I've got left, but practically, I've never done a single thing I've wanted to in my whole life! I don't know's I've accomplished anything except just get along."[18]

Ted and his wife, Eunice, have just accomplished something more daring than George Babbitt ever could. They eloped. In so doing, they accomplished an act of defiance to social convention in the city of Zenith. In truth, Babbitt saw himself as a man without accomplishments long before Ted and Eunice eloped:

> He saw the years, the brilliant winter days and all the long sweet afternoons which were meant for summery meadows lost in such brittle pretentiousness. He thought of telephoning about leases, of cajoling men he hated, of making business calls and waiting in dirty anterooms—hat on knee, yawning at fly-specked calendars, being polite to office-boys. "I don't hardly want to go back to work," he prayed. "I'd like to—I don't know."[19]

Babbitt could not look to his cohorts for assistance in his plight. They, too, were failing to lead lives of accomplishment. Paul Riesling, the Good Fellows, Babbitt's wife, Myra, and Tanis Judique and the aptly named Bunch were all stumped when it came to envisioning, much less living, lives of accomplishments. Indeed, some of Babbitt's cohorts did not understand the ideas of accomplishment and autonomy in the first place.

I draw inspiration for accomplishments, one's autonomy stakes, from what a number of contemporary writers have accomplished in their own thinking about accomplishments. These sources of inspiration include:

1. Each person's "call to be more than they presently are," as John Cowan puts it[20];

2. A life of "absorbedness—in defiance of death," as Donald Hall portrays his fervor to write[21];
3. "Being-in-relation," as Judith Jordan and her colleagues name one feminist perspective on putting together one's own psychological life[22];
4. Independence as a human capacity to practice what Nona Lyons and her colleagues term a "morality of care"[23];
5. Self-creation, and the associated fear that we might let ourselves become mere replicas of someone else, as Richard Rorty portrays a pragmatist version of private life[24];
6. Each person's concern with "the point of my life," as Charles Taylor describes authenticity[25];
7. The specter of a "nihilistic threat" among black Americans that, Cornel West worries, can render human beings utterly powerless in their own everyday spheres[26];
8. The moral autonomy that marks one's passage into adulthood, as Elizabeth Wolgast argues.[27]

What I am able to accomplish with accomplishments, one's autonomy stakes, is homage to what Cowan, Hall, Jordan and Lyons and their respective colleagues, Rorty, Taylor, West, and Wolgast have accomplished. They enable me to nominate Ray Kinsella and George Babbitt as heroic figures in my project to retrieve corporate strategy by means of accomplishments, one's autonomy stakes.

VII

The second proposition of Strategy Through Convention is:

> If we want to take seriously, through our accounts about business and ethics, each person's distinctive worldly contribution, then it stands to reason that we must create a lasting place in those stories for each person's worldly life, and we can do this by creating a lasting place in those stories for each person's belonging on particular pieces of common ground that are each shared and jointly shaped with another distinctive person, memberships by which each person lives in this world.

I call the central idea in this proposition, *common grounds, contingent memberships.* Common grounds, contingent memberships, is a second building block of my Strategy Through Convention story. With the idea of common grounds, contingent memberships, I create a lasting place for centers in my particular story about business and ethics.

Membership on common ground is a center through which a human being seeks to live a life of accomplishment. Accordingly, common ground is where a person can accomplish something that is a contribution to the world. By this idea of common ground, a human being accomplishes something always in relation to another human being, and only in relation to another human being.[28] There is no "going it alone." There is, instead, for each person a life of memberships on different pieces of common ground.

By this second proposition of Strategy Through Convention, each membership on common ground is a different experience for a person. Each piece of common ground bears the distinct imprint of what two particular human beings bring to their common ground, what they do on that common ground, and what their neighbors are doing on their own pieces of common ground. Hence, Strategy Through Convention is a story of a life of belonging to common ground that is contingent on what persons are doing on, and in the vicinity of, the place that they share in time. What I try to accomplish through this proposition is a story about business and ethics that contains a fascinating array of distinctive lives unfolding over time in a fascinating array of common grounds. Common grounds, contingent memberships, is an idea that further advances a Pragmatist Ethics of Differences, Centers, and Margins. With it, I can extend my new story about business and ethics to emphasize relationships as places where persons can make their contributions to the world.

Strategy Through Convention is a story in which each human being activates the idea of common grounds, contingent memberships, by living in search of answers to this question:

> Given the search for accomplishments that I conduct, and my anticipation of your response to that search, and given the search for accomplishments that you conduct, and your anticipation of my response to that search, what kind of common ground can we come to share and shape over time as something that is ours to which we belong as members?

I call this a Contingent Memberships Through and Through Question. No matter which way the characters of Strategy Through Convention turn, they deal unavoidably with this question and, hence, they live with the ethical matter of centers clearly in mind. In this way, a particular ethical concern with centers already runs "through and through" their worldly existences. Common grounds, contingent memberships, already runs through and through the lives of Ray Kinsella and George Babbitt.

The novel *Shoeless Joe* moves inexorably toward the time when Ray Kinsella and his father share some common ground. The father, Johnny Kinsella, makes the first move by participating in the baseball games on the field that Ray constructed. Ray Kinsella finally summons the courage to make a gesture of interest in membership with Johnny. He finds that courage, in no small way, as a consequence of the memberships that he helps solidify on common grounds with his wife, Annie, with a reclusive writer, and with an aging ballplayer who lives nearby. Throughout the story, Kinsella the novelist makes it possible for us to visit many common grounds. Each piece of common ground is under constant revision through the joint efforts of the inquisitive characters who meet there.[29]

The fictitious George Babbitt was the quintessential belonger. He held membership in every civic institution that would have him in the fictitious Zenith.[30] But none of that participation prepared Babbitt for the existential crisis that shook his life to the very core. Contingent membership on common ground was something that Babbitt and his Good Fellow comrades very much feared. They wanted an assured kind of common ground. They wanted the complexities of the world to stay away.

It took a crumbling friendship with Paul Riesling and a period of estrangement from Babbitt's wife, Myra, for George Babbitt to realize that he was inescapably accountable for what happened on each plot of common ground that he shared with another human being. In the end, he was "saved" from that lesson in contingent memberships. Babbitt's Good Fellow comrades welcomed him back into their cocoon.

I draw inspiration for common grounds, contingent memberships, from what a number of contemporary writers have accomplished in their own thinking about common grounds. These sources of inspiration include:

1. The "telltales" of what a relationship could entail, as John Cowan calls the "small decencies" of human exchange[31];
2. Moral problems as "fractures" of the common grounds that two persons share, as Nona Lyons and her colleagues put it[32];
3. The "worst day" when, as Donald Hall frets, the possibility is very real that two human beings will never again share the common ground that they have shared[33];
4. Each "us" into which we can welcome another human being whom we previously considered one of "them," as Richard Rorty proposes a pragmatist might lead a public life[34];
5. Attentiveness and responsiveness to others as a blueprint for "all of life activity," as Janet Surrey and her colleagues frame a life in relation to specific other human beings[35];
6. The modern carelessness about common grounds that Charles Taylor terms a willingness to accept a politics of "soft despotism"[36];
7. The jazz metaphor that Cornel West uses to sketch a "grass roots" recovery from racial tensions in America[37];
8. Justice as a concept that we learn only through the particular common grounds that are our life histories, as Elizabeth Wolgast conceives of justice.[38]

What I am able to accomplish with common grounds, contingent memberships, is homage to what Cowan, Hall, Lyons and her colleagues, Rorty, Surrey and her colleagues, Taylor, West, and Wolgast have all accomplished. They enable me to nominate Ray Kinsella and George

Babbitt as heroic figures in my project to retrieve corporate strategy with the idea of common grounds, contingent memberships.[39]

VIII

The third proposition of Strategy Through Convention is:

> If we want to take seriously, through our accounts about business and ethics, each person's distinctive worldly contribution, then it stands to reason that we must create a lasting place in those stories for each person's life of making contributions, and we can do this by creating a lasting place in those stories for each person's self-restrained acts of belonging, acts of accomplishment that happen to make a difference for the connections—(a) on each piece of common ground between the two distinctive persons who share that common ground and (b) on neighboring pieces of common ground between the two distinctive persons who share each of those pieces—that can be conducive for each to accomplish what one autonomously prefers to accomplish, self-restrained accomplishments by which each person lives a life of contributions to the lives of other human beings.

I call the central idea in this proposition, *conducive connections, self-restrained accomplishments*. Conducive connections, self-restrained accomplishments, is a third building block of my Strategy Through Convention story. With the idea of conducive connections, self-restrained accomplishments, I create a lasting place for margins in my particular story about business and ethics.

Connection is crucial for the two human beings who belong to a piece of common ground. By the second proposition of Strategy Through Convention, what happens on that common ground is inevitably a joint endeavor; it is a matter of what I do *and* you do. By this third proposition of Strategy Through Convention, the difference between, on one hand, a context that is conducive for the accomplishments that each member seeks to make in life and, on the other hand, a context that is frustrating for those pursuits is found in the strength of their continuing ties to each other. This means that the difference between each person's own accomplishment and own frustration is the relative strength of what they hold in common on their common ground. The margin—the deciding factor that each helps shape—is the strength of their solidarity as human beings.[40]

The strength of connection between members of a piece of common ground is their joint responsibility.[41] That follows from the second proposition of Strategy Through Convention. Given the utmost importance of their connection, it is plain to see that each must seek his and her own accomplishments in a manner that strengthens the connection. Self-restrained accomplishment is the name that I give to that kind of search.

This practice of self-restrained accomplishment is crucial in two settings. One is a local one.[42] On any given piece of common ground, if each person there can accomplish something important to her in a way that also contributes to the continuation of one's ties on each person's common ground, then a life of accomplishment, not frustration, for those two parties is better assured.

The second context is a neighborhood. The third proposition of Strategy Through Convention is predicated on the premise that what happens on one piece of common ground can readily spill over onto what happens to the two persons who belong to a "nearby" piece of common ground. If both can live a life of self-restrained accomplishment that enables their neighbors to do likewise, the reasoning goes, then the pathway is cleared for members and neighbors alike to make their distinctive worldly contributions. In both settings, self-restrained accomplishment makes all the difference in the world.

In my Strategy Through Convention story, accomplishment is inextricably linked with contribution. By conducive connections, self-restrained accomplishments, accomplishment is a practice of voluntary self-restraint. One accomplishes only insofar as one contributes to lives of others who share membership on pieces of common ground. What I try to accomplish through this proposition is a story about business and ethics that contains a fascinating array of distinctive persons engaged in self-restrained searches for things to accomplish, through which they strengthen their ties to one another, now and for times of accomplishment ahead. With this idea about conducive connections, as idea that further advances a Pragmatist Ethics of Differences, Centers, and Margins, I can enhance a new story about business and ethics to celebrate a world of human connections.

Strategy Through Convention is a story in which each human being activates the idea of conducive connections, self-restrained accomplishments, by living in search of answers to this question:

> What understanding do I and you in the course of our ongoing, mutually contingent interaction, and I and her in the course of that ongoing, mutually contingent interaction, and you and him in the course of that ongoing, mutually contingent interaction, create through our respective interactions, ratify and reaffirm every time we seek accomplishments in our lives and thereby participate on our common grounds, and without which neither I nor you nor she nor he could continue participating on our respective common grounds?

I call that a Self-Restrained Accomplishments Through and Through Question. No matter which way the characters of Strategy Through Convention turn, they deal unavoidably with this question and, hence, they live in constant awareness about the ethical matter of margins that spell the difference between accomplishment and frustration. This particular ethical concern with margins already runs "through and through" their worldly existences.

The characters of Strategy Through Convention answer my Self-Restrained Accomplishments Through and Through Question in terms of particular understandings that can be conducive to their searches for accomplishments. These understandings are evidence for the ties that two members share on their common ground. These understandings are the "names" that two persons can give to the contingent memberships that they share and that are crucial for their lives of accomplishment. These understandings are the particular margins through which human beings accomplish whatever they accomplish in Strategy Through Convention. The lives of Ray Kinsella and George Babbitt are vivid cases in point.

The fictitious Ray Kinsella and Annie Kinsella share an understanding that their farm and farm life is, as Annie says, "perfect."[43] Through their distinct lives of accomplishment, Ray and Annie each restrain what they do in order to sustain that understanding. As they do, they strengthen what some readers might consider an unconventional marriage. Strengthening this understanding as they go, Ray and Annie are each able to make headway against a significant challenge to his or her life of accomplishments. For Annie, that challenge involves a truce with her bullying brother. For Ray, the challenge is to keep the ballplayers returning to the ballfield night after night.

The fictitious George Babbitt prospered as a real estate agent as long as he restrained himself, as he went about accomplishing his business dealings, to honor a certain understanding about conformity. Babbitt and Vergil Gunch, a prominent Good Fellow, strengthened their connections around this understanding, and each prospered accordingly. However, when George Babbitt began to question what he was and was not accomplishing, that particular understanding was of no use to him anymore. Indeed, it became a trap for Babbitt. A tragedy in *Babbitt* is that the character Babbitt could find no one with whom he could shape a new common ground and a new kind of conducive understanding. Thus, his rebellion was doomed. The Good Fellows welcomed Babbitt back to common grounds where a longtime understanding looked very soothing to him.[44] Babbitt's search for conductive connections was his undoing. There were none to be found on the common grounds available to him.

I draw inspiration for conducive connections, self-restrained accomplishments, from what a number of contemporary writers have accomplished in their own thinking about conducive connections. These sources of inspiration include:

1. The "shared glory" of a goal scored in an ice hockey game, as John Cowan tells the story[45];
2. A private life of ties to others from which, Donald Hall argues, the "best day" can materialize in the life of a writer[46];

3. Responsibility as the "glue" that we help apply to human ties as we listen and respond to another person, as Janet Mendelsohn and her colleagues put it[47];
4. The kind of human solidarity that can emerge, Richard Rorty argues, through the "imaginative" acts of ordinary human beings who value solidarity enough to stay out of each other's way[48];
5. The mark made by two human beings who, as Janet Surrey and her colleagues term it, "care for and take care of the relationship between them"[49];
6. Dialogue as a crucial avenue along which each of us can travel in search of authenticity, as Charles Taylor emphasizes[50];
7. A "politics of conversion," as Cornel West outlines a kind of local effort in which human beings each create an alternative to the specter of nihilism[51];
8. An approach to punishment through which, as Elizabeth Wolgast argues, those meting out the punishment and those receiving it can remain members of a community that is stronger for the practice of punishment.[52]

What I am able to accomplish with conducive connections, self-restrained accomplishments, is one more expression of homage to what Cowan, Hall, Mendelsohn and her colleagues, Rorty, Surrey and her colleagues, Taylor, West, and Wolgast have all accomplished. They enable me to nominate Ray Kinsella and George Babbitt as heroic figures in my project to retrieve corporate strategy with the idea of conducive connections, self-restrained accomplishments.

IX

Accomplishments, one's autonomy stakes; common grounds, contingent memberships; and conducive connections, self-restrained accomplishments are the key ideas that comprise my vocabulary for retrieving corporate strategy.[53] With these ideas, I have begun to sketch a particular Pragmatist Ethics of Differences, Centers, and Margins with which we can create a lasting place for each person's distinctive worldly contribution in a story about business. This ethical framework is depicted in Figure 4–2. With this framework, I am now prepared to show exactly what it is about corporate strategy that I am retrieving.

X

I want to retrieve the idea of corporate strategy because a retrieved conception of corporate strategy is an idea with which we can talk more and more hopefully about each person's distinctive worldly contribu-

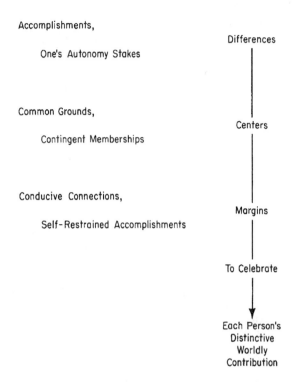

STRATEGY THROUGH CONVENTION

Figure 4–2.   Strategy Through Convention

tions.[54] I also want to retrieve corporate strategy because the idea has become a proxy for modern business talk. It is difficult to carry on a conversation about business without mentioning strategy and such related ideas as policies, goals, and corporate missions and credos. Business people and business professors alike talk routinely about marketing strategy, human resource strategy, takeover strategy, antitakeover strategy, tax strategy, information strategy, manufacturing strategy, and the like. For all these reasons, I choose corporate strategy as the opportunity for retrieving "of course we want business to be more ethical."

I predicate my hopes for corporate strategy on three specific links between a commonplace vocabulary of corporate strategy and my vocabulary of accomplishments, one's autonomy stakes; common grounds, contingent memberships; and conducive connections, self-restrained accomplishments. These three points of linkage are shown in Figure 4–1 in the column of dots titled "Retrieved Vocabulary of Corporate Strategy." The importance of these links is captured in the Strategy Through Convention designation.

XI

Students of management practice have long been accustomed to talking about corporate strategy with a vocabulary of strategy formulation, strategy implementation, and strategic fit. This trinity is a commonplace vocabulary of corporate strategy today. Every textbook about strategy is homage to these three ideas. The point of strategy formulation, strategy implementation, and strategic fit was proclaimed several decades ago by Kenneth Andrews as the basis for

> the fact that a business enterprise guided by a clear sense of purpose rationally arrived at and emotionally ratified by commitment is more likely to have a successful outcome, in terms of profit and social good, than a company whose future is left to guesswork and chance.[55]

Students of management might be surprised to learn their vocabulary of strategy formulation ("enterprise guided by a clear sense of purpose rationally arrived at"), strategy implementation ("emotionally ratified by commitment"), and strategic fit ("a successful outcome") and the vocabulary of Strategy Through Convention hold something in common. In fact, three points of linkage connect these vocabularies. These linkages are crucial, if the idea of corporate strategy is to play a central part in the "of course we want business to be more ethical" campaign. It is through these linkages that I am able to retrieve corporate strategy—rather than discard it in an act of "root-and-branch condemnation," as Charles Taylor puts it—as a useful ethical idea. The accomplishments in accomplishments, one's autonomy stakes; the common grounds in common grounds, contingent memberships; and the conducive connections in conducive connections, self-restrained accomplishments are all ideas that students of management will find familiar.

Strategy formulation is nothing but sustained, intelligent attention to accomplishments. Strategy formulation is the production of a plan in which the strategist specifies a "clear sense of purpose rationally arrived at" that will be his guide to accomplishing something purposeful in the marketplace.[56] Accomplishments are very important to the strategic bullies who populate the competitor selection, strategic groups, collective, and game theory for managers frameworks of corporate strategy. Strategic bullies want to accomplish some sort of position of strength in the marketplace, knowing that others are trying to do that for themselves.[57]

My Autonomy Through and Through Question is likewise an invitation to practice sustained, intelligent attention to accomplishments. Those who talk in terms of strategy formulation share a kinship with those who talk in terms of the accomplishments in accomplishments, one's autonomy stakes. It is at this intellectual juncture that I begin to retrieve—yet neither praise uncritically nor condemn to the roots and branches—the idea of corporate strategy. Because a corporate strategist could answer my Autonomy Through and Through Question with what he calls a corporate strategy, and because each human being could use that question as a guide to fashioning a life of accomplishments, "strategy" is the opening part of the Strategy Through Convention designation.

Strategy implementation is nothing more than sustained, intelligent attention to common grounds. Strategy implementation is the production of a policy about the common ground on which the members of an organization pledge ("emotionally ratified by commitment") to carry out the strategic plan for accomplishment. For the strategic bully, the common ground is the colony that he arranges for his stakeholders. The colony is where he hopes to accomplish what he sets out to do.[58]

My Contingent Memberships Through and Through Question is likewise an invitation to practice sustained, intelligent attention to common grounds. Those who talk in terms of strategy implementation share a kinship with those who talk in terms of common grounds, contingent memberships. It is at this intellectual juncture that I begin to retrieve—yet neither praise uncritically nor condemn to the roots and branches—the idea of "game." A game is common ground in which two human beings seek to accomplish something while being alert to each other's responses to their respective actions toward accomplishment.[59] Because a corporate strategist could answer my Contingent Memberships Through and Through Question with a description of a game through which he seeks to bully his way toward accomplishing something, and because two human beings can use the question to appreciate the rich contingency of their ties to one another, "strategy through" comprises two-thirds of the Strategy Through Convention designation. Each character in Strategy Through Convention accomplishes whatever she accomplishes through memberships in games.

Strategic fit is nothing more than sustained, intelligent attention to conducive connections.[60] Strategic fit involves a twin accomplishment: accomplish strategy formulation and strategy implementation in order to accomplish a connection between the firm and its environment. The strategic bully hopes to connect his firm to favorable "hooks" in the business environment. This is why strategy content, environmental scanning, corporate social responsibility, and joint ventures are such important ingredients in the practice of strategic fit.[61]

My Self-Restrained Accomplishments Through and Through Question is likewise an invitation to practice sustained, intelligent attention to conducive connections. Those who talk in a vocabulary of strategic fit share a kinship with those who talk in terms of the conducive connections in conducive connections, self-restrained accomplishments. It is at this intellectual juncture that I begin to retrieve—yet neither praise uncritically nor condemn to the roots and branches—the idea of strategic convention (which I shorten here to "convention").

A convention is a particular understanding that is shared by two human beings on their common ground. With that convention, the human beings who share common ground are able to make some degree of progress toward what it is they each seek to accomplish there.[62] Because a corporate strategist can answer my Self-Restrained Accomplishments Through and Through Question in terms of a shared understanding that he finds conducive to his bullying practices in a colony that he runs, and because a convention could also provide an opportunity for each person to make a distinctive worldly contribution, convention is the culminating part of my Strategy Through Convention designation. By Strategy Through Convention, conventions are crucial factors that make a difference between a strategist's accomplishments and a strategist's failures to accomplish. A convention is a significant margin in each strategist's life.[63]

I have gone to these lengths simply to stake my claim that Strategy Through Convention is a vocabulary about corporate strategy. The linkages among the trinity of strategy formulation, implementation, and fit and my Strategy Through Convention framework go no further than this. Those who accord the strategic bully heroic status in their accounts of corporate strategy have little to say about the "other half" of each of the three building blocks of Strategy Through Convention. Indeed, that is the way I want it to be.

The strategic bully is unwelcome in Strategy Through Convention. He is unwelcome because he does not take seriously the modifiers that I attach to accomplishments, common grounds, and conducive connections, respectively. He is unwelcome because he does not hear the Autonomy Through and Through, Contingent Memberships Through and Through, and Self-Restrained Accomplishments Through and Through questions as friendly queries. Put boldly, if a retrieved corporate strategy is to be useful in the "of course we want business to be more ethical" effort, then the strategic bully must be evicted from stories about corporate strategy.[64] I can do that quite readily as I bring this chapter to a close with a recapitulation of what I have done with the ideas of one's autonomy stakes, contingent memberships, and self-restrained accomplishments.

XII

Strategy Through Convention is an account about business and ethics in which each person lives a search for meaning about accomplishments and autonomy. Each lives a life guided by the ethical idea of accomplishments, one's autonomy stakes. That idea is part of each person's existence as she and he search for answers to an Autonomy Through and Through Question. For participants in the Strategy Through Convention story, theirs are lives of "ethics already through and through."[65]

The strategic bully is scared to death of accomplishments, one's autonomy stakes. Bullies shudder at the thought that someone else's accomplishments, defined autonomously by that person, should have the same standing as their own efforts. Strategic bullies do not like competition.[66] They want their accomplishments to take priority. Thus, the strategic bully is interested in a proposition that reads something like: "Accomplishments, my autonomy but not your autonomy."

What I have shown through comparative argument in this book is that the strategic bully's interpretation of accomplishments is ethically unacceptable. I made that point by:

1. retrieving the idea of corporate strategy with a meaning of accomplishments with which we can celebrate differences among human beings; and
2. retrieving accomplishments, in turn, from the belief that the accomplishments pursued by the "outsiders"—usually, corporate officers— acting above the moral malaise of business—are superior to the accomplishments pursued by everyone else.

With this retrieval of corporate strategy, I create an account in which corporate strategists and stakeholders alike acknowledge that each person occupies a unique place in the world. That unique place is defined, in part, by each person's accomplishments and the unique identity that follows from those accomplishments. This is a key first step on the way toward ensuring, in our accounts about business and ethics, a lasting place for each person's distinctive worldly contribution.

As a logical consequence of this first part of my retrieval effort, Strategy Through Convention is a way to discard the distinction between strength and weakness that permeates corporate strategy and, more generally, a logic of "ethics from the outside." Without that distinction, the strategic bully is lost.[67] Without that distinction, the strategic bully has no place—much less a heroic place—in a story about corporate strategy. That much is all for the good.

Strategy Through Convention is also an account about business and ethics in which each person lives a search for meaning about common grounds and contingent memberships on those common grounds. Each person lives a life guided by the ethical idea of common grounds, contingent memberships. Each person does this by living in search of answers to a Contingent Memberships Through and Through Question. Every time she ponders this question, a corporate strategist is living a life that is already a matter of "ethics through and through."

The strategic bully is scared to death of the idea of common grounds, contingent memberships. It is the idea of sharing and shaping common grounds that the bully finds most frightening. Both sharing and shaping sound like acts of weakness to the strategic bully, who thrives on interfering with others' accomplishments. The strategic bully wants compliant victims, not partners who have any substantial influence on what happens on a given piece of common ground. Hence, the strategic bully prefers an idea that reads something like: "Common grounds, membership on my terms."

What I have shown through comparative argument in this book is that the strategic bully's interpretation of common grounds is ethically unacceptable. I made this point by:

1. retrieving the idea of game with a meaning of common grounds with which we can celebrate the centers that pairs of human beings jointly shape; and
2. retrieving common grounds, in turn, from the belief that "outsiders" should approach their relationships with everyone else—particularly the "insiders" who populate the ethically starved world of business—with an eye to maintaining as much independence from "insiders" as possible.

As a logical consequence of this second part of my retrieval effort, Strategy Through Convention is a way to discard the distinction between "outsider" and "insider" that permeates the idea of corporate strategy and, more generally, a logic of "ethics from the outside." By the idea of common grounds, contingent memberships, there is no "outside" and no "inside."[68] Rather, Strategy Through Convention is a story of persons who are already deeply enmeshed in lives of centers shared with one another. There are only common grounds that a pair of persons jointly shape from yesterday to today and the prospects for future common grounds that they will jointly shape. Without this distinction between outside and inside, the strategic bully is lost. Without this distinction, there is no place—much less a heroic place—for the strategic bully in a story about corporate strategy. So be it.

Strategy Through Convention is, further still, an account about business and ethics in which each person searches for meaning about conducive connections and self-restrained accomplishments. Each lives a life guided by the ethical idea of conducive connections, self-restrained accomplishments. Each does this by living in search of answers to a Self-Restrained Accomplishments Through and Through Question. Each time she uses this question in her pursuits, the participant in Strategy Through Convention affirms that she is living a life of "ethics already through and through."

The strategic bully is scared to death of the idea of conducive connections, self-restrained accomplishments. He is frightened that the idea that self-restraint might actually apply to him. The strategic bully prospers if his victims know the rules of the common ground they share with the bully, follow those rules, and accept their due punishments for breaking those rules. This, of course, is the way any colonial governor simultaneously placates his colonists and holds over their heads the threat of punishment. Hence, as the strategic bully prefers to interpret it, the continuation of the colony has nothing to do with his self-restraint. The strategic bully prefers an idea that reads something like: "Conducive connections, restrain yourself so that I can appropriate gains from our connection, or else I will make sure that you do."

What I have shown through comparative argument in this book is that the strategic bully's interpretation of conducive connections is ethically unacceptable. I made this point by:

1. retrieving the idea of strategic convention with a meaning of self-restraint with which we can celebrate what human beings can create together as joint understandings that are the margins between lives of accomplishment and frustration; and
2. retrieving self-restraint, in turn, from the belief that, since they are in the Right, corporate "outsiders"—again, corporate officers—are under no obligation to restrain themselves, while there is an ever-present need to restrain the many "insiders" in the business world, since those "insiders" are inevitably in the Wrong.

As a logical consequence of this third part of my retrieval effort, Strategy Through Convention is a way to discard the distinction between strategic accomplishment and corporate responsibility. This distinction is an idea that permeates corporate strategy and, more generally, a logic of "ethics from the outside." By Strategy Through Convention, that distinction disappears. Any corporate strategy is an act of responsible behavior in some measure. By Strategy Through Convention, every time a corporate strategist seeks answers to questions about accomplishments, one's autonomy stakes; about common grounds, contingent memberships; and about conducive connections, self-restrained accomplishments, she is automatically dealing with questions about responsible behavior. The strategic bully is stranded without that distinction. He needs to believe that there is some outlet by which he can express occasional regret about what it is he must do in the name of business. That outlet is corporate social responsibility. Without this distinction, there is no place—much less a heroic one—for the strategic bully in a story about corporate strategy. "Good riddance" is what I say.

XIII

The upshot is that Strategy Through Convention is a vocabulary with which I can retrieve corporate strategy is a way that celebrates each person's distinctive worldly contribution. Because corporate strategy is so central to our modern vocabulary of business, I am able to retrieve "of course we want business to be more ethical" as a consequence of retrieving the idea of corporate strategy. Even more, in the course of creating a retrieved corporate strategy, I have shown just how unnecessary it is to keep talking about business with a logic of "ethics from the outside."

XIV

I could not have written this chapter in this way without receiving "assistance," which I recalled years later, from my student Searcher. She made her contribution to my thinking in a way that goes far beyond whether she bought the idea of affirmative action, or not. Searcher was wrestling, at my urging in that course, with the proposition that business can be an intellectual activity. She was analyzing hiring and promotion practices not merely as components in the profit equation, but as intellectual puzzles. She was working through those puzzles with ideas such as merit, dignity, educational opportunity, historical circumstance, and the American Dream.

Throughout this chapter, I have argued that corporate strategy is an intellectual activity. Strategy Through Convention is one example of what we can do if we take seriously the idea that corporate strategy can be an intellectual endeavor. The participants in Strategy Through Convention practice strategy as intellectuals. They do so simply by asking questions about accomplishments and autonomy stakes, common grounds and contingent memberships, and conducive connections and self-restrained accomplishments. More than she will ever know, Searcher helped me get this far in the argument because she wrestled with business practices as intellectual puzzles. Moreover, as I recall working through my doubts after class that day, I realize now that her influence extends to two more implications for this book.

First, affirmative action *is* an example of a successful intellectual retrieval, and that success has been an impetus for the retrieved idea that I call Strategy Through Convention. Affirmative action is affirmative evidence that intellectual retrieval is possible in the business world. Affirmative action is affirmative evidence that we need not apologize for thinking about business as an intellectual pursuit in a day and age when many people want to turn business studies into training for industrialized life and many others want to turn business education into orientation for membership in the Chamber of Commerce.

Affirmative action can be understood as a retrieval of the idea of merit from the clutches of those who talk in a vocabulary of objective test scores, hard work as a sufficient avenue for opportunity, an American racial history that is best forgotten, and a society stratified on a scale from strong to weak.[69] If we value the possibilities for living more interesting lives through lasting ties with others who are unlike us, then the foregoing vocabulary is useless at best. Strategy Through Convention is a retrieval of corporate strategy from the clutches of a comparably useless vocabulary about business and ethics.

Second, the storm over affirmative action in the mid-1990s is a vivid reminder that intellectual retrieval is not something that is achieved once-and-for-all, but rather is an accomplishment that must be strengthened intellectually over time. After all, any retrieved vocabulary is, in Richard Rorty's words, only "half-formed," and the "nuisance" vocabulary that it replaces does not automatically disappear. Proponents of affirmative aciton know that all too well. There is likely a grain of truth in the proposition that affirmative action proponents might well have run out of new defenses for the idea.[70] Thus, even as I sketch a framework for the idea of Strategy Through Convention, I am readying myself to meet disagreements with the way I have tampered with the idea of corporate strategy.

One such project of intellectual defense for Strategy Through Convention occupies the final chapter of this book. In Chapter 5, I add one more layer of meaning to the idea that corporate strategy should be retrieved in a way that enables us to celebrate each person's distinctive worldly contribution. With that layer, I strive to make Strategy Through Convention a little less "half-formed." With that layer, I hope to make Strategy Through Convention progressively more distinct from the "nuisance" stories in which the strategic bully prospers and stakeholders do his bidding.[71]

In all, I consider affirmative action a vivid reminder of the responsibilities that go with living an educated life. We can either commit ourselves to participating in the ongoing process of creating new meanings for ideas that have become "nuisances," or we can satisfy ourselves by reiterating ideas with which we are comfortable. We can either retrieve ideas based on our worldly experiences together, or we can let each other down. Affirmative action is evidence that we can make that choice. I offer Strategy Through Convention as one more way to act on that choice. Searcher, wherever she is, is always "sitting" in my classroom, always reminding me and my students of that choice.

5

Strategy Through Convention

I

Thank you, Bryan Burrough and John Helyar, for writing *Barbarians at the Gate*. Thank you for making available a story that has been one of the most useful case studies I have ever used in an undergraduate course about corporate strategy.[1] Thank you as well, Messrs. Burrough and Helyar, for your unintended assistance in my efforts to retrieve the idea of corporate strategy from the nuisance that it has become.[2] For a book with "barbarians" in the title, *Barbarians at the Gate* has been a most useful way to retrieve corporate strategy with a meaning that has something to do with our humanity. Thank you, many times over.

II

Each year, many of my students—seniors who are busily making final preparations for Commencement weekend—are positively captivated with the story that Burrough and Helyar tell in *Barbarians at the Gate*. From year to year, I have noticed a remarkable continuity in the objects of their fascination. Seniors come, and seniors go, yet many in each graduating class read *Barbarians at the Gate* enthusiastically as a story about:

1. RJR Nabisco stock prices;
2. Ross Johnson and his obsession with RJR Nabisco stock prices;
3. The opportunities in investment banking to win big and to lose big;
4. Henry Kravis and the financial clout of Kohlberg Kravis Roberts;
5. Lucrative fees that investment bankers can earn for taking part in merger deals and buy-out deals;
6. Ross Johnson and his obsession with RJR Nabisco stock prices;
7. The information resources that investment bankers can command;
8. The lucrative fees available to investment bankers for merely participating in preliminary talks about mergers and buy-outs;

9. The orderly bidding process managed by Charles Hugel and Peter Atkins;
10. The tactics used by Ross Johnson to oust his executive rivals along the way;
11. Ross Johnson and his obsession with RJR Nabisco stock prices;
12. Corporate restructuring opportunities at RJR Nabisco;
13. The cleverness of junk-bond financing;
14. The opportunities in investment banking to win big and to lose big;
15. Cash flows from cookies and cigarettes;
16. Ross Johnson and his obsession with RJR Nabisco stock prices;
17. The unlimited budgets that Ross Johnson managed to exceed;
18. Ross Johnson and his fleet of corporate jets;
19. Sports celebrities on the RJR Nabisco payroll;
20. Recurring opportunities in investment banking to join the "big leagues" of dealmakers;
21. Ross Johnson and his obsession with RJR Nabisco stock prices;
22. Ted Forstmann's refusal to take part in the final bidding;
23. The financial clout of Kohlberg Kravis Roberts;
24. RJR Nabisco stock prices; and
25. Ross Johnson and his obsession with RJR Nabisco stock prices.[3]

Every time I hear this interpretation of *Barbarians at the Gate*, I grow more convinced that we can draw a powerful conclusion about the way we are accustomed to talking about business. The many students who are fascinated with these aspects of *Barbarians at the Gate* are probably on their way, if not already there on the eve of Commencement Day, to missing a central point about what a college education can mean for their lives.

Every one of these students has had the opportunity to receive a liberal education. With each passing year, I am more convinced than ever that most of them are not only missing that opportunity, but have been systematically dissuaded from receiving a liberal education. Their enthusiasm for *Barbarians at the Gate* is occasion for sadness. But this kind of enthusiasm is also an opportunity to do something about what students are taught in undergraduate business programs and about what we say when we talk about business.

III

Many of my students are captivated by *Barbarians at the Gate* because they are good and ready for reassuring stories about their world. Commencement Day looms for these seniors. Many of them have gotten over the seductive myth that the transition from college into the workplace will be as smooth and full of options as was the transition from high school to college. They now know better than that. For some, that lesson was accompanied by a dose of anxiety. Many shades of gray color these students' lives near Commencement Day as they contemplate, await, and even fear what happens the day after they receive their diplomas.

As much as anything, I have learned, these men and women want assurance about the business world. They are looking for stories that confirm everything that they believe about business. They want this assurance because they have already bought into a story that I call the Future of Enlistment in Business.

Many of these young people will soon move from the college campus to the corporate workplace. They have come to subscribe wholeheartedly to the belief that one goes to college to get a business degree to enter the corporate workplace where that degree will earn them chance after to chance to prosper in the business world. They have spent the better part of four years preparing to turn themselves over to the world of business. Now, on the eve of Commencement Day, they face their decision to buy into a Future of Enlistment in Business and to live as enlistees.

We should not be surprised that many of these young people are entertaining at least a few second thoughts about their enlistment in business. Many of them have, in fact, not yet reached their twenty-second birthdays. This is where the appeal of *Barbarians at the Gate* comes into play.

Barbarians at the Gate can be such a comforting story to someone facing what looks like a lifetime of enlistment in the business world. The book can be a comprehensive, entertaining, delicious, and timely confirmation of everything that many of my students believe about business. With their meticulous reporting, Burrough and Helyar trace the steps of businessmen who are doing the things that, according to the lessons my students have been taught, businessmen ordinarily do.[4] Burrough and Helyar acquaint us with men who do the things that my students have learned to recognize as finance, marketing, accounting, business law, operations, business-level strategy, human resource management, and business policy. What many of these students find even more comforting is that the principals in *Barbarians at the Gate* appear to have themselves enlisted in the business world. To many of my seniors, the principals in the book are "all business."[5] That is good news to my group of enlistees.

The point is that my students open the cover of *Barbarians at the Gate* fully expecting to read what I call the Story of Business Administration. In the Story of Business Administration, businessmen command a knowledge of finance, marketing, accounting, business law, operations, business-level strategy, and human resource management, and then tie up all this knowledge into one coherent package with their command of business policy.[6] Whether they rave about the book or not, my students expect this story line because every case study that they have analyzed thus far in their undergraduate business courses is a story about people doing these things. And, lo and behold, they discover this story in what Burrough and Helyar have published. No wonder that I walk into a classroom full of eager discussants that week! Some of them feel such exhilaration that they even remove their baseball caps for class.

Look at the list of the truths that fascinate many of my students. Stock price, restructuring, high-profile marketing images, budgets and budget controls, executive power, financial leverage, information resources, functioning markets, cash flow, debt instruments, and shareholder value are all truths about business. These are the truths that make up the Story of Business Administration. These are truths that my students expect to find in every case about business. As prospective long-term enlistees in this story, many of my seniors want assurance that it is safe to invest their lives in this perspective about how the world "really works."[7] Thanks to Bryan Burrough and John Helyar, my students' days are a little brighter and their steps are a little livelier once they read the book. *Barbarians at the Gate* is serendipity for them.

IV

I am no longer surprised by this kind of enthusiastic response to *Barbarians at the Gate*. Still, I am continually disappointed by this annual rite. I am disappointed because this enthusiasm is a telltale sign that these students are going to accomplish less in their college years than they could have accomplished. Three levels of disappointment are pertinent to what I am trying to accomplish in this chapter.

First, this prospect of lesser accomplishment is simply unnecessary. Many of my seniors leave college eager to do something that they need not go to college to do. They are eager to turn their lives over to others and follow the rules that those others set. In the case of a Future of Enlistment in Business, the others are the people who have already enlisted and re-enlisted in the world of business. If someone wanted simply to enlist in a cause generally, he need not go to college to do that. All one need do is listen long enough to certain radio and television talk shows, for instance. Enlistment opportunities exist across the dial. There is no reason why the undergraduate experience anywhere should be reduced to an apprenticeship in conformity.[8]

Second, it is through no fault of their own that many of my students see enlistment as the only reason—indeed, as a natural and inevitable reason—for going to college. The Story of Business Administration leaves them no room for any other conception of college and their futures. The Story of Business Administration is, in other words, a prime suspect here.[9] The principals in the Story of Business Administration prosper by following the rules of finance, marketing, accounting, human resource management, business policy, and the like. If they do not follow those rules, then they will likely fail, according to the Story of Business Administration. What is disappointing here is that the story of a Future of Enlistment in Business, which is all about following rules in the corporate workplace, is reinforced by the Story of Business Administration, which is all about following rules in business.

Third, college can be a time when young men and women grow into a very different perspective about living their lives. That perspective is known as liberal education. My *Barbarians at the Gate* fans have missed an opportunity at liberal education, because the Story of Business Administration gets in the way. Liberal education is an alternative to the story of a Future of Enlistment in Business and an antidote to what is lost in a lifetime of enlistment. This is where Strategy Through Convention enters the picture as a useful framework. Here is one place where Strategy Through Convention "vaguely promises great things," as Richard Rorty heralds the creation of any new vocabulary.[10] Here, too, is where the versatility of *Barbarians at the Gate* is so apparent.

V

I am one of those educators who believe that four years of undergraduate study can be a time for human beings to grow into a way of living that is commonly called liberal education.[11] I am also an educator who is very particular about what we mean by liberal education. I take the "liberal" in liberal education to mean much more than an academic transcript that shows a sprinkling of courses bearing such different labels as Chemistry, History, German, Political Science, Philosophy, Environmental Science, Economics, Psychology, and Business Administration. I am also an educator who takes liberal education to be something other than a warmup act that students perform before getting down to the "real" business of majoring in some field of study.[12] I am an educator who believes that liberal education is more than some ritual process by which students become mysteriously sensitized before they get down to the real business of a major field of study. Finally, I am an educator who has experienced—firsthand and vicariously in the lives of many of my students— liberal education as a way human beings can choose to live.

A liberally educated person can grow to value a curiosity about the world, a curiosity that can sustain one confidently and autonomously for the rest of one's life. A person can grow into a practice of criticism, rather than obedient citizenship, as Henry Giroux draws the distinction.[13] A liberally educated person can grow to appreciate what the power of ideas has wrought for better and for worse in human history. College is a time and place where all this intellectual foment and fervor can begin and evolve for a person. Students can set their sights on leaving a formal liberal education with the beginnings of a story that they have to tell about the world and, in particular, about the place for humanity in their world.[14] A formal liberal education is a point of departure for a lifetime of liberal education, a lifetime of living inquisitively about human beings.

I detect no enthusiasm for this kind of living in the fascination that many of my students hold for *Barbarians at the Gate*. For them, liberal education was some phase that they were required to endure several years before they encountered the book. For these fans of *Barbarians at the Gate*, liberal education went into total eclipse when the Story of Business Administration came into their lives.

VI

The purpose of this chapter is to add a layer of meaning to the framework of Strategy Through Convention that I created and defended in Chapter 4. In this layer of meaning, the participants in Strategy Through Convention are a curious bunch. They are inquisitive about their own humanity and the humanity of corporate strategists whom they get to know along the way, and they live with this curiosity every step of the way.

Corporate strategists in Strategy Through Convention are curious about where the idea of accomplishments, one's autonomy stakes, might lead. They practice this curiosity by seeking answers to an Autonomy Through and Through Question (see Chapter 4). These corporate strategists are curious about where the idea of common grounds, contingent memberships, might lead. They practice this curiosity by seeking answers to a Contingent Memberships Through and Through Question. The corporate strategists in Strategy Through Convention are curious about where the idea of conducive connections, self-restrained accomplishments, might lead. They practice this curiosity by seeking answers to a Self-Restrained Accomplishments Through and Through Question.

The human beings who participate in Strategy Through Convention are liberally educated men and women, inquisitive as they are about humanity.[15] In so doing, they follow a trail blazed by the fictitious Ray Kinsella and George Babbitt, both of whom are fascinated with humanity, and they set their own course for sustaining such curiosity. Kinsella and Babbitt are, in their own distinctive ways, liberally educated men.[16]

In charting this kind of intellectual life for themselves, the corporate strategists in Strategy Through Convention do what the principals in the Story of Business Administration could never hope to do: They eagerly and daringly live with the idea of humanity. They live lives of curiosity and inquisitiveness about their own humanity and the humanity of other distinctive human beings. To the human beings who believe in this genre of liberal education, humanity is truly something about which they can lead a life of intellectual fascination.

The Story of Business Administration, by contrast, is not a story about inquisitive human beings, much less a story about human beings who are inquisitive about humanity—their own humanity, their neighbor's humanity, the humanity of ancestors and strangers who lived in eighteenth-century Europe and Africa, the humanity of Native Americans who lived on and with the land that we know as the Great Plains, and so on. What we get with the Story of Business Administration is what Charles Taylor bemoans as "flattened" horizons on the world.[17] The corporate strategists in Strategy Through Convention live each day in search of precisely the opposite of horizons that are flattened into truths about finance, marketing, human resources management, and business policy. As a story populated by inquisitive human beings, Strategy Through Convention is one contribution to liberal education. Strategy Through Convention is not only an antidote to the Story of Business Administration; it is also a rebellion against that story, and any story, that seduces human beings into living flattened lives.

In this chapter, I introduce five new metaphors for the corporate strategist. Each is a metaphor for a person living inquisitively about humanity. One metaphor deals with the idea of accomplishments, one's autonomy stakes. Two more deal with the idea of common grounds, contingent memberships. The remaining two deal with the idea of conducive connections, self-restrained accomplishments. These five metaphors for the corporate strategist are the glue in this new layer of meaning for Strategy Through Convention.

Barbarians at the Gate is where these five new metaphors for corporate strategist make their debut. I fully intend two ironies in that. First, I interpret these five new metaphors in the very same book in which many of my seniors find comfort about their enlistment in the corporate workplace. Second, *Barbarians at the Gate* is a tale in which we can meet human beings who—as curious as they are about their humanity and others' humanity—act as anything but barbarians.

VII

A corporate strategy in the Strategy Through Convention story is a pattern of answers to an Autonomy Through and Through Question, a Contingent Memberships Through and Through Question, and a Self-Restrained Accomplishments Through and Through Question. Every sentence in this kind of corporate strategy is a statement of curiosity about humanity. Each corporate strategist who creates, and acts according to, such a corporate strategy commits himself and herself to a life of inquisitiveness about human beings.[18] In the next section, I create one sketch of what a corporate strategist might include in a corporate strategy of this kind. What follows is certainly a complicated statement. It is a complicated statement because humanity is a complicated matter, and the corporate strategist in Strategy Through Convention savors the opportunity to live a complicated life.

VIII

Each corporate strategist in Strategy Through Convention begins to reason and act according to the following logic:[19]

PART A

I take action X-1, and not action X-2, contingent on the kind of unique, focused, and exemplary identity that I seek for myself (called "stakes of distinction") and the kind of identity that I will not permit myself to seek (called a "stakes threshold"), given what I value as meaningful about my past and in view of the capabilities that I can reasonably expect to muster as I move into a future that I can have a hand in shaping by taking action X-1,

and

You take action Y-1, and neither action Y-2 nor action Y-3, contingent on the kind of unique, focused, and exemplary identity that you seek for yourself (called "stakes of distinction") and the kind of identity that you will not permit yourself to seek (called a "stakes threshold"), given what you value as meaningful about your past and in view of the capabilities that you can reasonably expect to muster as you move into a future that you can have a hand in shaping by taking action Y-1.

and

PART B

I take action X-1, and not X-2, and you take action Y-1, and neither action Y-2 nor action Y-3, at the intersection where my doing X-1 and your doing Y-1, brings us together on some common ground that we share and shape over time around a particular question on the common ground (called a "question of interdependence") that is ours to answer jointly through my doing X-1 and your doing Y-1, and a question from which action X-1 and action X-2 logically follow and from which action Y-1, action Y-2, and action Y-3 logically follow, a joint action that is called the "we game" to which I and you belong.

and

PART C

I take action X-1, and not action X-2, in anticipation that you will take action Y-1, and neither action Y-2 nor action Y-3, and you take action Y-1, and neither action Y-2 nor action Y-3, in anticipation that I will take action X-1, and not action X-2, such that you and I shape, by my taking action X-1 and your taking action Y-2, a particular understanding (called a "local convention") as an answer to the question of interdependence to which we belong in a "we game," *and*

PART D

that particular understanding bears important consequences in two nearby contexts in which:

(In one nearby context) I take action M-1, and not action M-2, contingent on the kind of unique, focused, and exemplary identity that I seek for myself (called "stakes of distinction") and the kind of identity that I will not permit myself to seek (called a "stakes threshold"), given what I value as meaningful about my past and in view of the capabilities that I can reasonably expect to muster as I move into a future that I can have a hand in shaping by taking action M-1,

and

"Second" You take action N-1, and neither action N-2 nor action N-3, contingent on the kind of unique, focused, and exemplary identity that Second You seek for yourself (called "stakes of distinction") and the kind of identity that you will not permit yourself to seek (called a "stakes threshold"), given what Second You value as meaningful about your past and in view of the capabilities that Second You can reasonably expect to muster as Second You move into a future that Second You can have a hand in shaping by taking action N-1.

and

I take action M-1, and not M-2, and Second You take action N-1, and neither action N-2 nor action N-3, at the intersection where my doing M-1 and your doing N-1, brings us together on some common ground that we share and shape over time around a particular question (called a "question of interdependence") that is ours to answer through my doing M-1 and your doing N-1, and a question from which action M-1 and action M-2 logically follow and from which action N-1, action N-2, and action N-3 logically follow, a joint action that is the "we game" to which I and Second You belong,

and

(In another nearby context) You take action P-1, and not action P-2, contingent on the kind of unique, focused, and exemplary identity that you seek for yourself (called "stakes of distinction") and the kind of identity that you will not permit yourself to seek (called a "stakes threshold"), given what you value as meaningful about your past and in view of the capabilities that you can reasonably expect to muster as you move into a future that you can have a hand in shaping by taking action P-1,

and

"Third" You take action Q-1, and neither action Q-2 nor action Q-3, contingent on the kind of unique, focused, and exemplary identity that Third You seek for yourself (called "stakes of distinction") and the kind of identity that Third You will not permit yourself to seek (called a "stakes threshold"), given what Third You value as meaningful about your past and in view of the capabilities that Third You can reasonably expect to muster as Third You move into a future that Third You can have a hand in shaping by taking action Q-1.

and

You take action P-1, and not P-2, and Third You take action Q-1, and neither action Q-2 nor action Q-3, at the intersection where your doing P-1 and Third You doing Q-1 brings you and Third You together on some common ground that you two share and shape over time around a particular question (called a "question of interdependence") that is yours to answer jointly through your doing P-1 and Third You doing Q-1, and a question from which action P-1 and action P-2 logically follow and from which action Q-1, action Q-2, and action Q-3 logically follow, a joint action that is the "we game" to which you and Third You belong,

and

I and you interact around the particular question of interdependence in the "we game" to which I and you belong, and I and Second You interact around the particular question of interdependence in the "we game" to which I and Second You belong, and you and Third You interact around the particular question of interdependence in the "we game" to which you and Third You belong, in such a way that what is happening (in what is called a "web of we games") in one of these "we games" bears important consequences (and thus becomes a shadow game) for what is happening in another of these "we games," or several of these "we games,"

and

PART E

in the course of the search by you and I for a stable common understanding about the particular question of interdependence that I and you address jointly in the "we game" to which I and you belong, and joint search by I and Second You for a stable common understanding about the particular question of interdependence that I and Second You address jointly in the we game to which I and Second You belong, and the joint search by you and Third You for a stable common understanding about the particular question of interdependence that you and Third You address jointly in the "we game" to which you and Third You belong, I, you, Second You, and Third You seek a stable common understanding about, and across, our respective stable common understandings, and understanding about understandings (called a "convention of local conventions") by which I, you, Second You, and Third You can each act toward shaping the particular identity (called "stakes of distinction") that I, you, Second You, and Third You value for our respective lives, and by which I, you, Second You, and Third You can avoid living (as what is called a "member under a stakes threshold") in circumstances that I *and* you *and* Second You *and* Third You will not tolerate,

hence

I, you, Second You, and Third You practice an ethics throughout corporate strategy and I, you, Second You, and Third You practice (corporate) Strategy Through Convention.

In this layer of meaning for Strategy Through Convention I create room for five new metaphors for the corporate strategist.[20] These corporate strategists show up time and again in *Barbarians at the Gate*.

IX

In Part A above, each corporate strategist answers an Autonomy Through and Through Question. Metaphorically, the strategist does this as an amateur. "Amateur" is one metaphor for corporate strategist in Strategy Through Convention.

The amateur pays close attention to matters of accomplishment and autonomy. As David Halberstam shows us in his book *The Amateurs*, each amateur knows full well that she and he is an unfinished product when it comes to accomplishment and autonomy.[21] An amateur is someone who lives for the opportunity to improve, relative to some standard of his or her own past accomplishments.[22] Every Olympic year we have an opportunity to appreciate this commonplace meaning of amateurism.

The amateur corporate strategist is not a narcissist.[23] She thinks about herself as an amateur and assumes that each other corporate strategist is also an amateur. Stakes of distinction and stakes threshold are ideas that each amateur corporate strategist uses as reminders of each other's amateurism.

Amateur corporate strategists are so keenly interested in humanity that they are intrigued by the specific, mutually exclusive actions available not only to them but also the specific, mutually exclusive actions that other human beings can take.[24] Indeed, they are so intent on learning about these other persons that they attribute a greater range of alternative actions—Y-1, Y-2, and Y-3, that is—to others than they do to themselves.[25] Amateur corporate strategists begin to commit themselves to a life of curiosity about humanity by living inquisitively about stakes of distinction and stakes thresholds.

Amateur corporate strategists are everywhere in *Barbarians at the Gate*, if we go looking for them.[26] Burrough and Helyar make it possible for us to get to know every principal player in the RJR Nabisco drama as someone who thinks very carefully about what he could accomplish through the deal. These men also pay careful attention to what their rival bidders could accomplish through the deal. Hence, persons are paying attention to stakes of distinction throughout the story. Moreover, the authors introduce us to several investment bankers who agonize over whether, by participating in the bidding, they might be tempted to become the kind of persons they do not want to become. For them, a stakes threshold appears to be a very active ingredient in their strategic efforts. In all, what Burrough and Helyar tell us about the RJR Nabisco leveraged buy-out is an instructive case of human beings taking stakes of distinction and stakes thresholds quite seriously.

X

In Part B outlined above, which includes Part A, the corporate strategist answers a Contingent Memberships Through and Through Question. Metaphorically, he does this as a neighbor. "Neighbor" is a second metaphor for corporate strategist in Strategy Through Convention.

A neighbor pays close attention to what other human beings are doing in the vicinity of his life. As each of Jane Smiley's characters do in her novel *A Thousand Acres,* a neighbor looks for regularity in a pattern of interaction with another human being,[27] and distinguishes among those who are merely "passing through" and those with whom one can share some common ground. The neighbor is an amateur, concerned with accomplishments and autonomy, who also values common ground.

The neighbor corporate strategist looks at his world in terms of bilateral relationships on pieces of common ground. He belongs to that common ground, which he and his neighbor come to define in terms of their question of interdependence. A question of interdependence is a problem that these two corporate strategists must jointly address on their common ground. As a neighbor, each corporate strategist takes actions with this question clearly in mind.[28] As a result, the "we game" that two neighbor corporate strategists share as a center in their lives is very much a contingent matter. To each neighbor corporate strategist, a "we game" is the only place where strategic action can occur. That is why amateur corporate strategists are also neighbor corporate strategists.

Neighbor corporate strategists are everywhere in *Barbarians at the Gate.* Several pairs of investment bankers belong to, and shape, "we games" around some version of the following question of interdependence: How do we keep Ross Johnson interested in what has become an increasingly complicated bidding process?[29] Several pairs of RJR Nabisco board members belong to, and shape, "we games" around some version of this question of interdependence: In the wake of revelations of huge payments going to the buy-out management team, how do we deal with the public uproar?[30] Several pairs of financiers belong to, and shape, a question of interdependence such as: What is the future of junk-bond financing?[31] Burrough and Helyar make it possible, as well, to interpret a we game between Johnson and Henry Kravis around this question of interdependence: How do we move the bidding process to a speedy conclusion? In all these cases, two amateur corporate strategists acknowledge, in a saga of action and response and response to responses, that neither of them can solve the question of interdependence by himself. That admission by the neighbor corporate strategist sets the stage for an idea about self-restraint in Strategy Through Convention.

XI

In Part C above, which includes Parts A and B, each corporate strategist answers a Self-Restrained Accomplishments Through and Through Question. Metaphorically, strategists do this as members. "Member" is a third metaphor for corporate strategist in Strategy Through Convention.

A member belongs to a local convention that she and another distinctive human being share. Each local convention is a particular answer, in their "we game," to the question of interdependence through which they share common ground.[32] As we can read repeatedly in *At the Highest Levels*, by Michael Beschloss and Strobe Talbott, an account of the end of the Cold War, a member is an amateur who believes that she cannot accomplish anything without, and outside of, a local convention on a piece of common ground.[33] For George Bush and Mikhail Gorbachev in *At the Highest Levels*, one such convention appears to be that "perestroika is an experiment that deserves every chance to last for another day, week, and month."[34]

A member is acutely aware of the link between her pursuits as an amateur and her actions as a neighbor. Because a local convention is the margin that makes a difference between her accomplishments and her failures to accomplish, the member corporate strategist voluntarily restrains her amateur actions.[35] The strategist wants a local convention to endure; thus, she does her part as a contributor to the connections that can be conducive to each neighbor on the common ground. This is what I mean by conducive connections, self-restrained accomplishments. It is possible to conclude from *At the Highest Levels* that both Bush and Gorbachev would be lost, paralyzed as statesmen and diplomats, without their local convention.

Member corporate strategists are everywhere in *Barbarians at the Gate*, if we go looking for them and for the local conventions to which they willfully belong.[36] "Let's do this deal by the numbers" is one local convention that several pairs of investment bankers, lawyers, and executives try to sustain. In each case, the two member corporate strategists tailor this connection to the particular circumstances on their common ground.[37] Within the Kohlberg Kravis Roberts organization, we meet pairs of men who contribute to some version of the local convention, namely "We will move toward the brink in this deal very carefully after considerable debate."[38] Pairs of RJR Nabisco directors appear to follow some variation on the local convention: "We will bend over backwards to make the bidding process a fair one for any credible bidder who wants to be heard." At least one prominent investment banker wants to join others in this convention: "We will make junk bonds a public issue." However, it is apparent in the story that Burrough and Helyar tell that no one else wants to live in that neighborhood.[39] In each instance, member corporate strategists accomplish whatever they accomplish through the local understandings that they consciously work to sustain. Here is where the Strategy Through Convention designation originates.

XII

In Part D above, which includes Parts A, B, and C, each corporate strategist develops a more complicated answer to a Contingent Memberships Through and Through Question than he or she does as neighbors. Metaphorically, each does this as a student. "Student" is a fourth metaphor for corporate strategist in Strategy Through Convention.

A student lives through multiple common grounds. At least one of those common grounds involves what we commonly call "education." Indeed, the whole point of education can be for two persons to flourish on a common ground and in their local convention in ways that spill over to their memberships in other neighborhoods. Those two persons can be instructor and student or student and student. In either case, they go to school to become something other than what they were before. They are amateurs, after all.

As do the leaders of the Marthatown Council in Sheri Tepper's novel *The Gate to Women's Country*, a student willfully places herself in multiple neighborhoods at the same time.[40] For women like Morgot, those common grounds involve her daughters, her servitor, leaders of the warrior garrison, and leaders of other towns in Women's Country.[41] In so doing, Morgot, whom we can know as a student corporate strategist, is constantly on the lookout for "we games" whose members live under the influence of what is going on in one or more other we games.

"Shadow game" is the name that I give to such a source of influence.[42] The student corporate strategist sees her life as a complicated life that she lives through a web of "we games" that shadow other "we games."[43] It is with high hopes that such spillovers can be positive for her life as an amateur, neighbor, and member that the student decides to go to school in the first place.[44]

We can read *Barbarians at the Gate* as a story in which the members of two different "we games" interact in ways that cast long shadows on other "we games."[45] First, we can interpret one shadow game that is the common ground shared by Ross Johnson and Peter Cohen. Johnson and Cohen, we might conclude, share this question of interdependence: "How much of the RJR Nabisco deal do we share with others?" Several student corporate strategists are able to move ahead with their bids owing to the way Johnson and Cohen interact around this question.

Second, as Burrough and Helyar tell it, the entire bidding process changes when the principals at Kohlberg Kravis Roberts show some interest in RJR Nabisco. To any number of student corporate strategists in the story, the we game between Henry Kravis and Ross Johnson—around the question of interdependence, namely "How quickly will the bidding come to a conclusion?"—casts a long, long shadow. In sum, student corporate strategists see their lives in terms of webs and shadows that are inhabited by amateur, neighbor, member corporate strategists like themselves.

XIII

In Part E above, which includes Parts A, B, C, and D, each corporate strategist interprets a more complicated answer to a Self-Restrained Accomplishments Through and Through Question than she and he do as members. Metaphorically, each develops such an answer as a teacher. "Teacher" is a fifth metaphor for corporate strategist in Strategy Through Convention.

A teacher accomplishes something whenever someone else, with whom she belongs to a local convention, is able to accomplish something that that person could not have previously done.[46] Local conventions, the teacher knows, make for conditions that are conducive to the experience of each member. A teacher is a member of many such local conventions at the same time. This web is something that we commonly call a "class" or a "course section."

For a teacher to be a contributing member of so many local conventions, she and her students each need an understanding about their respective understandings. This is what I call a "convention of local conventions." A convention of local conventions is a conducive kind of connection across the common grounds on which many pairs of persons belong to their particular local conventions. A class or course is held together, on this view, through a convention of local conventions.

Father Frank Healy, in Jon Hassler's novel *North of Hope,* experiences firsthand the fear that a student somehow gets overlooked.[47] This is one of a teacher's greatest fears, and it is what happens when a convention of local conventions is missing from a web of "we games." To ensure that no one student is overlooked, the teacher corporate strategist supplements her concern about a convention of local conventions with attention to what I call a "member under a stakes threshold."

Father Healy deals with many desperate men and women on the fictitious Basswood Reservation in northern Minnesota. At times, it takes all of his physical and emotional energy to deal, as a member, with any one of these persons.[48] It takes that much more for him to become the teacher that he is, someone who accomplishes a rescue of every member under a stakes threshold except one in the narrative that Hassler creates.

Barbarians at the Gate is a story with which we can appreciate why member under a stakes threshold and convention of local conventions are ideas that must go together, if we take seriously each person's distinctive worldly contribution.

On one hand, we could conclude from the wealth of information provided by Burrough and Helyar that the principals in the RJR Nabisco buy-out act as conscientious teacher corporate strategists. We can explain the fact that the entire bidding process is conducted in the private sector in terms of these businessmen belonging to the following convention of local conventions: "We will not conduct the bidding for RJR Nabisco in any way that might jeopardize the future of this cozy little market, which we have arranged and refined, for megadeals."[49] This might be the work of pairs of member corporate strategists who, in the course of contribution to their own local conventions, also contribute to this convention of local conventions. But there is a reason why I hesitate in praising the principals in the *Barbarians at the Gate* story for their actions as teacher corporate strategists.[50]

I hesitate because members who are living near, or under, their stakes thresholds are difficult to find in *Barbarians at the Gate*. We learn from Burrough and Helyar that one RJR Nabisco executive is excluded from the management buy-out group. He appears to land on his feet. But other than him, human beings for whom the RJR Nabisco deal jeopardizes conducive connections—in a "we game" and across a web of we games—are not prominent in the book. The teacher corporate strategist does not let herself commit such an act of omission in her web of games.

I come to an ironic conclusion here. It is precisely because of this silence about members under a stakes threshold that *Barbarians at the Gate* is so useful a book. Teacher corporate strategists always check whether there is anyone in the web of "we games" who is living under a stakes threshold. In effect, she takes it as her responsibility to "count noses."[51]

In a web of "we games" in which the members live in a conducive connection of conducive connections, each corporate strategist is a teacher who counts noses. Barbarians believe that such self-restraint is a bother. Barbarians do not care about a member who has fallen on hard times, a person who is excluded from the chance to flourish through a convention of local conventions.[52] Burrough and Helyar tell us a story with which we can draw a distinction that we would all do well to remember: A barbarian cannot be a teacher.

I summarize this layer of meaning for Strategy Through Convention, five metaphors for corporate strategist and nine associated concepts in all, in Table 5–1.

XIV

"Be practical; reduce uncertainty for business people" is dogma in the modern business school and in modern business talk. It is imperative there that business school professors, in particular, reduce such uncer-

Table 5–1. A layer of meaning for Strategy Through
Convention (STC)

STC Idea	Metaphor for Corporate Strategist	New Concepts in Vocabulary of STC
Accomplishments, one's autonomy stakes (Differences)	Amateur	Stakes of distinction
		Stakes threshold
Common grounds, contingent memberships (Centers)	Neighbor	Question of interdependence
		"We game"
Conducive connections, self-restrained accomplishments (Margins)	Member	Local convention
Common grounds, contingent memberships (Centers)	Student	Shadow game
		Web of "we games"
Conducive connections, self-restrained accomplishments (Margins)	Teacher	Convention of local conventions
		Member under a stakes threshold

tainty.[53] This dogma is so entrenched that one business school professor after another feels compelled to comment on "implications for managers" in their research papers, even after treating managers as mere data points in their research. This dogma is so entrenched that some go so far as to offer advice to managers at the end of research papers in which testable hypotheses do not contain the slightest trace of humanity.[54]

When keepers of the "be practical; reduce uncertainty for business people" dogma are feeling underappreciated or threatened, they often feel compelled to direct their unhappiness at persons like me who write about business language.[55] You see, at the modern business school, uncertainty is the bane of business practice.[56] Those who write essays and critiques, especially comparative critiques as pragmatists, ostensibly add to the uncertainty of business.

It might come as a surprise then that I will happily oblige the keepers of "be practical; reduce uncertainty for business people." I can think of few more useful cues for summarizing this chapter and this book than this dogma. "Be practical; reduce uncertainty for business people" is a useful way for me to call attention to four implications of my "half-formed new vocabulary" about corporate strategy.[57] What follows are four things that you—particularly the "you" who wave the flag of the Story of Business Administration—can now do that you could not do before it was possible to use a vocabulary of Strategy Through Convention, even as half-formed as it is.

First, you no longer need to talk about stakeholders.

Every person in the Strategy Through Convention story is a stakeholder and recognizes every other person as a stakeholder.[58] Thus, it would be redundant to keep talking about stakeholders in this new vocabulary about corporate strategy. This will come as welcome news to those business professors and journalists and managers who have had difficulty fitting stakeholders into the Story of Business Administration. It will come as especially wlecome news to those business professors and journalists and managers who consider "stakeholder" to be the equivalent of an obscenity. With Strategy Through Convention, the stockholder-stakeholder ambiguity simply goes away. I reduce uncertainty for business people by that much.

Second, you no longer need to worry about keeping up with the latest case studies about what business people are really doing.

Strategy Through Convention is a story about accomplishments, one's autonomy stakes; common grounds, contingent memberships; and conducive connections, self-restrained accomplishments. You can read many stories to deepen your appreciation of these three concepts. I have introduced six such stories in this chapter. These stories are listed in Table 5–2.

These stories are part of a new case study for talking about business. Some of these stories are works of fiction. Some are works of nonfiction.

Table 5–2. Six case studies for Strategy Through Convention (STC)

Metaphor for Corporate Strategist in STC	Case Studies
Amateur	*Barbarians at the Gate* *The Amateurs*
Neighbor	*Barbarians at the Gate* *A Thousand Acres*
Member	*Barbarians at the Gate* *At the Highest Levels*
Student	*Barbarians at the Gate* *The Gate to Women's Country*
Teacher	*Barbarians at the Gate* *North of Hope*

Some could be works of drama and poetry.[59] By Strategy Through Convention, you can keep up with business by teaching yourself and each other about the nuances of accomplishments, common grounds, and conducive connections. In this way, you can worry less about whether you know about the latest "hot" case studies of business practice. With Strategy Through Convention, you can instead read about corporate strategy in a new way that you can apply to the particular business practices that interest you. That is a reduction in uncertainty.

Third, you no longer need to worry about "turf battles" between salespeople and "bean counters," between marketing and product design, and between financiers and "touchy-feely" managers.

There is no place in the vocabulary of Strategy Through Convention for the business functions per se. Finance, marketing, accounting, operations, and human resource management are among the functional areas that are organizing elements of the Story of Business Administration. They are not organizing features of Strategy Through Convention.

Instead, with Strategy Through Convention you can use accomplishments, one's autonomy stakes; common grounds, contingent memberships; and conducive connections, self-restrained accomplishments, to begin to cut across functional boundaries. With common grounds, contingent memberships, for instance, you can think about what is common, not antagonistic, about certain activities that are now segregated into finance, marketing, and human resource management.[60] Cross-functional ambiguity simply goes away once you start talking with a vocabulary of Strategy Through Convention. That seems like a way to reduce uncertainty about business.

Fourth, you no longer need to worry about finding and maintaining a balance between business and ethics.

By Strategy Through Convention, every sentence about corporate strategy is also a sentence about ethics. Strategy Through Convention is a vocabulary in which each corporate strategist takes responsibility for respecting the dignity of each human being with whom one interacts.[61] Hence, *a corporate strategy in Strategy Through Convention is an ethical principle*.[62] Hence, dilemmas about balancing business and ethics simply disappear.[63] By creating Strategy Through Convention in a way that makes this disappearance possible, I take one more practical step to help reduce uncertainty for business people.

XV

Strategy Through Convention is a vocabulary about business that is also a vocabulary with which we can take human solidarity a little more seriously than we could before.[64] Strategy Through Convention is a vocabulary of common grounds, conventions on those common grounds, and meanings of "us" in those conventions. Today, there is no shortage of vocabularies about walls between "them" and "us."[65] In our times, there is no shortage of vocabularies in which the heroes are barbarians who take *them* over, defeat *them*, outperform *them*, and restructure the lives of *them*.[66] Strategy through Convention is a challenge to such barbarism.

With Strategy Through Convention, I offer a retrieved conception of corporate strategy as a metaphor that can pertain to human institutions more widely. Strategy Through Convention is a vocabulary with which we can celebrate the possibility of each person's distinctive worldly contribution through—that is, by means of —a retrieved corporate strategy. This is a subtle meaning of the theme that I develop in this book.

With Strategy Through Convention, I argue that "of course we want business to be more ethical" is a shorter version of the proposition "of course the choice is between more common grounds where 'us' flourishes and more common grounds marked by 'us versus them.'"[67] The Story of Business Administration is a story of "us versus them." So, too, an Ethics of Deadbeats, Dullards, and Derelicts' Disasters Driving the World Into Moral Decline and the Stakeholder Containment Imperative are "us versus them" stories.

With Strategy Through Convention, I argue that it is time to put an end to the intellectual isolation of business discourse, business schools, and business curricula.[68] Ethics through corporate strategy is one way to accomplish that, beginning the minute after you finish this paragraph. After all, we all live on common grounds. Moreover, barbarism is optional. Who could possibly argue with that?[69] I am waiting.

NOTES

CHAPTER 1.

1. If you see half-filled rather than half-empty glasses when it comes to the influence that business ethics teaching and research has had on modern business discourse, I recommend that you read the best-selling book in which Michael Hammer and James Champy make their case for the practice of "business reengineering." The ethical undertones are sobering. After sketching a novel description of the corporation as an evolving composite of discontinuous processes, each of which is the product of agreement among a particular cadre of movers and shakers, Hammer and Champy resort to tired cliches when it comes time to describe how to practice as a reengineer. Among these cliches is a caricature of employees as malleable, marginally moral, beings without personal lives and histories:

> An organization's management systems—the ways in which people are paid, the measures by which their performance is evaluated, and so forth—are the primary shapers of employees' values and beliefs.

M. Hammer and J. Champy, *Reengineering the Corporation: A Manifesto for Business Revolution* (New York: HarperCollins, 1993), 75. This is a key premise in their account because "Changing values is as important a part of reengineering as changing processes." Ibid., 76. Then, when a basic question of distributive justice attends the "radical" degree of change that they openly advocate, Hammer and Champy throw up their hands with this cliche:

> Reengineering isn't to everyone's advantage. Some employees do have a vested interest in current operations, some people will lose their jobs, and some workers may be uncomfortable with their jobs post-reengineering. Trying to please everyone is a hopeless ambition that will either devalue reengineering to a program of incremental change or delay its implementation into the future.

Ibid., 212. It is sobering that *Reengineering the Corporation*, an argument with far-reaching implications, shows no evidence at all of being influenced by business ethics teaching and research. For an extensive critique of the Hammer-Champy argument, see D. Gilbert, Jr., "Management and Four Stakeholder Politics: Corporate Reengineering as a Crossroads Case," *Business & Society* 34, no. 1 (1995):90–97.

2. Many words have been written and many volleys of arguments have been exchanged regarding whether business ethics is a discipline, a field of study, and so on. Two excellent introductions to this debate are N. Bowie, "Business Ethics as a Discipline: The Search for Legitimacy," in R. E. Freeman, ed., *Business*

Ethics: The State of the Art (New York: Oxford University Press, 1991), 17–41, and R. De George, "Will Success Spoil Business Ethics?," in Freeman, *Business Ethics,* 42–56.

Much less attention, however, has been given to the possible relationships between those who teach and write about business ethics and those engaged in management practice. Thomas Mulligan's interpretation of "two cultures," one a "business culture" and one a "humanities culture," in higher education gives impetus to practicing business ethics education as an act of criticism. Mulligan proposes that the humanities culture, of which ethical inquiry is a part, can serve as a "counterbalance" to the business culture. See T. Mulligan, "The Two Cultures in Business Education," *Academy of Management Review* 12 (1987):593–599. R. Edward Freeman and I drew inspiration from Mulligan as we argued that Business and Society educators must adopt the marginal role of "crits." See R. E. Freeman and D. Gilbert, Jr., "Business, Ethics and Society: A Critical Agenda," *Business & Society* 31, no. 1 (1992):9–17.

A disappointing treatment of this subject recently appeared in A. Stark, "What's the Matter with Business Ethics?," *Harvard Business Review* (May–June 1993):38–48. In an account that is as uncritical as it is acritical, Stark reviews a number of business ethics texts that

> point to the gulf that exists between academic business ethics and professional management and suggest that business ethicists themselves may be largely responsible for this gap.

Ibid., 38. To Stark, business ethics education is unquestionably the metaphorical construction subcontractor destined to provide "concrete assistance" (p. 38) to business executives. His entire review of business ethics research turns on this premise, for which he offers nary a clue of justification. The fact that criticism might be another genre of "concrete assistance," as in the arts, eludes Stark completely.

Still another impediment to broader conversations between business ethics educators and management practitioners is self-imposed in certain quarters of the business school community. The problem is manifest in the tired cliche that moral philosophers converse in an inaccessible language and, hence, cannot be admitted to normal discourse about business. One example is expressed in R. Buchholz, *Fundamental Concepts and Problems in Business Ethics* (Englewood Cliffs, NJ: Prentice-Hall, 1989), xiv. I have called attention elsewhere to how this cliche is self-defeating in Buchholz's argument. See D. Gilbert, Jr., "Rogene A. Buchholz, *Fundamental Concepts and Problems in Business Ethics*" (book review), *Journal of Business Ethics* 9 (1990):472, 518. This particular criticism notwithstanding, I argue there that Buchholz's project is useful as a way to convince management educators about the relevance of ethics for management discourse.

My principal concern is that Buchholz unwittingly gives those untutored in ethical theory, such as Stark, one more reason to separate themselves and their analyses from business ethics educators and their arguments. Stark, once again, undermines his own analysis with this generalized characterization of moral philosophy as

> a discipline that tends to place a high value on precisely those kinds of experiences and activities where self-interest does *not* rule.

Stark, "What's the Matter with Business Ethics?," 40. He certainly did not read Chapters 3 and 8—both faithful applications of contractarian moral philosophy—in one target of his complaints: R. E. Freeman and D. Gilbert, Jr., *Corporate Strategy and the Search for Ethics* (Englewood Cliffs, NJ: Prentice-Hall, 1988).

Another vivid example of what happens when ethical theory is summarily dismissed from analysis of human interaction can be found in A. Dixit and B. Nalebuff, *Thinking Strategically: The Competitive Edge in Business, Politics, and Everyday Life* (New York: W.W. Norton, 1991). It is curious that Dixit and Nalebuff *open* their book by posing an ethical question, which they then avoid answering: "How should people behave in society? Our answer does not deal with ethics or etiquette." Ibid., 1. Shortly thereafter, they further distance themselves from moral reasoning (emphasis added): "Our theme, although *less lofty,* affects the lives of all of us *just as much as do morality* and manners." Ibid. Evidently, ethics is such a remote subject that it is expendable in a story about conflict among people, which happens to be prime territory for ethical analysis. Dixit and Nalebuff move later from silence about ethics to offer apologies for sidestepping ethical questions. Ibid., 60 (*), 120. However, such self-criticism is gratuitous. Their account does not require it.

If we interpret business concerns and ethical concerns as antitheses, and Stark and Dixit and Nalebuff do just that, then those who want to say "business ethics is an oxymoron" will continue to be taken seriously. This book is part of my campaign to doom that statement to extinction.

3. As I weave this account of persons creating or falling behind, but never "idling in neutral," I plead guilty to writing under the influence of Ayn Rand, Charles Taylor, Henry Giroux, and Richard Rorty. Rand's biographies of the architects Howard Roark and Peter Keating are one source of inspiration here. See A. Rand, *The Fountainhead* (New York: New American Library, 1971). Taylor uses the metaphor "poet" to describe the person seeking to create his or her own unique identity:

> My self-discovery passes through a creation; the making of something original and new. Self-discovery requires *poiesis,* making.

C. Taylor, *The Ethics of Authenticity* (Cambridge, MA: Harvard University Press, 1991), 62. Giroux writes about ethics as a "continual engagement": in "everyday life." See H. Giroux, "Liberal Arts Education and the Struggle for Public Life: Dreaming about Democracy," in D. Gless and B. H. Smith, eds., *The Politics of Liberal Education* (Durham, NC: Duke University Press, 1992), 134. Richard Rorty portrays the poet as a self-creating person who labors under a never-ending "anxiety of influence, each poet's fear that no proper work remains for him to perform." R. Rorty, *Contingency, Irony, and Solidarity* (Cambridge: Cambridge University Press, 1989), 25. On Rorty's view, the self-creator lives in ironic recognition of his or her self:

> Anyone who spends his life trying to formulate a novel answer to the question of what is possible and important faces the extinction of that answer.

Ibid., 23. Roark *and* Keating would nod in assent. These characters are liberal ironists, in Rorty's terms, because each grasps the possibility of creating his own identity and the possibility that that identity will not always prove stable, useful, and original. Moreover, they both need to believe in one possibility to believe the other. See Rorty, *Contingency, Irony, and Solidarity,* 73–78. Roark is capable of finding delightful inspiration in such irony. Keating, like Sinclair Lewis's George Babbitt character, can only acknowledge it in despair.

David Knights and Glenn Morgan give an account of corporate strategy in which lives are under construction due to what they see as the inevitability of power relations. See D. Knights and G. Morgan, "Corporate Strategy, Organizations, and Subjectivity: A Critique," *Organisation Studies* 12, no. 2 (1991):251–273. Although it might come as a shock to postmoderns like Knights and Morgan, it is possible to write a story about corporate strategy in which power is not part of the vocabulary. This volume is one case in point.

4. There remains considerable question, however, about how much of an advance the concept of corporate social responsibility (CSR) does offer to discourse about management and business. For an argument about the potential ambiguity of CSR, see Freeman and Gilbert, *Corporate Strategy and the Search for Ethics,* 88–105. I have chided several principal CSR researchers for treating CSR, ironically, as both a mature concept and a vulnerable concept. See D. Gilbert, Jr., "Corporate Social Responsibility Reconsidered," discussant's remarks presented at the Academy of Management, Atlanta, Georgia, 1993.

5. I take this distinction from Rand's writings. Roark, Rand's creator exemplar, says this about the borrowers he calls "second handers":

> "They don't ask: 'Is this true?' They ask: 'Is this what others think is true?' Not to judge, but to repeat. Not to do, but to give the impression of doing. Not creation, but show. Not ability, but friendship. Not merit, but pull."

Rand, *The Fountainhead,* 607. In my teaching, I challenge a conventional interpretation that Roark and John Galt (one of Rand's protagonists in *Atlas Shrugged*) are heroes for their individual stands against "the collective." I argue instead that Roark and Galt can be heroes because of the kind of human connection that they advocate and help construct, in contrast to the kinds of community that, in *The Fountainhead,* Ellsworth Toohey and Gail Wynand seek to perpetuate.

It is worth clarifying that I am concerned about autonomous action with this choice, as opposed to action as a follower or sheep or bison or any other herd animal. It is also worth clarifying that I take a search for human connection to be the antithesis of a search for independence. Oftentimes, autonomy and independence are taken for synonyms. I resist this interpretation in view of my aims in this book. I resist, in particular, the proposition that a person's self-directed (autonomous) search for a self must interfere with the search for a conducive context (connection) for self-creation. Jean Baker Miller wants us to talk less about autonomy, it seems, for fear of such interference. J. B. Miller, *Toward a New Psychology of Women,* 2nd ed. (Boston: Beacon Press, 1986), 95.

6. Thus, with the condition "however attentively," I depict self-improvement as a highway that can be traveled using many different forms of transportation. Take *The Fountainhead* narrative, once again, as a case in point. Ellsworth Toohey and Peter Keating lead lives of self-improvement by borrowing and appropriating gains from others' ideas. Avinash Dixit and Barry Nalebuff—notwithstanding their disavowal about making moral claims—paint a vivid picture of self-improvement through the practice of ethical egoism. They tell us, "It is better to be a good strategist than a bad one." Dixit and Nalebuff, *Thinking Strategically,* 1. They even alert us to the consequences of seeking

self-improvement as a "good strategist" who engages others practicing self-improvement:

> We warn you that some of the strategies that are good for achieving these goals may not
> earn you the love of your defeated rivals.

Ibid., 4. I will use this elastic concept of self-improvement as part of a context in which I will critically compare the logics of "ethics from the outside" and "ethics through and through."

7. See, for example, R. Rosenblatt, "How Do Tobacco Executives Live with Themselves?," *New York Times Magazine*, 20 March 1994:34–41, 55, 73–76.

8. The point is that we can interpret values not as fixed and pithy slogans, but rather as specific reasons by which distinct human beings take an action or refrain from that action. In this way, the concept of *value* is liberated from the bedrock foundations of society and placed in the minds and hands of people like you and me. For two introductions to this liberal pragmatist project, see A. Rosmarin, *The Power of Genre* (Minneapolis: University of Minnesota Press, 1985), and R. E. Freeman, D. Gilbert, Jr., and E. Hartman, "Values and the Foundations of Strategic Management," *Journal of Business Ethics* 7 (1988):821–834. A brief case example—taken from my Bucknell teaching experiences—can help us differentiate between values as slogans and values as usable guides for taking action. Consider the hypothetical case of a retailer who doubles the price of a key building supply in the aftermath of a natural disaster in his market area. Many of my students want to raise, and quickly clinch, their objection to this pricing policy by appealing to the retailer's violation of the moral value called "fair play." I then encourage them to critique "fair play" as an idea that they can see themselves enacting in their own lives. What emerges, with respect to the retailer, is another kind of statement of moral values, one of which runs something like this: One should not derive a benefit from dealing with another person whose sole opportunity to recover from a major loss involves an exchange with you, relative to the benefit you would have received in such an exchange under normal circumstances. I ask my students, "Which of these two statements of moral values is more accessible?" Through this exercise, "fair play" means a great deal more than a slogan taken for granted.

9. Certainly this statement leaves open the door to many different genres for celebrating the idea of personhood. We can celebrate the personhood of virtue-seeking beings, altruists, narcissists, and members of a particular cultural group, for example. For a thoughtful account of personhood and cultural identity, see C. Taylor, *Multiculturalism and the Politics of Recognition* (Princeton, NJ: Princeton University Press, 1992). Alternatively, the worth of one's personhood is an idea alien to a broad swath of strategic management research. See D. Gilbert, Jr., *The Twilight of Corporate Strategy: A Comparative Ethical Critique* (New York: Oxford University Press, 1992).

10. If we locate relationships, and exchanges within such relationships, at the center of ethical criticism, then we can begin to think of ethical values as a kind of "social glue." See D. Gilbert, Jr., "Why Worry about Ethics?," paper presented to the Direct Marketing Association Spring Conference, Anaheim, California, 1992. My view clashes sharply with the belief, familiar to those who practice by "ethics from the outside," that ethical values should be clubs wielded in the vicinity of people's heads. By the time this book ends, you will see why I believe

that we should stop talking—in business ethics education and management education more generally—about such noted business figures as Ivan Boesky and Michael Milken. To rehash their professional biographies is to miss the point about an affirmative link between the discourses of business and ethics. All that rehashing does is confirm the "ethics from the outside" way of thinking.

11. By posing this question, I distance myself from those such as Alasdair Macintyre who would have us return to emphasizing an ethics of virtue. See A. MacIntyre, *After Virtue: A Study in Moral Theory,* 2nd ed. (Notre Dame, IN: University of Notre Dame Press, 1984). My reason for talking about an ethics of relationships is a straightforward pragmatist one. Contemporary business discourse can proceed as a story about exchange. Exchange in the marketplace, exchange within organizational hierarchies, exchange of signals among rivals, and regulatory impediment to exchange are all familiar elements of that language. I write this book to talk with those who live in that language. That is, in a postmodern pragmatist spirit, I want to meet these persons in the historical and social circumstances "where they are."

Quite ironically, here is a place where I agree with Stark that, for any conversation about business practice and ethics practice to be useful for the participants, they must find a language that they can share. Stark, "What's the Matter with Business Ethics?," 46. This is my project in Chapter 1. What Stark does not seem to understand is that the language game that dominates "the institutional world inhabited by most managers" is not the only possible way to talk about business. Ibid. We need not put ourselves in businesspersons' back pockets or volunteer for indentured servitude in order to talk with them.

12. Stark seems to take the view that debate about ethical values—a process which he labels "absolutist"—is the antithesis of offering "practical" advice. Ibid., 38. There is a non sequitur in that proposition which, at the very least, requires explanation if such a picture of practical assistance is to make any sense. Absent such a justification, all Stark offers his readers is speculative complaint. Many executives would probably be very surprised to learn that their debates about such matters as the proper bounds on customer service qualify as "absolutist" exercises. To philosophical pragmatists like me, life is a never-ending intellectual search for a contest, debate, or showdown between alternative ways of talking and acting. That does not sound very "absolutist."

13. Rorty, *Contingency, Irony, and Solidarity,* 9. For my purposes, I take "vocabulary" to refer to a particular way of expressing the pattern of meanings that a community of persons adopt as their language. In this regard, I follow Elizabeth Wolgast's distinction between a term (part of a vocabulary) and the grammatical context (language) in which the term is put into practice. Thus,

> the grammar of a term includes a wide variety of practices connected with its use and the criteria and background conditions that govern its normal application.

E. Wolgast, *The Grammar of Justice* (Ithaca, NY: Cornell University Press, 1987), x. For the most part, I will use vocabulary and language interchangeably. At times, I will stress the former when I want to call attention to particular components of my new story about corporate strategy. Nothing in my aims here requires any further distinction between the two concepts.

14. See Gilbert, *Twilight of Corporate Strategy,* 147–165.

15. See Rorty, *Contingency, Irony, and Solidarity,* 12.

16. I am grateful to Bill Frederick for his assistance over the years as I have tried to make sense of the corporate social responsibility idea.

17. I follow Stanley Fish's distinction here between (a) doing and (b) talking about doing. S. Fish, *Doing What comes Naturally: Change, Rhetoric, and the Practice of Theory in Literary and Legal Studies* (Durham, NC: Duke University Press, 1989), 372–398. My first justification is an appeal to you in the realm of "your doing," that subjective experience that only you can live. As a liberal pragmatist, all I can logically do—and should ethically do—is talk about how you might "do" a life of differences, centers, and margins. If I persuade you, the rest of the justification is up to you. With my second justification, I reach out to a certain group of intellectual neighbors. These neighbors, by virtue of their particular past and ongoing efforts at "talking about doing," could join me in talking about an ethics of differences, centers, and margins. Fish makes the distinction between doing and talking about doing with a masterful analysis of a brief, yet telling, conversation about pitching strategy between major league pitcher Dennis Martinez and Earl Weaver, Martinez's one-time manager. Ibid. On Fish's account, "Once you start down the anti-formalist road," as I do, you must give up the idea that you can use theory to live another's life as he experiences it. Instead, all (!) you can do is try to strike up a conversation with him, hopefully en route to authentic progress for him and you. Ibid., 2.

My project in this book is analogous to how a structural engineer might weigh two alternative bridge designs, how an orthopedist might choose between two approaches for treating a knee injury, how a detective might sift through competing trails of clues left by a clever suspect, and how a literary critic might compare a writer's earlier and later works. Each of these persons can practice the kind of critical interpretation that I conduct here. Like each of these persons, I am interested in the intellectual integrity of a way of seeing and acting, in criteria with which I can evaluate a way of seeing and acting, and in reasons with which I can justify a critical preference for one alternative over another. My objects of analysis are possible meanings for "we want business to be more ethical." My data are what others have said about ethics and business. Concerned as I am with the meaningfulness of accounts written by some human beings about other human beings, I act formally as a literary and ethical critic in this book. For a detailed account of researcher-as-literary-critic, see Gilbert, *Twilight of Corporate Strategy*, 29–54.

18. Those few people are the moral leaders whose presence has won widespread acceptance in modern business discourse about business ethics and CSR. My proposition is that this elite corps of moral leaders is not some Truth of Nature, but rather a literary and rhetorical device perpetrated by those who faithfully teach the so-called Harvard Policy language of business. See D. Gilbert, Jr., E. Hartman, J. Mauriel, Jr., and R. E. Freeman, *A Logic for Strategy* (New York: Ballinger, 1988). While I leave it to some enterprising doctoral student to trace the genealogy of "ethics from the outside" (Hint: go back at least to the writings of Herbert Simon and Alfred Sloan), I want to focus on the ethical baggage that goes along with assigning executives the heroic role of ethics expert. For stinging critique of the idea of moral leadership, see B. DeMott, "Choice Academic Pork," *Harper's* 287, no. 1723 (1993):61–62, 64, 66–68, 72, 77.

It has taken me some time, and now the occasion of this book, to work out this interpretation of "ethics from the outside." I am indebted to Ed Freeman for his advice over this period. For a collection of earlier attempts to critique this "external" premise, see D. Gilbert, Jr., "Diane Vaughan, *Controlling Unlawful Organizational Behavior: Social Structure and Corporate Misconduct*" (book review), *Journal of Business Ethics* 7 (1988):800–802; D. Gilbert, Jr., "*Executive Integrity: The Search for High Human Values in Organizational Life*, by Suresh Srivastva and Associates" (book review), *Business Horizons*, July–August 1989:80–81; and D. Gilbert, Jr., "Respect for Persons, Management Theory, and Business Ethics," in Freeman, *Business Ethics*, 111–120. I am quite aware that it might not be a popular tack to call attention to such a disparaging conception of human beings. Several reviewers have chided me for doing so. But, as Rorty, Fish, and Wolgast—among others—remind us, to act as a critic is to work within the languages that we have inherited and shaped ourselves.

19. I have in mind no fixed rule for determining which layer(s) of organizational hierarchy constitute this privileged position above the immoral fray. As I am critiquing the arguments made by those who write and talk in accordance with "ethics from the outside," I willingly take their cues as to where they draw the boundary between "outsider" and "insider." If that logic runs, say, four levels deep into the hierarchy, so be it.

20. Thus, my distinction between "outside" and "inside" does not square with conventional business discourse. On that account, one resides inside the organization if one receives a paycheck, E-mail, and voice mail at that organizational address. By contrast, the formal organization per se is not my point of reference.

There are many places in the management literature where this alienation-from-the-ethical-life theme burns brightly. Oliver Williamson's premise about opportunism is a case in point. See O. Williamson, *Markets and Hierarchies: Analysis and Antitrust Implications* (New York: Free Press, 1975), 26–30, 53–54. Another story where persons' "natural" moral unreliability is taken as an axiom is conventional game theory. Dixit and Nalebuff assert the following about the parties to the Prisoner's Dilemma, one game-theory narrative:

> The underlying problem is the players' incentive to cheat on any agreement. Therefore, the central questions are, How can such cheating be detected? What prospect of punishment will deter it?

Dixit and Nalebuff, *Thinking Strategically*, 95. I will take a close critical look in Chapter 3 at the Prisoner's Dilemma, which seems to be one of the game-theorist's favorite stories. For another perspective on the moral improverishment of game theory, see Chapter 5 in R. Solomon, *Ethics and Excellence: Cooperation and Integrity in Business* (New York: Oxford University Press, 1992). I thank Edwin Hartman for bringing Solomon's argument to my attention.

21. I thank Ed Freeman for pointing out how my concept of "ethics from the outside" bears a resemblance to Straussian political philosophy. For one challenge to a Straussian view, see R. Rorty, "Two Cheers for the Cultural Left," in Gless and Smith, eds., *Politics of Liberal Education*, 235.

22. This is an opportunity for each human to be treated with dignity. Charles Taylor shows how a universalized concept of "dignity" has replaced selective eligibility for "honor" in modern political discourse and institutions. See Taylor, *Ethics of Authenticity*, 46–47. For a more extensive treatment of this historical turn, see Taylor, *Multiculturalism and the Politics of Recognition*. A current debate about the reach of dignity and the respect for one's uniqueness involves deafness,

which historically has been treated as a physical and social problem to overcome. See E. Dolnick, "Deafness as Culture," *The Atlantic Monthly*, 272, no. 3 (1993):37–53. Throughout my argument here, the continuing influence of John Rawls's "justice as fairness" is strong. See J. Rawls, *A Theory of Justice* (Cambridge, MA: Harvard University Press, 1971).

23. Another way to put the point is this: To practice the logic of "ethics from the outside" is to give priority to reinforcing the power positions of senior executives. Although enacting "ethics from the outside" programs and policies might swell the pride these individuals have about their own virtue, such practice offers little support for the idea of human dignity, and hence *each* person's moral sensitivities and capabilities regardless of organizational membership. For an extensive argument based on this particular outside-insider distinction, see R. Frank, *Passions Within Reason: The Strategic Role of Emotions* (New York: W. W. Norton, 1988).

24. My discussion about personal growth through ties to others draws on the feminist arguments made by Carol Gilligan and her colleagues and Jean Baker Miller and her colleagues. See, in particular, C. Gilligan, *In a Different Voice: Psychological Theory and Women's Development* (Cambridge, MA: Harvard University Press, 1982); C. Gilligan, N. Lyons, and T. Hanmer, eds., *Making Connections: The Relational Worlds of Adolescent Girls at Emma Willard School* (Cambridge, MA: Harvard University Press, 1990); J. B. Miller, *Toward a New Psychology of Women;* and J. Jordan, A. Kaplan, J. B. Miller, I. Stiver, and J. Surrey, *Women's Growth in Connection: Writings from the Stone Center* (New York: Guilford Press, 1991). Consequently, I develop my argument with a more prominent place for the value of connection than Richard Rorty provides with his laissez faire account of human solidarity. Rorty wants to describe a world where liberal self-creators worry about "how to equalize opportunities for self-creation and then leave people alone to use, or neglect, their opportunities." Rorty, *Contingency, Irony, and Solidarity,* 85. I follow the premise advanced by Gilligan, Miller, and their colleagues that staying out of each other's way is not quite enough for self-creation. I thank Ed Freeman, Norman Bowie, Craig Dunn, and Robbin Derry for their advice in this regard.

In order to make margins—that is, joint opportunities to think and act contingently—central features of my argument, I do not treat *relationship* and *connection* as synonyms. Rather, I assume that the latter is a special case of the former. The usefulness of this premise will become clear in Chapter 5. Once again, the different worlds in which Roark and Toohey move in Ayn Rand's *The Fountainhead* are cases in point. Toohey, I argue, forges relationships that serve to undermine human connection, the kind of psychological bond that Jordan and colleagues discuss and advocate. Hence, while I am persuaded by the form of life that Jordan and others advocate, I do not want to go straight to the "punch line." There is critical work to be accomplished before that, namely the critical disposal of "ethics from the outside."

My argument is influenced here by not only Rorty, Taylor, Jordan, Kaplan, Miller, Stiver, and Surrey, Gilligan, Wolgast, and Fish, but also by John Rawls and his recent work on political liberalism. See J. Rawls, *Political Liberalism* (New York: Columbia University Press, 1993).

25. My principal sources here are D. Lewis, *Convention: A Philosophical Study* (Cambridge, MA: Harvard University Press, 1969); T. Schelling, *Micromotives*

and Macrobehavior (New York: W. W. Norton, 1978); I. Kantrow, *The Constraints of Corporate Tradition: Doing the Correct Thing, Not Just What the Past Dictates* (New York: Harper & Row, 1987); A. Schotter, *The Economic Theory of Social Institutions* (Cambridge: Cambridge University Press, 1981); and H. Leibenstein, *Inside the Firm: The Inefficiencies of Hierarchy* (Cambridge, MA: Harvard University Press, 1987). There is irony in my reference to Leibenstein's work, for he argues that conventions can threaten a firm's efficiency. That sounds like one more appeal to "ethics from the outside." Additionally, I should note that I depart from Elizabeth Wolgast, among others, who talk about conventions as some force transcending the actions of the parties to them. Wolgast, *Grammar of Justice*, 212. I want to argue that we can choose to live as postmoderns and to live through conventions, too.

26. Throughout this book I concentrate on a discourse about *corporate* strategy. I do this to acknowledge the dominance of corporate/business discourse in modern Western societies. Still, the line between corporate strategy and strategy "unmodified" is neither very important nor very permanent. With the non-business examples that I use throughout the book, I set the stage for erasing that boundary altogether. That is, I hope that this book can foster conversations about Strategy Through Convention in contexts ranging from education to government to sports to the family to military operations and to business.

27. I prefer the preposition "through" to "in" when talking about Ethics Through Corporate Strategy and Strategy Through Convention. "Through" implies, it seems to me, greater consequence and potential for one's growth than is the case when one is simply "in" a relationship with another person. "Through" also implies a time dimension. I want to talk about lives and relationships that have a past, a present, and a possible future. A richer conception of personal originality thus becomes available. By talking in this way, I am also taking care to avoid the modern trap of "instrumental reason," as Charles Taylor describes and bemoans the practice of making choices solely on the basis of the net economic gains available to the chooser. Taylor, *Ethics of Authenticity*, 4–8. When it comes to associating with others, a practitioner of instrumental reason is a transient. Since 1976, more than a few major league baseball players (free agents) have been accused of acting in this way. Thus, while relationships *are* instrumental to the characters in my account—as they are in Taylor's—precisely because they are fertile fields for one's becoming authentic, they are not readily disposable. Ibid., 28–29, 45–49. I think that "through," better than "in," enables me to distance my argument from the shortcomings of an ethic of instrumental reason. Hence, I read Taylor as a polestar for my argument.

28. In his critiques of stakeholder research, Ed Freeman refers to this as the "separation" theory. On a separation view, there are matters of the ethical kind and there are (real) matters of the business kind. See R. E. Freeman, "The Politics of Stakeholder: Some Future Directions," *Business Ethics Quarterly* 4 (1994):409–421. It is this belief that enables Andrew Stark to arrive at his astonished conclusion about the "myopia" of those who try to make sense of business through moral philosophy filters: "In other words, business ethics means acting within business for nonbusiness reasons." Stark, "What's the Matter with Business Ethics?," 40. What Stark does not consider is the moral cost of believing that such separation is a useful way to live in the business world.

29. This then is a way to bridge the traditional chasm between business and the humanities. I maintain that it is business academics, and not humanities

educators, who are responsible for the gulf between cultures that Thomas Mulligan has rightfully bemoaned. See D. Gilbert, Jr., "Management, Literary Criticism, and What We Could Say About the Matter of Control Over Others," paper presented at the Social Issues in Management Research Workshop, Academy of Management, Anaheim, California, 1988. That paper has been transformed into D. Gilbert, Jr., "A Critique and a Retrieval of Management and the Humanities," *Journal of Business Ethics* 15 (1996), in press. I have been working through this proposition with the encouragement of Ed Freeman, Kate Rogers, Gordon Meyer, Larry Shinn, John Miller, Elaine Garrett, Teresa Amott, Eugenia Gerdes, and Pushkala Prasad.

One way to bridge this gap is to create new metaphors for business. On the subject of new metaphors generally, see Rorty, *Contingency, Irony, and Solidarity*, 9. If I had to choose an epigraph for a story about my doctoral studies, Rorty's discussion is it. A turning point in my thinking about metaphors and management theory was a series of conversations with Todd Hostager and Ed Freeman. Another turning point was an impatient commentary, from an anonymous reviewer, in response to my first attempt at critiquing metaphors used in management theory. The spirit of that paper, and of the "hatchet job" done to it, permeates this book. For an account of the contingency of metaphors, see C. Schine, "Dying Metaphors Take Flight," *New York Times Magazine*, 8 August 1993:14.

30. The distinction here involves what we choose to include in what Richard Rorty calls our "final vocabulary," which one reaches at this margin of conversation:

> If doubt is cast on the worth of these words, their user has no noncircular argumentative recourse. Those words are as far as he can go with language; beyond them these is only helpless passivity or a resort to force.

Rorty, *Contingency, Irony, and Solidarity*, 73. "Ethics from the outside" is a popular final vocabulary that, as Andrew Stark's analysis shows, gives priority to the business status quo. "Empirical" support for the logic of "ethics from the outside" is a project designed to reinforce that status quo discourse. With "ethics already through and through," I hope to construct a new doorway through which can pass creators of many different final vocabularies in which personal originality through human connection—and not a vocabulary concluding with cash flow, annual global sales growth, numbers of white collar crimes, and so on—is as far as we can travel.

Daniel Quinn provides a creative twist on this idea, in terms of "the myth of Mother Culture." See D. Quinn, *Ishmael* (New York: Bantam/Turner, 1992), 34–52. Quinn's protagonist is Ishmael, a gorilla. Ishmael patiently guides his human pupil through self-scrutiny about the story of "how things came to be this way" that dominates the pupil's society. Ibid., 40. One of my projects, with this book and elsewhere, is to set traps for those who want to deny their "final vocabulary," much less the ethical implications of both that denial and that vocabulary. Recently, in a paper on using literature to teach about business ethics, Tony McAdams worries that

> this suggested use of stories risks a charge of indoctrination in that one is necessarily teaching a particular content and probably a particular point of view, thus violating the neutrality that we normally seek in moral education.

T. McAdams, *"The Great Gatsby* as a Business Ethics Inquiry," *Journal of Business Ethics* 12 (1993):659. On my pragmatist account, the "probably" makes no sense, and the "violation" is a nonviolation. As Stanley Fish puts it, we are unavoidably "in a point of view." Fish, *Doing What Comes Naturally,* 12. See also Gilbert, "A Critique and a Retrieval of Management and the Humanities."

31. To the pragmatist, "talking" refers to a complex, contingent, ironic con- coction of word, deed, history, relationships, and aspirations that is a defining act of living. This seems to be a very practical notion. Concerns about language become impractical only if we sever the link between how we talk and how we act. If we subscribe to a final vocabulary based on that severance, then, of course (a) concerns with language are "absolutist," per Andrew Stark; (b) criticism of lan- guage is "politically correct" quibbling; (c) the separation between strategy for- mulation (talking) and strategy implementation (doing) is clean; (d) business ethics (talking) is a nuisance to the real business of the world (doing); and so on. To the pragmatist, and to the liberal contractarian pragmatist in particular, this kind of separation is dangerous nonsense.

CHAPTER 2.

1. I draw inspiration here from Richard Rorty's suggestion about whom we should consider to be the leading cultural critics in a world of pragmatists:

> This process of coming to see other human beings as "one of us" rather than as "them" is a matter of detailed description of what unfamiliar people are like and of redescription of what we ourselves are like. This is a task not for theory but for genres such as ethnography, the journalist's report, the comic book, the docudrama, and, especially, the novel.

R. Rorty, *Contingency, Irony, and Solidarity* (Cambridge: Cambridge University Press, 1989), xvi. For an account that explains changes in American society in terms of contemporary popular culture, see D. Halberstam, *The Fifties* (New York: Villard, 1993).

2. The specific sources here are "Calvin & Hobbes" by Bill Watterson, distrib- uted by Universal Press Syndicate; "Rocky & Bullwinkle" by Jay Ward, distrib- uted in video by Buena Vista Home Video, a division of the Walt Disney Com- pany; "Blondie" by Dean Young and Stan Drake, distributed by King Features Syndicate, Inc.; W. Kinsella, *Box Socials* (New York: Ballantine, 1991); G. Jen, *Typical American* (New York: Plume, 1992); and D. Coupland, *Generation X: Tales for an Accelerated Culture* (New York: St. Martin's Press, 1991). In commenting on these six sources, I write as a reviewer. I make no attempt to ascertain or divine or explain the "true" intent behind what each of these creators has accomplished. Rather, I take their works as significant cases with which I can fashion a particu- lar point of my own creation. In this sense, I think of a reviewer as someone who practices rhetorical, rather than someone who seeks special insights into an au- thor's mind. For several examples of such a pragmatist kind of critical review, see the following reviews published when the Walt Disney Co. first released "Rocky & Bullwinkle" in video cassettes: D. Kaplan, "Rocky and Bullwinkle Brave the Comeback Trail," *New York Times,* 7 May 1989, Section 2:31, 41; C. Rickey, "Rocky and Bullwinkle Hit the Silver Screen," *Philadelphia Inquirer,* 21 April 1990:3C; S. Rea, "Hokey Smokes! It's Rocky on Video," *Philadelphia Inquirer,*

and the Practice of Theory in Literary and Legal Studies (Durham, NC: Duke University Press, 1989), 372–398.

11. I fully intend the reference here to men. "Deadbeat" businesswomen are all but invisible in the business media. I am ironist enough to admit that there is more to say some day about gender and corporate strategy.

12. This particular ethics is a genre that I create for purposes of this analysis. For an earlier attempt to interpret this ethics, see D. Gilbert, Jr., *"Can Ethics Be Taught? Perspectives, Challenges, and Approaches at Harvard Business School,* by Thomas Piper, Mary Gentile, and Sharon Daloz Parks" (book review), *International Journal of Organizational Analysis* 2, no. 4 (1994):433–436. I thank Diane Swanson for her encouragement and good humor as I completed that book review.

13. I use "ethical" here as an adjective to refer to serious matters that involve a person's life prospects and projects. From that encompassing usage of "ethical," it is then possible to move to use "ethical" in the more local sense of saying, "Action A in Case C is ethical/not ethical." Those researchers who are determined to equate ethics with prevention collapse these two meanings of "ethical." As a consequence, they discourage the kinds of discussions that any two critics can have about matters of right and wrong. If we ignore the first meaning of "ethical,"we are guilty of ignoring the context in which human beings move.

14. This is a decidedly narrower focus than, say, the costs imposed on third parties who are helpless in the face of a deadbeat's actions. The political message in such a narrower concept of "deadbeat" is unmistakable. Supporters of this conception of "deadbeat" say, in effect, "we in the business world must protect our own franchise before strangers come in and do it (ignorantly) for us. Thus, the deadbeat is a threat to us and to our franchise." The appeal to self-governance here is admirable. Nonetheless, the willful disregard of what happens along the boundary between the business franchise and the larger world is ripe for criticism, on a liberal pragmatist view.

15. Dereliction, as I use the concept here, should be understood as a possible conclusion that one could reach if one used an ethical assumption that employees should be loyal agents of senior management. That ethical assumption is part of a prevention perspective. Hence, I do not use "dereliction" to cast aspersion on a particular person's character. That meaning of dereliction makes sense in a different ethical tradition.

16. I am grateful to Douglas Sturm for his counsel on this point, and many other points about undergraduate teaching.

17. G. Trudeau, "Doonesbury," *Philadelphia Inquirer,* 17 November 1993:G7. Indeed, Trudeau has long been on the lookout for deadbeats. For an early expose, see G. Trudeau, *Guilty, Guilty, Guilty!* (New York: Holt, Rinehart & Winston, 1973).

18. G. Trudeau, "Doonesbury," *Philadelphia Inquirer,* 1 June 1994:G9, regarding the "Carcinogen Seven."

19. I began to work out this rhetorical place for the antihero in Gilbert, *"Can Ethics Be Taught?,"* book review. Jay Ward and his creative collaborators on "Rocky & Bullwinkle" have influenced me considerably with regard to antiheroes. It was not very difficult for me, as an eight-year-old watching "Rocky & Bullwinkle" on prime-time afterschool television, to figure out that Boris Badenov, Natasha Fatale, and Fearless Leader epitomized the "antihero."

20. The entire advertisement, which was sent through the mail, reads: *"Business Ethics. The only business magazine for the good guys. For those who are changing the way business does business."*

21. See "The Rewards of Doing It Right: Ethics in American Business," *Forbes* (28 March 1994, advertising supplement):1–4. These awards were jointly sponsored by the American Society of CLU & ChFC and *Forbes*.

22. R. Buchholz, *Business Environment and Public Policy*, 4th ed. (Englewood Cliffs, NJ: Prentice-Hall, 1992), 1–2, 42–43, 68–69, 89–90, 116–118, 211–212, 278–279, 313–314, 350–351, 412–413, 486–487.

23. I. Kesner, B. Victor, and B. Lamont, "Board Composition and the Commission of Illegal Acts: An Investigation of *Fortune* 500 Companies," *Academy of Management Journal* 29 (1986):789–799.

24. W. Davidson III and D. Worrell, "The Impact of Announcements of Corporate Illegalities on Shareholder Returns," *Academy of Management Journal* 31 (1988):195–200.

25. L. K. Trevino and B. Victor, "Peer Reporting of Unethical Behavior: A Social Context Perspective," *Academy of Management Journal* 35 (1992):38–64.

26. M. Baucus and J. Near, "Can Illegal Corporate Behavior Be Predicted? An Event History Analysis," *Academy of Management Journal* 34 (1991):9–36.

27. M. Bommer, C. Gratto, J. Gravander, and M. Tuttle, "A Behavioral Model of Ethical and Unethical Decision Making," *Journal of Business Ethics* 6 (1987):265–280.

28. A. Mitchell, T. Puxty, P. Sikka, and H. Willmott, "Ethical Statements as Smokescreens for Sectional Interests: The Case of the U.K. Accountancy Profession," *Journal of Business Ethics* 13 (1994):39–51. Publication of this paper, along with other articles that I cite, is indicative of not only what interests management researchers, but also what interests journal editors, their editorial boards, and the reviewers on whom they call for advice. In this sense, the interest in business deadbeats can be explained in terms of how Michel Foucault defines the modern author. See M. Foucault, "Who Is an Author?," in J. Harrar, ed., *Textual Strategies: Perspectives in Post-Structuralist Criticism* (Ithaca, NY: Cornell University Press, 1979), 141–160. I do not agree, however, with Foucault's suggestion that what happens in academic communities can be explained as simply a matter of power elites holding the high ground against the pressures from those who do not hold such power. A framework of voluntary agreements is another way to think about academic communities.

29. S. Zahra, "Unethical Practices in Competitive Analysis: Patterns, Causes and Effects," *Journal of Business Ethics* 13 (1994):53–62.

30. S. Grover and C. Hui, "The Influence of Role Conflict and Self-Interest on Lying in Organizations," *Journal of Business Ethics* 13 (1994):295–303.

31. P. Simpson, D. Banerjee, and C. Simpson, Jr., "Softlifting: A Model of Motivating Factors," *Journal of Business Ethics* 13 (1994):431–438.

32. The point here is not that this is a "representative sample of research," but rather that this is a diverse set of commentaries that might not ordinarily be called a genre. For an explanation of this distinction, see the discussion of what I call a "test of breadth" in Gilbert, *Twilight of Corporate Strategy*, 51–53, 69–73. Consider the range of perspectives and cases in the following recent research about business deadbeats: M. Salem and O. -D. Martin, "The Ethics of Using Chapter XI as a Management Strategy," *Journal of Business Ethics* 13 (1994):95–

104; P. Lansing and D. Hatfield, "Corporate Control Through the Criminal System—An Alternative Solution," *Journal of Business Ethics* 4 (1985):409–414; M. Pearson, "Auditor Independence Deficiencies & Alleged Audit Failures," *Journal of Business Ethics* 6 (1987):281–287; L. Hosmer, "The Institutionalization of Unethical Behavior," *Journal of Business Ethics* 6 (1987):439–447; D. Dalton and I. Kesner, "On the Dynamics of Corporate Size and Illegal Activity: An Empirical Assessment," *Journal of Business Ethics* 7 (1988):861–870; A. Parkman, B. George, and M. Boss, "Owners or Traders: Who Are the Real Victims of Insider Trading?," *Journal of Business Ethics* 7 (1988):965–971; L. K. Trevino and G. Ball, "The Social Implications of Punishing Unethical Behavior: Observers' Cognitive and Affective Reactions," *Journal of Management* 18 (1992):751–768; S. Payne, "Organization Ethics and Antecedents to Social Control Processes," *Academy of Management Review* 5 (1980):409–414; and E. Szwajkowski, "Organizational Illegality: Theoretical Integration and Illustrative Application," *Academy of Management Review* 10 (1985):558–567.

33. A. Bennett, "Ethics Codes Spread Despite Skepticism," *Wall Street Journal,* 15 July 1988:17.

34. B. Feder, "Helping Corporate America Hew to the Straight and Narrow," *New York Times,* 3 November 1991, Section 3:5.

35. J. Byrne, "The Best-Laid Ethics Programs . . . Couldn't Stop a Nightmare at Dow Corning. What Happened?," *Business Week,* 9 March 1992, 68–69.

36. Volume 1, Number 1, of *Corporate Conduct Quarterly* appeared in the summer of 1991. This periodical is published by The Forum for Policy Research at Rutgers, The State University of New Jersey, Camden campus.

37. One implication then of my critical analysis of this ethics about deadbeats, dullards, derelicts, and declines is that it might be worthwhile to critique the time-honored proposition that senior executive leadership is the "way out" of our modern ethical dilemmas in organizational life. For one analysis of the anti-dullard campaign, see R. Mitchell, "Managing Values: Is Levi Strauss' Approach Visionary—Or Flaky?," *Business Week,* 1 August 1994, 46–52. Mitchell's answer is "yes, on both counts." This should not be surprising. His subtitle gives away the destination that he has in mind. Mitchell assumes that anti-dullard campaigns should be subordinate to stockholder wealth. For one analysis of the anti-deadbeat campaign, see the commentary about "sleazebags" and their cousins in B. O'Reilly, "J&J Is on a Roll," *Fortune,* 26 December 1994, 178–192. My criticism here is directed at Mitchell and O'Reilly and the interpretive community in which they can be considered members in good standing. I am saying nothing here, on the other hand, about persons acting as agents for the corporations that Mitchell and O'Reilly analyze.

38. See T. Piper, M. Gentile, and S. D. Parks, *Can Ethics Be Taught? Perspectives, Challenges, and Approaches at Harvard Business School* (Boston: Harvard Business School, 1993).

39. Ibid., 121.

40. Ibid., 168.

41. See their claim to "our fundamental responsibility." Ibid., 11. I refer to the argument made by Piper, Gentile, and Parks as an expression of a "politics of reassertion" in Gilbert, *"Can Ethics Be Taught?,"* book review. Reassertion refers to the ostensibly rightful place that American business executives should occupy as moral exemplars. It is "reassertion," because Piper, Gentile, and Parks proceed

from the assumption that this rightful place has been tarnished, if not occupied by impostors, in recent years. The campaign against the business dullard is waged outside Boston, too. For an account about a venture of this kind at the Wharton School, University of Pennsylvania, see T. Dunfee and D. Robertson, "Integrating Ethics Into the Business School Curriculum," *Journal of Business Ethics* 7 (1988):847–859.

Processes for transforming the beliefs of the business dullard is a common focus in academic research. A recent article in this spirit by LaRue Hosmer could readily be retitled, "Strategic Planning as if the Divine Right of Managers to Shame and Eradicate Business Dullards Mattered." See L. Hosmer, "Strategic Planning as if Ethics Mattered," *Strategic Management Journal* 15 (1994):17–34. In the campaign against the dullard, see the discussion about ethics as something that is "instrumental to valued consequences," in R. Morgan, "Self- and Co-Worker Perceptions of Ethics and Their Relationship to Leadership and Salary," *Academy of Management Journal* 36 (1993):200–214. That paper is an excellent example of the logic of "ethics from the outside." According to two other authors, "there is an ethical person profile." R. O'Neal and D. Pienta, "Economic Criteria Versus Ethical Criteria Toward Resolving a Basic Dilemma in Business," *Journal of Business Ethics* 13 (1994):71–78. Another researcher claims: "The pedagogic concern is to find effective methods of incorporating ethics into the fabric of business education." K. Brown, "Using Role Play to Integrate Ethics Into the Business Curriculum: A Financial Management Example," *Journal of Business Ethics* 13 (1994):105–110. The campaign against the business dullard is waged further in G. Mellema, "Business Ethics and Doing What One Ought to Do," *Journal of Business Ethics* 13 (1994):149–153; R. Peterson, "Depiction of Idealized Youth Lifestyles in Magazine Advertisements: A Content Analysis," *Journal of Business Ethics* 13 (1994):259–269; P. Primeaux and J. Stieber, "Profit Maximization: The Ethical Mandate of Business," 287–294, (see their comment about "the good ethics of the majority"; Ibid., 287); and L. Newton, "The Internal Morality of the Corporation," *Journal of Business Ethics* 5 (1986):249–258. Newton refers to "the excellences of the corporation." Ibid., 252–254.

In all these papers, a high moral ground is in the spotlight. The difficulties in reaching such high moral ground are discussed in L. Pitt and R. Abratt, "Corruption in Business—Are Management Attitudes Right?," *Journal of Business Ethics* 5 (1986):39–44, and H. R. Smith and A. Carroll, "Organizational Ethics: A Stacked Deck," *Journal of Business Ethics* 3 (1984):95–100. Smith and Carroll note that "the deck is frequently 'stacked' against higher levels of ethical behavior." Ibid., 95.

42. K. Andrews, *The Concept of Corporate Strategy*, rev. ed. (Homewood, IL: Richard D. Irwin, 1980), 10–11.

43. See S. Srivastva and associates, *Executive Integrity: The Search for High Human Values in Organizational Life* (San Francisco: Jossey-Bass, 1988); C. Walton, *The Moral Manager* (Cambridge, MA: Ballinger, 1988); R. Golembiewski, *Men, Management, and Morality: Toward a New Organizational Ethics* (New York: McGraw-Hill, 1965); and K. Goodpaster, "Ethical Imperatives and Corporate Leadership," in R. E. Freeman, ed., *Business Ethics: The State of the Art* (New York: Oxford University Press, 1991), 89–110.

44. "The Best of 1993," *Business Week*, 10 January 1994, 122–125.

45. Many articles have appeared in the business media on this subject. For a

comprehensive survey, see N. Ramsey, "What Companies Are Doing," *Fortune*, 29 November 1993, 142–162. See also N. Perry, "School Reform: Big Pain, Little Gain," *Fortune*, 29 November 1993, 130–138.

46. For a recent review of the tradition of corporate social responsibility that has been practiced in Minnesota, and Norman Bowie's efforts to sustain that tradition, see, W. Swanson, "Saving the SR CEO," *Minnesota* (July–August 1994):38–43. *Minnesota* is published by the University of Minnesota Alumni Association. For another angle on this Minnesota tradition, see L. Inskip, "Laudable Corporate Responsibility Program Is Back on Track," *Minneapolis Star Tribune*, 27 June 1994:11A. See also N. St. Anthony, "Payless Chief Balances Bottom Line, Social Issues," *Minneapolis Star & Tribune*, 16 January 1987:1M, 9M.

47. P. Shrivastava, "Are We Ready for Another Three Mile Island, Bhopal, Tylenol," *Industrial Crisis Quarterly* 1 (1987):2.

48. One way to think about crises is in terms of the rights of the parties involved. Interpreted as a prevention campaign, so-called crisis management amounts to an assertion that senior management's rights to direct the affairs of the firm take priority. All that crisis management entails, on this view, is an extension of the priority that senior managers have claimed for themselves all along—and that management researchers have faithfully accorded senior managers all along. If this sounds to you like business politics as usual, you earn an *A* for your ethical critique of crisis management. See D. Gilbert, Jr., "Rights and Crises," paper presented at the Second International Conference on Industrial and Organizational Crisis Management, New York, November 1989.

49. P. Slovia, "Ripples in a Pond: Forecasting Industrial Crises," *Industrial Crisis Quarterly* 4 (1987):34–43.

50. K. Weick, "The Vulnerable System: An Analysis of the Tenerife Air Disaster," *Journal of Management* 16 (1990):571–593.

51. I. Mitroff, C. Pearson, and T. Pauchant, "Crisis Management and Strategic Management: Similarities, Differences and Challenges," in P. Shrivastava, A. Huff, and J. Dutton, eds., *Advances in Strategic Management*, Volume 8 (Greenwich, CT: JAI Press, 1992), 235–260.

52. See Volume 4 of *Journal of Management Studies* 25 (1988); and Volume 2 of *Journal of Business Administration* 9 (1978).

53. *Time*, 25 May 1987. See the cover story, "What's Wrong," *Time*, 25 May 1987, 14–17. See also, "Looking to Its Roots," *Time*, 25 May 1987, 26–29.

54. "Ethics Pays," *Wall Street Journal*, 29 December 1987:1.

55. *Newsweek*, 13 June 1994. See the cover story, "The Virtuecrats," *Newsweek*, 13 June 1994, 30–36.

56. I am indebted to Douglas Sturm, Joe LaBarge, and Jeff Turner for their ncouragement as I first worked out this idea in the course of our discussions as)art of the Professional Ethics Study Group at Bucknell.

57. M. Magnet, "The Decline & Fall of Business Ethics," *Fortune*, 8 December 986, 65–66, 68, 72; and K. Labich, "The New Crisis in Business Ethics," *Fortune*, !0 April 1992, 167–168, 172, 176.

58. F. F. Church, " A Modest Revival in Business Ethics?," *New York Times*, !2 December 1985, Section 3:3.

59. W. Neikirk, "Ethics Comeback Can't Be Ignored," *Chicago Tribune*, !8 May 1989, Section 7:3.

60. "Businesses Are Signing Up for Ethics 101," *Business Week*, 15 February 1988, 56–57.

61. B. Hager, "What's Behind Business' Sudden Fervor for Ethics," *Business Week*, 23 September 1991, 65.

62. See T. Boling, "The Management Ethics 'Crisis': An Organizational Perspective," *Academy of Management Review* 3 (1978):360–365. Boling gives another accessible rendition of the logic of "ethics from the outside." See also G. James, "The Crisis of American Business," *Journal of Business Ethics* 1 (1982):285–291.

63. "Crisis in Ethics," *Business Insights* 5 (1989). *Business Insights* is published by the School of Business Administration, California State University at Long Beach.

64. See Goodpaster, "Ethical Imperatives and Corporate Leadership."

65. D. Miller, "Organizational Pathology and Industrial Crises," *Industrial Crisis Quarterly* 2 (1988):65.

66. T. Pauchant and I. Mitroff, "Crisis Prone v. Crisis Avoiding Organizations. Is Your Company's Culture Its Own Worst Enemy in Creating Crisis?," *Industrial Crisis Quarterly* 2 (1988):53–63.

67. A driving imperative for this ethics is the deeply entrenched belief that The Organization must be preserved. The concept of corporate social responsibility, for example, is one management truth that would make no sense if not for this apology for the status quo.

68. I teach my students about this split with the help of Brent Wade's novel *Company Man*. Wade's protagonist is cast as a "bad" person in no fewer than three communities in which he struggles for acceptance as a human being. See B. Wade, *Company Man* (Chapel Hill, NC: Algonquin Books of Chapel Hill, 1992).

69. Eliza Collins nominates corporate executives as leaders in the campaign against love among managers in the corporate workplace. Office romances, Collins wants us to believe, must be prevented before amorous managers become derelict in their duties to the organization and the organization's power structure. See E. Collins, "Managers and Lovers," *Harvard Business Review* 83, no. 5 (1983):142–153. Collins pronounces love between managers to be a "dangerous" thing. Ibid., 143.

70. One reason why corporate executives might find this generalized "we" to be an "unfriendly" notion is that they might not be enamored with the very idea of "we" in a modern democracy. For a provocative essay on this political matter, see C. Lasch, "The Revolt of the Elites," *Harper's* 289, no. 1734 (1994):30–49.

71. Crisis management has been defined conventionally as a systems problem for which systems solutions must be found. Human beings, on that view, foul up systems. I thank Sajay Samuel for helping me clarify this point.

72. I am paying a pragmatist compliment here as I trace the evolution of my thinking. If I am able to make an argument stronger by linking, say, "Rocky & Bullwinkle" and a pragmatist contractarian ethics, then I want to pay a compliment to the scholars who have helped create the latter account. They deserve praise for telling a story that I can, in turn, use to create a story that I share with you about everyday life in a democracy. Although some might consider my effort to link popular culture and ethical theory as an insult to "serious" scholars of the latter, I am actually doing something else: redefining "serious" in a pragmatist way. Richard Rorty and Ed Freeman have influenced my thinking in this respect.

73. Such personal and "local" connection with one's institutions, of course, is the last thing that the advocates of an Ethics of Deadbeats, Dullards, and Derelicts' Disasters Driving the World Into Moral Decline want to encourage. After all, "ethics from the outside" works only if we everyday folk are subject to whatever in is that institutions and institutional leaders ordain as the appropriate ways for us to live. It is this belief that enables Robert Frank to propose that his model of rationality can help "personalize" people's ties to their institutions. See R. Frank, *Passions Within Reason* (New York: W. W. Norton, 1988):248. I have in mind here that institutions are patterns of practices and beliefs in which we move and on which we leave our fingerprints as we interact with one another. Consider an example. For me, Little League baseball, on this pragmatist account about institutions, was what my teammates and coaches and parents and I created in our own "local" setting in Bethlehem, Pennsylvania, rather than what was structured and ordered by Little League Baseball's headquarters in Williamsport, Pennsylvania.

74. David Halberstam tells a story about four men who epitomize this claim to distinctiveness, as he recounts the Olympic rowing hopes of Tiff Wood, Joe Bouscaren, John Biglow, and Bard Lewis. See D. Halberstam, *The Amateurs* (New York: Penguin, 1986). Valerie Miner introduces us to four other exemplars of this claim to distinctiveness. They are the fictitious Moira Finlayson, Teddy Fielding, Wanda Nakatani, and Ann(a) Rose(enzweig). See V. Miner, *All Good Women* (Freedom, CA: The Crossing Press, 1987). On the subject of listening, I am one of Robbin Derry's many students.

75. Kinsella, *Box Socials*, 139.

76. Robert Coles quotes William Carlos Williams on the matter of placing human beings into taxonomies and the like. Williams wrote: "Who's against shorthand? No one I know. Who wants to be shortchanged? No one I know." R. Coles, *The Call of Stories: Teaching and the Moral Imagination* (Boston: Houghton Mifflin, 1989), 29.

77. In making this statement, I travel a very different road from the one traveled by many researchers who believe that business ethics research should consist of counting the differences in people's beliefs. One quintessential example of such a "science of business ethics" is H. Becker and D. Fritzsche, "Business Ethics: A Cross-Cultural Comparison of Managers' Attitudes," *Journal of Business Ethics* 6 (1987):289–295. Someone would make a major contribution to business ethics research if he or she brought together every business ethics scientist, posed the question "Why are these differences useful for management education?," and forbade the answer "because we did not know this before." Business ethics scientists can take a cue from Thomas Donaldson and Thomas Dunfee that there is more to differences than the *fact* of differences. Donaldson and Dunfee observe that different central norms are used in different human communities. They use that assumption—which they label, unfortunately, "moral free space"—as part of their justification for a social contracts interpretation of the business world. Unlike the business ethics scientists, Donaldson and Dunfee do not stop at the "fact" of difference. They move through it to another destination. See T. Donaldson and T. Dunfee, "Toward A Unified Conception of Business Ethics: Integrated Social Contracts Theory," *Academy of Management Review* 19, no. 2 (1994):252–283. If the destination that business ethics scientists have in mind is something like "the fact of differences is a precursor to controlling

unwelcome differences," then they, too, are vulnerable to critique as members of the ethics-of-prevention campaign.

78. B. Watterson, *The Essential Calvin and Hobbes: A Calvin and Hobbes Treasury* (Kansas City, MO: Andrews and McMeel, 1988), 239. I recognize that some readers might object to my using "Calvin & Hobbes" to argue for a politics of inclusion and institutional transformation. One objection might be that Calvin's parents fail to teach their son so-called family values. If this, or some other, is your objection, then I ask you this pair of questions: From what politics do you create your objection and why is that politics preferable?

79. See B. Watterson, "Calvin & Hobbes," *Philadelphia Inquirer*, 9 June 1994:F17. In that strip, Calvin's mother muses that, since she has not seen Calvin for fifteen minutes, "That probably means he's getting in trouble."

80. I recognize that some readers might object to my using "Rocky & Bullwinkle" to argue for a politics of inclusion and institutional transformation. One objection might be that Ward and his colleagues are "really" trying to spoof the Cold War combatants. If this, or some other, is your objection, then I ask you this pair of questions: From what politics do you create your objection and why is that politics preferable?

81. Kinsella, *Box Socials*, 199.

82. Ibid. I recognize that some readers might object to my using *Box Socials* to argue for a politics of inclusion and institutional transformation. One objection is that Kinsella is "really" writing about the suffocation—material and intellectual— of small-town life, in the tradition of Sinclair Lewis. Another objection might be that baseball is "frivolous." If either of these, or some other, is your objection, then I ask you this pair of questions: From what politics do you create your objection and why is that politics preferable?

83. Jen, *Typical American*, 67. I recognize that some readers might object to my using *Typical American* to argue for a politics of inclusion and institutional transformation. One objection might be that Jen tells a one-sided story about the American Dream and, accordingly, tarnishes that ideal by narrating the Changs' failures. If this, or some other, is your objection, then I ask you this pair of questions: From what politics do you create your objection and why is that politics preferable?

84. See, for example, the "Goof Gas" caper perpetrated by Boris and Natasha in "The Adventures of Rocky and Bullwinkle, Volume 3: Vincent Van Moose." Copyright Buena Vista Pictures Distribution Inc. Copyright Jay Ward Productions Inc.

85. I draw inspiration here from S. Tepper, *The Gate to Women's Country* (New York: Bantam, 1988). Tepper brilliantly portrays Stavia, for example, living distinctively *in* relationship with Margot and Joshua of Women's Country, and with Chernon from the garrison.

86. I recognize that some readers might object to my using "Blondie" to argue for a politics of inclusion and institutional transformation. One objection might be that Young and Drake perpetuate a stereotype of suburban American marriage and that Blondie is trapped as a victim of that way of life. If this, or some other, is your objection, then I ask you this pair of questions: From what politics do you create your objection and why is that politics preferable?

87. See D. Young and S. Drake, "Blondie," *Sunbury Daily Item*, 19 February 1994:21, regarding a television weathercaster; and D. Young and S. Drake,

"Blondie," *Philadelphia Inquirer*, 5 August 1994:E11, regarding one of Dagwood's masterpiece sandwiches.

88. Coupland, *Generation X*, 5. I recognize that some readers might object to my using *Generation X* to argue for a politics of inclusion and institutional transformation. One objection might be that Coupland's protagonists have no one but themselves to blame for their aimlessness, because they have rejected the so-called American family values and work ethic that could see them through their struggles. If this, or some other, is your objection, then I ask you this pair of questions: From what politics do you create your objection and why is that politics preferable?

89. Ibid., 93–96.

90. For this epic moment in the life of Blondie and Dagwood, see D. Young and S. Drake, "Blondie," *Sunbury Daily Item*, 6 September 1992. This episode is also a vivid portrayal of the common-law doctrine of at-will employment. This particular comic strip is a handy device for teaching that concept.

91. "Enduring deficiency" is the concept that I coined in my doctoral dissertation to describe such jointly produced traps. Enduring deficiency seems to apply to all parties to the Major League Baseball strike, except perhaps the lawyers.

92. Jen, *Typical American*, 200.

93. Kinsella, *Box Socials*, 85–126.

94. See Gilbert, *Twilight of Corporate Strategy*, 166–180.

95. See "The Adventures of Rocky and Bullwinkle, Volume 5: La Grande Moose." Copyright Buena Vista Pictures Distribution Inc. Copyright Jay Ward Productions Inc.

96. Kinsella, *Box Socials*, 125.

97. Ibid., 124.

98. For a primer on this proposition, see Tepper, *Gate to Women's Country*. For an application of this margins perspective to management education, see Gilbert, "A Critique and A Retrieval of Management and the Humanities."

99. Jen, *Typical American*, 142.

100. The influences of John Rawls and Richard Rorty are significant here. So, too, is the commentary about "making a difference in combating domestic tyranny" provided in H. Giroux, "Liberal Arts Education and the Struggle for Public Life: Dreaming about Democracy," in D. Gless and B. H. Smith, eds., *The Politics of Liberal Education* (Durham, NC: Duke University Press, 1992), 122.

101. Coupland, *Generation X*, 8.

102. See Rosmarin, *The Power of Genre*, regarding the logic of developing a genre in such a pragmatist way.

103. Richard Rorty uses "liberal ironists" to describe those who believe this. Rorty, *Contingency, Irony, and Solidarity*, 73–74. Two characters who consciously lead lives of liberal irony are Christy Mathewson and Yakov (Jackie) Kapinski in E. R. Greenberg, *The Celebrant* (New York: Penguin, 1986).

104. C. Taylor, *The Ethics of Authenticity* (Cambridge, MA: Harvard University Press, 1991), 65.

105. Ibid., 4–7.

106. Ibid., 23, 45.

107. Rorty, *Contingency, Irony, and Solidarity*, xiv–xv. See also Rorty, "Trotsky and the Wild Orchids."

108. Rorty, *Contingency, Irony, and Solidarity*, 23–25.

109. Ibid., 196.

110. See Rorty, "Texts and Lumps, *New Literary History* 17, no. 1 (1985):1–16.

111. Rorty, *Contingency, Irony, and Solidarity,* 45.

112. Fish, *There's No Such Thing as Free Speech,* 9.

113. Ibid., 12.

114. Ibid., 16.

115. J. Jordan, A. Kaplan, J. B. Miller, I. Stiver, and J. Surrey, *Women's Growth in Connection* (New York: Guilford Press, 1991).

116. Ibid., 52. Janet Surrey is credited by her co-authors with writing the chapter from which this passage is quoted.

117. C. West, *Race Matters* (Boston: Beacon Press, 1993), 12–17.

118. Ibid., 15.

119. Ibid., 18–19.

120. Ibid., 20.

121. Differences, centers, and margins form a framework with which we can understand the work of a number of critics in a larger liberal community as well. What these critics of modern democratic institutions hold in common is a primary concern with what I call the centers through which distinctive human beings can live. John Rawls and Vaclav Havel are prominent in this liberal circle.

Rawls deals with the principle of justice as fairness against a backdrop of two kinds of centers in modern liberal states. One is an overarching consensus about such things as each human being's basic opportunities to lead a good life. J. Rawls, *Political Liberalism* (New York: Columbia University Press, 1993), xvi–xxvii, 4–15. The other is a set of local consensuses around which particular human communities cohere. Rawls refers to the latter as a set of "comprehensive doctrines" that constitute a "normal result" of democracy. Ibid., xvi. Political liberalism is a complicated practice, Rawls claims, because these comprehensive doctrines are numerous, because they are incompatible, and because they are "reasonable" doctrines. Ibid., xx. Political liberalism thus becomes a search for a center among centers:

> How is it possible for there to exist over time a just and stable society of free and equal citizens, who remain profoundly divided by reasonable religious, philosophical, and moral doctrines?

Ibid., 4.

Havel argues that the era of modernity—in which science is the unquestioned access to, and arbiter of, truth—has been marked by a growing separation among persons of distinctive cultures. See V. Havel, "Our Troubled Quest for Meaning in a Post-Modern World," *Philadelphia Inquirer,* 6 July 1994:A17. (The article is an excerpt of Havel's speech in Philadelphia on July 4, 1994.) Modernity, as an intellectual center, has left us wholly unprepared, he argues, to create bonds with different human beings around the world. We are unprepared to create new centers, he argues, because science has disconnected us from our sense of self-worth. Havel proposes that we reinterpret our searches for distinctive identities as pursuits of something that transcends our own lives. He names "self-transcendence" as an antidote to the supreme self-confidence that "objective" science will make our lives more meaningful. Ibid. Self-transcendence is a way of seeing ourselves as actors meeting on margins, rather than as pagans awaiting the verdicts of the priests of science.

122. I pose this question under the influence of Richard Rorty, who advocates criticism as

a picture of intellectual and moral progress as a history of increasingly useful metaphors rather than of increasing understanding of how things really are.

Rorty, *Contingency, Irony, and Solidarity*, 9. I have focused on metaphors in this pragmatist spirit in a seminar that I recently led with a group of first-year Bucknellians. The seminar was titled "The Idea of Management: A Century of Controversy." ("Controversy" refers to both the idea and the century.) Over the course of a semester, we developed several dozen metaphors for "manager," all of which began with the letter "m." These metaphors ranged from mastermind to monarch to mogul to militarist. My aim was to remove management from the familiar milieu of social science and astrology and relocate it in a rich cultural setting. For their support of my efforts here, and with Bucknell's (unfortunately named) Foundation Seminar concept more generally, I thank Nancy Weida, Chris Zappe, and Eugenia Gerdes.

123. For a classic account that spells out an ethics of prevention and punishment, see H. Fayol, "General Principles of Management," in H. Merrill, ed., *Classics in Management* (New York: American Management Association, 1960), 217–241.

124. Two exhilarating accounts of experimentation are D. Hall, *Life Work* (Boston: Beacon Press, 1993), and J. Cowan, *Small Decencies: Reflections and Meditations on Being Human at Work* (New York: Harper Business, 1992). I am grateful to Kate Rogers for recommending Cowan's writings to me. Calvin gives one expression of his experimental approach to play when he muses about his options on a rainy day. See B. Watterson, "Calvin & Hobbes," *Philadelphia Inquirer,* 30 March 1994:G7.

125. One way to comprehend the historical appeal of an Ethics of Deadbeats, Dullards, and Derelicts' Disasters Driving the World Into Moral Decline is to read M. Foucault, *Discipline and Punish: The Birth of the Prison* (New York: Vintage, 1979). Foucault traces a shift in punishment from violence done to the body to violence done to the soul, in the name of a rehabilitation favored by those who control institutions. Regarding a "new political anatomy," see ibid., 103. I am grateful to Ed Freeman for suggesting that one chapter of Foucault's book would put corporate social responsibility and corporate ethics campaigns in a whole new light. I learned that lesson by reading Foucault's book on a snowbound evening in Staunton, Virginia. I pass that advice along to any student of management and organizations.

126. I first used the reference to mice in D. Gilbert, Jr., "Some Questions That Robert Frank (and Very Few Others, for That Matter) Encourages Us to Ask About the Prisoner's Dilemma," paper presented at the Society for Business Ethics Annual Meetings, Dallas, Texas, August 1994.

CHAPTER 3.

1. A thoughtful opportunity to consider Americans' penchant for medals and awards is available in the clever "Rocky & Bullwinkle" cartoons created a generation ago by Jay Ward and his associates. Rocky and Bullwinkle are the only

characters in that series who are not impressed by, or enamored with, medals or titles. The villains Boris and Natasha, by contrast, are constantly seeking tangible signs of approval from their superiors. So, too, are the military officers in the series. They wear uniforms that are routinely weighted with medals. It is a big day, for example, when the fictitious Dudley Do-Right wins the Canadian Pretty Good Conduct Medal. See "Dudley Do-Right Digs for Gold to Win Nell's Heart," on "The Adventures of Rocky and Bullwinkle," Volume 3, Buena Vista Home Video. Copyright B. V. Pictures Distribution, Inc., Copyright Ward Productions, Inc.

2. I do not use "oop" to comment in any way on Al Capp's "Alley Oop" comic strip. Rather, I have in mind a commonplace meaning of "oop" and "oops" as an admission of one's own error. When I refer to "study management," I have in mind an act that can be committed by a group of persons that can include management researchers, social critics, practicing managers, journalists, politicians, business boosters, and, of course, students enrolled in college business courses. What qualifies someone as a student of management is simply an interest in the justifications for what can be done in the name of management. *Wall Street Journal* editors and reporters do that every day, for instance. They are keen and committed students of management, by my interpretation.

3. I deliberately designate this award for groups. I do this to signal my interest in genres of management thought, rather than in the solo efforts of any one student of management. Regarding genres of management thought, see Chapter 2 in D. Gilbert, Jr., *The Twilight of Corporate Strategy: A Comparative Ethical Critique* (New York: Oxford University Press, 1992). My premise there, and here too, is that we must trace ethical problems in the business world to the genres of management thought, and to the perpetrators of those genres, in which business and ethics are disconnected views of the world. I am grateful to Ed Freeman for his continuing encouragement as I seek new roads that I can travel with this premise.

4. The pool of candidates for this award will probably be small, now and for some time to come. Debates about property per se rarely appear in management research circles and in the business media. "It's the shareholders' property" is an assertion that wins nodding approval in these circles. However, the act of making that assertion does not qualify some group of management students for this award. A more daring intellectual step is required.

5. G. Larson, *The Far Side Gallery* (Kansas City, MO: Andrews, McMeel & Parker, 1984):146. I cite "The Far Side" here as a reviewer who is commenting on the rhetoric of discourse about management.

6. Larson's animals routinely question the ironies in their worldly existences while they continue to plug away in their little corners of the world. Theirs are rebellions in self-justification, not rebellions against social arrangements. I write this book on the assumption that, when it comes to ethics and business, we humans can rebel in both regards.

7. G. Larson, *Cows of Our Planet* (Kansas City, MO: Andrews and McMeel, 1992):28.

8. These relatively novel defenses include crisis management; transaction cost economics; corporate re-engineering; corporate social performance; virtual corporations; systems thinking; and intelligent enterprises. For primers on the latter two frameworks, see, respectively, P. Senge, *The Fifth Discipline: The Art & Prac-*

tice of the Learning Organization (New York: Currency Doubleday, 1990), and J. B. Quinn, *Intelligent Enterprise: A Knowledge and Service Based Paradigm for Industry* (New York: Free Press, 1992).

9. The pool of candidates for this award should be quite large. Managerial privilege is axiomatic in the politics of business education. For one detailed interpretation of that axiom, see D. Gilbert, Jr., "S. Prakash Sethi, *Multinational Corporations and the Impact of Public Advocacy on Corporate Strategy: Nestlé and the Infant Formula Controversy*," book review, *Academy of Management Review* 20, no. 1 (1995):225–229. A reaffirmation of the importance of orthodoxy about property is the so-called resource-based framework for strategic management. See B. Wernerfelt, "A Resource-Based View of the Firm," *Strategic Management Journal* 5, no. 2 (1984):171–180. This "hot" research topic is an ordinary defense of the traditional Business Policy model of corporate management. Wernerfelt admits this openly. Ibid., 172. Business Policy is a classic statement of managerial privilege. In this regard, see both D. Gilbert, Jr., E. Hartman, J. Mauriel, and R. E. Freeman, *A Logic for Strategy* (Boston: Ballinger, 1988), 39–54; and R. E. Freeman, D. Gilbert, Jr., and E. Hartman, "Values and the Foundations of Strategic Management," *Journal of Business Ethics* 7, no. 11 (1988):821–834. Indeed, Wernerfelt's paper has already been recognized with an award given in the same spirit as OOP-2. The *Strategic Management Journal* editors awarded the SMJ 1994 Best Paper Prize to Wernerfelt for his article. See E. Zajac, "SMJ 1994 Best Paper Prize to Birger Wernerfelt," *Strategic Management Journal* 16, no. 3 (1995):169–170.

10. C. Browne, "Hagar the Horrible," *Philadelphia Inquirer*, 12 April 1991: 24-D.

11. B. Watterson, "Calvin & Hobbes," *Philadelphia Inquirer*, 31 July 1992:D25.

12. Ibid. Watterson maintains a running story line about one example of such "ordinary" practice of privileged behavior. Calvin, mimicking a public opinion pollster, likes to announce periodic ratings of his father's performance as a father. With n = 1 (him), Calvin believes that he has special insights available from his privileged perch.

13. If this sentence astonishes you, go back to Chapters 1 and 2. Yes, I am defending a claim that the works of researchers such as Michael Porter can be interpreted as ethical commentaries and, more particularly, as applications of a contractarian ethics. For an extensive introduction to the justification for, and benefits from, such a reading, see Gilbert, *Twilight of Corporate Strategy*. Here, too, I thank Ed Freeman for his continuing encouragement.

14. I am honoring the rhetoric of the Original Orthodoxy on Property and the rhetoric of the Ordinary Ode on Privilege. In so doing, I write to students of management as persons who share and shape a particular language about business, not as persons who think that they can give managers expert advice about running a business. I do this under the influence of Donald McCloskey and Stanley Fish. This means that I do not see myself as a critic who is trying to help the Chamber of Commerce, or who is conversing with professors who see themselves as agents for the Chamber of Commerce. For a recent expression of the opposing view, See D. Schendel, "Notes from the Editor-in-Chief," *Strategic Management Journal* 16, no. 1 (1995):1–2. I hope that my argument in this book might qualify for the genre of "speculation, opinion, and clever journalism" that Schendel wants strategic management researchers to avoid. Ibid., 1.

15. See any strategic management textbook for evidence of sustained worship of these ideas.

16. Managerial privilege has received renewed support in two recent papers about ethics and business. See L. Hosmer, "Strategic Planning as if Ethics Mattered," *Strategic Management Journal* 15, Special Issue (1994):17–34; and A. E. Singer, "Strategy as Moral Philosophy," *Strategic Management Journal* 15, no. 3 (1994):191–213. Hosmer and Singer both want to move ethics and moral philosophy to the center of strategic management theory. Hosmer notes:

> In short, this article will question whether the "integrity of common purpose" should be included as an integral rather than a peripheral component in the strategic planning process.

Hosmer, "Strategic Planning as if Ethics Mattered," 18. That aim is commendable enough, but the kind of "common purpose" that Hosmer wants to move to the center of strategic planning is the privileged view of the firm that executives prefer. Thus, Hosmer gives us one more rendition of the age-old story of managerial privilege. This is plainly evident in his assumption that it is the organization's stakeholders who must be brought into line with management's privileged view. Consider his fourth proposition:

> It is possible to build trust, commitment and effort on the part of all of the stakeholders by including the ethical principles in the strategic decision processes of the firm.

Ibid., 28. This is nothing more than using ethical principles to extend the privilege of management. In short, the paper could be profitably retitled, "Strategic Planning as if the Divine Right of Managers Mattered."

Singer sets out to "redirect strategic thinking" that is located on the common ground now shared by concepts of strategy, rationality, and ethics." Singer, "Strategy as Moral Philosophy," 192. He intends to provide

> a new conceptual and rather integrated conceptual framework that sees strategy and moral-philosophy as not only related, but essentially the same subject.

Ibid., 193. Singer cleverly equates strategy and moral philosophy by arguing that both strategy and moral philosophy can be practiced by a so-called corporate moral agent. Singer enlists moral philosophy in the service of improving the "rationality" of this agent. True to the faith of managerial privilege, the only human agents in this organizational learning process are the executives who have the privilege of "knowing" this corporate agent. If the title of Singer's paper whets your appetite for new insights about human coexistence and human community, you will be disappointed. The paper could be profitably retitled, "Better Managerial Privilege Through Better Corporate Rationality."

17. This is moral relativism, plain as day. For a critique of various genres of moral relativism, see R. E. Freeman and D. Gilbert, Jr., *Corporate Strategy and the Search for Ethics* (Englewood Cliffs, NJ: Prentice-Hall, 1988), 21–41. By the doctrines of moral relativism, the only justification that a manager needs for his actions is his own resolve to carry them out. By that doctrine, there is no value in a public process of justification. As a corollary to this doctrine of managerial privilege, other human beings must justify their actions in relation to the privileged position of the self-justified manager. Hosmer enacts this corollary consistently. In his paper, the legitimacy of stakeholders' pursuits is always evaluated against

the standard of managerial purpose. By Hosmer's account, stakeholders are important, insofar as *their* trust and commitment and effort helps management run the firm more competitively! Hosmer, "Strategic Planning as if Ethics Mattered," 25–32. Singer also enacts this corollary. In his resurrection of corporate moral agency, stakeholders are merely "constraints." Singer, "Strategy as Moral Philosophy," 196. By Singer's argument, managers must give their full attention to the rationality of the corporate moral agent, which he describes metaphorically as, among other things, a "hired gun." Ibid., 202.

18. In Alfred Sloan's account of General Motors history, senior management has the privilege of defining the "logical way of doing business in accordance with the facts and circumstances of an industry, if you can figure it out." A. Sloan, *My Years with General Motors* (New York: Doubleday, 1972), 63. Senior managers have the privilege of "figuring it out" by virtue of their command of a decision-making structure and process. Ibid. 505–521. Sloan's book can be a very useful text for those who want to debate the pace of "paradigm shifts" in management theory. By reading his text alongside the papers published in the widely read management journals of 1995, one could conclude that there has been no "paradigm shift." Andrew Carnegie's claim to managerial privilege is nowhere clearer than in his recollection of the Homestead strike. He simply cannot understand why those he calls "the men" did not accept his new policies. A. Carnegie, *The Autobiography of Andrew Carnegie* (Boston: Northeastern University Press, 1986), 219–244. As a primer in managerial privilege, my students and I read and discuss the moving saga of three generations of the fictitious, steelworking Dobrejcak family in T. Bell, *Out of This Furnace* (Pittsburgh: University of Pittsburgh Press, 1976). Then I read to them excerpts from Carnegie's autobiography. It is difficult for many of them to believe at first that both Carnegie and Bell wrote about the very same time and place.

19. The hope for distinctive contributions made by human beings to their human communities is the last thing that is celebrated in two papers that recently received high praise in strategic management research circles. In his paper about the so-called resource-based view of corporate strategy, Birger Wernerfelt tells a story about strategists who, in Darwinian desperation, very much want others to leave them alone to their rent-seeking projects. B. Wernerfelt, "A Resource-Based View of the Firm." See also B. Wernerfelt, "The Resource-Based View of the Firm: Ten Years After," *Strategic Management Journal* 16, no. 3 (1995): 171–174. In their paper about the so-called dominant logic of a corporation, C. K. Prahalad and Richard Bettis propose a way for corporate strategists to improve the chances that their organization will adapt to a Darwinian environment. C. K. Prahalad and R. A. Bettis, "The Dominant Logic: A New Linkage Between Diversity and Performance," *Strategic Management Journal* 7, no. 6 (1986): 485–501. See also C. K. Prahalad and R. Bettis, "The Dominant Logic: Retrospective and Extension," *Strategic Management Journal* 16, no. 1 (1995):5–14.

20. Sustainable competitive advantage occupies a central place in the rhetoric of the times in strategic management research and teaching. Sustainability, competitiveness, and advantage are all unmistakable rhetorical emphases on the strategist's quest for a way to stay in the marketplace for a while. Tracy Kidder's "pinball" metaphor—the opportunity to play again and again—is a useful way to frame this approach to strategy. See T. Kidder, *The Soul of a New Machine* (New York: Avon, 1981), 228.

21. There is deliberate irony here with regard to who can teach us useful lessons about ethics and business. With the OOP-1 award, I am arguing, in effect, that the creators of what I call the Original Orthodoxy on Property point us toward a relatively more convincing avenue "if we want business to be more ethical" than do Hosmer and Singer, two researchers who use ethical reasoning to talk about business.

22. I draw inspiration from Richard Rorty and Jean Baker Miller as I make this point about strength and weakness. See R. Rorty, "Sex, Lies and Virginia's Voters," *New York Times,* 13 October 1994:A27. See also J. B. Miller, *Toward a New Psychology of Women,* 2nd ed. (Boston: Beacon Press, 1986). Miller's distinction between domination and subordination should be required reading for any course about management and business institutions—and modern life for that matter. I thank M. J. Grourke for helping me understand how Miller can speak to us in the latter regard. The difference between strength and weakness is crucial, even if it is left unstated, in the dominant logic and the resource-based frameworks for strategic management. Both are predicated on the importance of finding positions of strength for the firm under trying circumstances. Singer's "corporate moral agent" is clearly a dominant figure that is needed, by his account, to overcome the reasoning deficiencies that beset mere mortal managers. Indeed, Singer is so intent on emphasizing the dominating role of the corporate moral agent (CMA) that he throws down this challenge to others who try to link ethics and business:

> In sum, denial of CMA has now become an extreme, barely tenable position. It could perhaps be sustained by insisting upon strictly a-rational foundations for ethics, like intuitionism or divine command theory. The only remaining tactic for denying CMA is radical indeed; a rejection of large tracts of existing prescriptive strategic management theory.

Singer, "Strategy as Moral Philosophy," 202. I prefer to act by the "only remaining tactic."

23. The rhetorical tactic is a clever one. Set up the "everyday" man and woman as some kind of antihero found in Nature. Then predicate some regime of domination on the need to fight the antihero's influence. For a general critique of this tactic, see D. Gilbert, Jr., *"Can Ethics Be Taught? Perspectives, Challenges, and Approaches at Harvard Business School* by Thomas Piper, Mary Gentile, and Sharon Daloz Parks," book review, *International Journal of Organizational Analysis* 2, no. 2 (1994):433–436. I thank Diane Swanson for her encouragement with this book review. This rhetorical tactic is particularly popular in the organizational-change literature. The antihero there is the ubiquitous, yet nameless, character who has the annoying habit of resisting the changes that corporate executives want to impose. Corporate reengineering is one such exercise in domination. For a critique based on that premise, see D. Gilbert, Jr., "Management and Four Stakeholder Politics: Corporate Reengineering as a Crossroads Case," *Business & Society* 34, no. 1 (1995):90–97.

The same tactic for establishing strength over weakness is discernible in the stories told by Singer, Hosmer, and Prahalad and Bettis. Singer resurrects the idea that stakeholders are "constraints," an idea that he links to Igor Ansoff. Singer, "Strategy as Moral Philosophy," 196. Hosmer bemoans a crucial "fact" about a particular weakness of stakeholders: "It is difficult to motivate behavior

that is both cooperative and innovative by all of the stakeholders of the firm."
Hosmer, "Strategic Planning as if Ethics Mattered," 26. This situation can be
reversed, Hosmer concludes, through the actions of strong men who practice, via
"the ethical principles," a timeless kind of virtue:

> It is possible to build trust, commitment and effort on the part of all of the stakeholders
> by including the ethical principles in the strategic decision processes of the firm.

Ibid., 28. Evidently, these stakeholders pursue aims of such relative poverty that
they must wait for corporate strategist to act before they, the stakeholders, will
commit themselves to working diligently for the corporate strategist. This story
of domination and subordination is as old as the wind. So, too, is the way that
Prahalad and Bettis rely on the premise that only by following the "dominant"
logic can the firm adapt to changes in the larger world. It is, after all, the *dominant*
logic, and not a negotiated or shared or conventional or provisional logic.

24. The sources here are J. Kubicki, *Breaker Boys* (New York: Warner Books,
1986), and B. Wade, *Company Man* (Chapel Hill, NC: Algonquin Books of
Chapel Hill, 1992).

25. For another unflattering portrayal of a coal baron who runs a company
town, see J. Yount, *Hardcastle* (Dallas, TX: Southern Methodist University Press,
1992).

26. Kubicki, *Breaker Boys*, 359–360.

27. Wade, *Company Man*, 177.

28. I have in mind a company town as a fiefdom of a tyrant. Yes, it is always
possible that the residents of that town can live peaceful private and public lives
under such a regime. However, such an outcome would be a case of serendipity.
There is no place for such a way of life in the logic of running a company town,
because there is no place in that logic for the kind of human interaction that goes
into bargaining, joint self-governance, and other practices predicated on the
concept of democratic inclusion. If the foregoing practices were prevalent, there
would be no company town. Hosmer provides a vivid depiction of this logic. He
assigns, without a shred of defense, this colonial role to the corporate strategist:

> It is the responsibility of the senior executives of the firm to distribute those benefits and
> allocate those harms among the stakeholders of the company.

Hosmer, "Strategic Planning as if Ethics Mattered," 32. Once again, Hosmer's
stakeholders, like Carnegie's stakeholders, are doomed to wait for the largesse of
their strategic masters.

29. One of William ("Billy") Covington's colleagues, a man named Carl Rice,
tries to convince Covington to rebel against Haviland for running a metaphorical
plantation at Veratec. Wade, *Company Man*, 101–114. For a thought-provoking
account of an alternative to the plantation, see the case "Inland Steel Industries,"
Business Enterprise Trust, Palo Alto, California, 1992. In that case, Stephen
Bowsher is able to accomplish some things in collaboration with his colleagues
toward a kind of understanding that the fictitious Haviland could never imagine.

30. Wade, *Company Man*, 212.

31. Thus, Wade and Kubicki have written texts with which we can free ourselves to ask new questions about managerial privilege and corporate strategy,
using each person's distinctive worldly contribution as our standard for criticism.
For an explanation of this liberal pragmatist use of literature, see D. Gilbert, Jr.,

"A Critique and a Retrieval of Management and the Humanities," *Journal of Business Ethics* (1996), in press.

32. Kubicki, *Breaker Boys,* 306.

33. Wade, *Company Man,* 213.

34. Ibid., 123.

35. A clear rendition of this colonial imperative is available in the account of corporate strategy that Hosmer heralds as a "new paradigm" for strategic planning. Hosmer, "Strategic Planning as if Ethics Mattered." By this rendition, the strategist-colonial governor must figure out what kind of ethical behavior will earn the trust of the stakeholders of the firm. Once he does that, the logic goes, he can count on the continued commitment and hard work from the stakeholder-colonists. Hosmer's argument gives us reason, more broadly, to examine critically the belief, which is held widely in Business and Society circles, that managers should "balance" stakeholders' interests. After all, a colonial governor "balances" stakeholders' interests.

36. For an extensive study of colonialism, see A. Memmi, *The Colonizer and the Colonized* (Boston: Beacon Press, 1991). Memmi puts this dependence boldly:

> The colonialist realizes that without the colonized, the colony would no longer have any meaning.

Ibid., 66. The senior executive who treasures "human resources" could come to the same realization.

37. Kubicki, *Breaker Boys,* 4. In an inescapable and cruel irony, the right of the children of Jeddoh to receive a public education only serves to trap them further in Markham's colony. Kubicki's novel can serve as a useful case with which to consider the sufficiency of a rights-based conception of human community. The rights to education, worship, private property, and to participate in economic activity seem to provide little help to the residents of Jeddoh, other than Markham and his family.

38. Ibid., 138.

39. Ibid., 446.

40. Wade, *Company Man,* 14.

41. Ibid., 110.

42. For an account of this self-justification, as practiced by the colonizer, see Memmi, *Colonizer and the Colonized,* 75. I conduct my critique here on the liberal postmodern premise that bullying is one particular language of human relationships. In other words, human beings can prefer to create and sustain a language of bullying. I have worked with people who are masters at that. In Richard Rorty's terms about the critique of any language, bullying is the entrenched "nuisance" language that I want to challenge, en route to proposing an alternative. See R. Rorty, *Contingency, Irony, and Solidarity* (Cambridge: Cambridge University Press, 1989), 9.

43. This is the precisely the kind of regime that Hosmer proposes. If the corporate strategist follows the ethical principles that should go into strategic planning, the argument goes, then the stakeholders should have sufficient inducement to do the strategist's bidding. This ethical approach has value for the firm, Hosmer argues:

> It benefits that company by ensuring a cooperative, innovative and directed effort on the part of all of the stakeholders of the firm.

Hosmer, "Strategic Planning as if Ethics Mattered," 29. This is precisely the proposition that the fictitious John Markham believed that he was following in Kubicki's *Breaker Boys*.

It is worth my repeating the circumstances in which I use the term "victim." Recall from Chapter 1 that I choose to apply an ethical criterion of each person's distinctive worldly contribution in the course of my critique of corporate strategy. Hence, I argue that a human being is a victim insofar as someone deliberately interferes with his or her efforts at making a distinctive worldly contribution in relation to other human beings. The person bent on interference is the bully. The bully does not value the ethical standard that I have defended in Chapter 1 for this critical purpose.

Moreover, by my ethical standard of distinctive worldly contribution, the bully who practices extortion, for instance, can never justify the legitimacy of that practice. Extortion is a calculated attempt to interfere with at least one other human being's life of ties to other human beings. In this context, I can counter the bully's claim that he is doing something distinctive, worldly, and contributory. Bullies like to make that particular claim.

44. B. Watterson, *The Indispensable Calvin and Hobbes* (Kansas City, MO: Andrews and McMeel, 1992), 134.

45. The Containment Crew members win the OOP-1 and OOP-2 awards precisely because they accord a central place in their stories to this interplay between bullies and their victims. By emphasizing this drama, even as it undermines the ethical justification for their accounts, the Containment Crew members stand apart from their strategic management brethren who are busy creating stories in which stakeholders are silenced. Resource-based, dominant logic, and strategy process frameworks are stories in which stakeholders are silenced. For so daring a rhetorical move, the Containment Crew members deserve their awards.

46. In a classic admission that he commits such an act of interference, Paul Riesling says this to George Babbitt in Sinclair Lewis's *Babbitt*:

> "You know, my business isn't distributing roofing—it's principally keeping my competitors from distributing roofing. Same with you. All we do is cut each other's throats and make the public pay for it."

S. Lewis, *Babbitt* (New York: New American Library, 1980), 55. Ever the bully, Babbitt dismisses the charge that Riesling levels at himself and his friend. The members of a college faculty have good reason to be on the lookout for colleagues who practice such interference. The vitality of their community hangs in the balance. A faculty member who makes it his business to prevent others from practicing as educators is the bully whose influence must be mitigated. Intimidation of that kind is one of the worst threats to a faculty. For an account of faculty members wrestling with the vitality of their community, see P. F. Kluge, *Alma Mater* (Reading, MA: Addison-Wesley, 1993).

47. This is the kind of practice that Hosmer endorses with his "new paradigm" for strategic management.

48. M. Porter, *Competitive Advantage: Creating and Sustaining Superior Performance* (New York: Free Press, 1985), 228.

49. Ibid., 201.

50. Ibid., 212.

51. See Porter's remarks about the reconciliation of a competitor's goals. Ibid., 214.

52. For a different conception of competition and competitors, see S. Walton, with J. Huey, *Sam Walton: Made in America: My Story* (New York: Doubleday, 1992). It does not take very much prodding for my strategy students to interpret Walton's autobiography as a rich source of metaphors by which competitors can be understood as fellow human beings. Walton often talks about competitors as his teachers, for instance.

53. See K. R. Harrigan, "Entry Barriers in Mature Manufacturing Industries," in R. Lamb, ed., *Advances in Strategic Management*, Volume 2 (Greenwich, CT: JAI Press, 1983), 88–90. Nowhere in the competitor selection story is there any space given to a justification for why the "good" competitor must do the corporate strategist's bidding. Apparently, that colonial kind of relationship is just "the way it must be." For one amusing reminder about how seductive it can be to have others march to one's tune, see Calvin's self-assessment about thriving on change in B. Watterson, *Homicidal Psycho Jungle Cat* (Kansas City, MO: Andrews and McMeel, 1994), 98.

54. See, in this regard, the discussion about metagames in B. Dutta and W. King, "Metagame Analysis of Competitive Strategy," *Strategic Management Journal* 1 (1980):357–370. See also, with regard to a strategist's vigiliance in an industry, Porter, *Competitive Advantage*, 225.

55. Porter, *Competitive Advantage*, 201–228.

56. Ibid., 224.

57. For an account of the social interactions among competitors, see G. Easton, G. Burrell, R. Rothschild, and C. Shearman, *Managers and Competition* (Oxford: Basil Blackwell, 1993).

58. For other angles on strategic groups, see J. McGee and H. Thomas, "Strategic Groups: Theory, Research, and Taxonomy," *Strategic Management Journal* 7 (1986):141–160, and S. Oster, *Modern Competitive Analysis* (New York: Oxford University Press, 1990), 61–79.

59. The strategic management theorist might protest, per the conventional fascination with the proper form of a "good" theory, "But a theory can only cover so much." I am interested in something else. I ask simply, "Why does this theory make certain human beings prominent and other human beings invisible?" I am asking an ethical question, not a grammatical one.

60. See K. Cool and D. Schendel, "Strategic Group Formation and Performance: The Case of the U.S. Pharmaceutical Industry, 1963–1982," *Management Science* 33, no. 9 (1987):1102–1124.

61. See Michael Porter's discussion about favorable positions for the firm and the formulation of competitive strategy in M. Porter, *Competitive Strategy: Techniques for Analyzing Industries and Competitors* (New York: Free Press, 1980), 144–149.

62. Oster, *Modern Competitive Analysis*, 77. For an extensive critique of game theory for managers, or anyone else, see R. Solomon, *Ethics and Excellence: Cooperation and Integrity in Business* (New York: Oxford University Press, 1992), 48–64. Solomon notes that

the game theory metaphor, like so many systematically misleading metaphors in philosophy, needs not improvement but dismantling (as a model for business practices and, especially, for morality and business ethics; I certainly have no objection to the theory for its own sake, or as a powerful model *for games*). But game theory has now become the preferred way of doing both ethics and economics, and that is a very different matter.

Ibid., 63. I walk along some of the same critic's path in Solomon's footsteps. I could not agree more with the final sentence in the passage above. Still, we are headed toward different destinations in our accounts about business and ethics. Solomon sets up a choice between accepting game theory or "dismantling" it. As will become clear in Chapter 4, I see an opportunity to retrieve, for a number of ethical reasons, the game metaphor. My choices in that act of retrieval concern which pieces of game theory to retain and which pieces to discard.

63. This perpetual state of emergency, Memmi argues persuasively, also has the effect of "corrupting" the colonial governor. See Memmi, *Colonizer and the Colonized*, 147–151.

64. See Oster's discussion of factors that "can help shield incumbents from new entry and allow them to earn excess profits over protracted periods." Oster, *Modern Competitive Analysis*, 48.

65. In Hosmer's account, the corporate strategist can do this by incorporating ten "most basic or most widely accepted" ethical principles into a strategic planning process. Hosmer, "Strategic Planning as if Ethics Mattered," 18.

66. For a more extensive analysis on this point, see D. Gilbert, Jr., "The Thrill of Victory and the Agony of Having to Compete: An Ethical Critique of a Myth About Competition," in P. Shrivastava, C. Stubbart, A. Huff, and J. Dutton, eds., *Advances in Strategic Management*, Volume 12A (Greenwich, CT: JAI Press, 1995), 49–75.

67. B. Mascarenhas and D. Aaker, "Mobility Barriers and Strategic Groups," *Strategic Management Journal* 10 (1989):485.

68. By contrast, in both the resource-based and dominant logic frameworks there are no others into whose eyes a strategist might look.

69. E. Wolgast, *The Grammar of Justice* (Ithaca, NY: Cornell University Press, 1987), 1–27.

70. M. Dollinger, "The Evolution of Collective Strategies in Fragmented Industries," *Academy of Management Review* 15, no. 2 (1990):268.

71. W. G. Astley, "Toward an Appreciation of Collective Strategy," *Academy of Management Review* 9, no. 3 (1984):526–535.

72. Ibid., 533.

73. Dollinger, "Evolution of Collective Strategies in Fragmented Industries," 268.

74. R. Bresser and J. Harl, "Collective Strategy: Vice or Virtue?," *Academy of Management Review* 11, no. 2 (1986):425.

75. For a comprehensive and accessible introduction to game theory for managers, see A. Dixit and B. Nalebuff, *Thinking Strategically: The Competitive Edge in Business, Politics, and Everyday Life* (New York: W. W. Norton, 1991); J. K. Murnighan, *The Dynamics of Bargaining Games* (Englewood Cliffs, NJ: Prentice-Hall, 1991); and W. Poundstone, *Prisoner's Dilemma: John von Neumann, Game Theory, and the Puzzle of the Bomb* (New York: Doubleday, 1992). My earliest influences about the relevance of game theory for managers were D. Muzzio, *Watergate Games: Strategies, Choices, Outcomes* (New York: New York University Press, 1982), and S. Brams, *Biblical Games: A Strategic Analysis of Stories in the Old Testament* (Cambridge, MA: MIT Press, 1980).

76. Periodically, strategy researchers critique the worth of game theory for

strategic management theory. Those critiques are inevitably focused inward on the assumptions on which the game theorist tells his story. A common focus in those debates is whether corporate strategists are sufficiently "rational" to practice what game theorists think that strategists should do. Nowhere in that debate about rationality is anything about human community or human empathy. For a recent round of debate about the rationality requirements in game theory and the rationality capabilities of a strategist, see G. Saloner, "Modeling, Game Theory, and Strategic Management," *Strategic Management Journal* 12, Special Issue (1991):119–136; S. Postrel, "Burning Your Britches Behind You: Can Policy Scholars Bank on Game Theory?," *Strategic Management Journal* 12, Special Issue (1991):153–155; and C. Camerer, "Does Strategy Research Need Game Theory?," *Strategic Management Journal* 12, Special Issue (1991):137–152. Camerer writes, "The answer to my title question is: it wouldn't hurt." Ibid., 149. Saloner and Postrel seem to concur.

77. Dixit and Nalebuff, *Thinking Strategically*, 4. For a review of the story told by Dixit and Nalebuff, see D. Gilbert, Jr., *"Thinking Strategically: The Competitive Edge in Business, Politics, and Everyday Life* by Avinash Dixit and Barry Nalebuff," book review, *Journal of Business Ethics* 12 (1992):274, 280, 322, 338–340. I thank James Gaa for his support here.

78. Oster reminds us to "Remember now the efficient-market principle: Appealing situations do not in general last very long." Oster, *Modern Competitive Analysis,* 23.

79. Oster continues:

> In testing alternative strategies, we must constantly ask ourselves the fundamental market question: What protects my strategy against encroaching entry? And, if I am not protected, and entry does occur, what can I do to maintain good performance in the new era?

Ibid., 29. If anyone doubted the corporate strategist's profound distaste for the democratic flavor of free-market competition, Oster's arguments, like Porter's, should dispel such doubts. For one sketch of such a politics of corporate strategy, see D. Gilbert, Jr., "Corporate Strategy and Ethics," *Journal of Business Ethics* 5, no. 2 (1987):137–150. The corporate strategist who practices a resource-based approach must live in constant fear of such encroachment. Jay Barney writes:

> In general, firms seeking a sustained competitive advantage should choose strategies that exploit valuable, rare, inimitable, and nonsubstitutable resources.

J. Barney, "Integrating Organizational Behavior and Strategy Formulation Research," in P. Shrivastava, A. Huff, and J. Dutton, eds., *Advances in Strategic Management,* Volume 8 (Greenwich, CT: JAI Press, 1992), 44. Barney tries to soothe strategist's fears with the proposition that "nonsubstitutable socially complex organizational phenomena" can count as such a valuable resource. Ibid., 48. This vocabulary of "rare, inimitable, and nonsubstitutable" is a sure sign that the resource-based strategist would dearly love for the rest of the competitive world to disappear. This is a clear return to the Business Policy thinking that Alfred Sloan put into words.

80. R. Axelrod, *The Evolution of Cooperation* (New York: Basic Books, 1984).

81. Murnighan, *Dynamics of Bargaining Games,* 180–202. Murnighan closes a

long discussion of what can go wrong ethically in bargaining situations with four pieces of advice: "Learn from your mistakes"; "Use the mirror to look at yourself and see whether you like what you see"; "Put yourself in the other person's shoes and see how that other person sees you. (If the picture is a good one, you're probably doing fine)"; and "Be on guard." Ibid., 202. It is no wonder that game theorists cannot tell us much about getting along with others. These four adages have nothing to do with the other person per se, much less with any clear conception of human community. On this score, I agree wholeheartedly with Robert Solomon. Game theorists just do not seem to get the point that their very models of human interaction are the problem.

82. See R. Frank, *Passions Within Reason: The Strategic Role of the Emotions* (New York: W. W. Norton, 1988).

83. Porter, *Competitive Strategy*, 145–148.

84. See, for instance, Murnighan, *Dynamics of Bargaining Games*, 202.

85. Robert Frank shows us—without announcing the point—just how deeply ingrained in game theory is the premise that strategists will cheat on each other. He poses the dilemma of a restaurant patron who is about to depart a diner in a distant city that he will probably never visit again. The dilemma posed by Frank is whether the diner should tip or not. Frank, *Passions Within Reason*, 16–19. This supposedly is testimony to our propensity to try to get away with cheating. I argue that the story is testimony to something else: a distressing contempt that game theorists hold for human relationships. How we can learn anything useful, I wonder, about lasting human relationships when an important test case is one in which one human being is about to leave the company of another? In short, game theorists use a clever rhetoric. They set up, as an axiom, the fragility of human relationships to make a point about people's overriding interests in themselves. The whole case is a "setup."

86. A dirty little secret among the proponents of game theory for managers is that the managers to whom they are writing might also be tempted. However, that admission is something that, at best, you might find in the small print. It is always the other player's untrustworthiness that is in the spotlight.

87. See the military language, for instance, in Porter, *Competitive Strategy*, 75–87.

88. I develop this critique in greater detail in D. Gilbert, Jr., "The Prisoner's Dilemma and the Prisoners of the Prisoners Dilemma," *Business Ethics Quarterly* 5 (1996), in press.

89. I argue, ibid., that the Prisoner's Dilemma game is misdrawn in a way that masks the politics of the Prisoner's Dilemma genre. Once we redraw the prisoners' plight in terms of two simultaneous attempts by the jailer to coerce a confession, we can begin to ask some new questions about what we cannot, and should not, accomplish with the Prisoner's Dilemma device.

90. A milestone in management education would be a debate about the ethical justification for teaching the Prisoner's Dilemma at all. Management education would be that much stronger for such a period of self-scrutiny.

91. This position is occupied by the Corporate Moral Agent in Singer's account, the ten ethical principles in Hosmer's account, and the dominant logic in the story told by Prahalad and Bettis. Andrew Stark has recently posed the question, "What's the matter with business ethics?" In effect, Singer, Hosmer, and Prahalad and Bettis all reply to Stark, "Nothing that a resort to 'ethics from

the outside' cannot solve." See A. Stark, "What's the Matter with Business Ethics?," *Harvard Business Review* 71, no. 3 (1993):38–48.

CHAPTER 4.

1. Searcher is an actual person. I have fabricated certain descriptions of her background to protect her identity. None of those fabrications diminish the lesson that I take from that semester for my purposes in this chapter.

2. C. Taylor, *The Ethics of Authenticity* (Cambridge, MA: Harvard University Press, 1991), 23. For another example of intellectual retrieval, see what Donald Worster does with "the American West." D. Worster, *Under Western Skies: Nature and History in the American West* (New York: Oxford University Press, 1992).

3. "Pragmatism" is a practice of considering the comparative worth of ideas with which we can approach our lives. The pragmatist can choose, of course, from among many standards for conducting such an intellectual showdown. For example, in the course of weighing the comparative worth of ideas in relation to each person's distinctive worldly contribution, I practice as a contractarian, quasi-communitarian, feminist self-in-relation, liberal pragmatist. I could have conducted the same comparison from a very different pragmatist angle. Regarding a plurality of pragmatisms, see R. Rorty, "Trotsky and the Wild Orchids," in M. Edmundson, ed., *Wild Orchids and Trotsky: Messages from American Universities* (New York: Penguin, 1993), 29–50.

4. The distinction between retrieval and reiteration is my adaptation of a distinction that Ayn Rand makes in *The Fountainhead* between creators and so-called second-handers. Second-handers are masters of reiteration. This is what Rand's Howard Roark character says about them and their "deadliness":

> "They don't ask: 'Is this true?' They ask: 'Is this what others think is true?' Not to judge, but to repeat. Not to do, but to give the impression of doing. Not creation, but show."

A. Rand, *The Fountainhead* (New York: New American Library, 1971), 607. Retrieval is the thoroughly evaluative act of a critic who seeks to create new meanings. Howard Roark lives a life of retrieval as an architect.

Retrieval is something that we can each practice. Retrieving baseball is an important project for me these days. Baseball has been a constant in my life, an "ideal" in Charles Taylor's terms. Baseball has always been one of the first things that many family members and friends associate with me. Still, baseball has also been a changing "ideal" for me through the years. I am very conscious of that these days, as certain chapters on my baseball ideal are closing.

Former Philadelphia Phillies' stars Mike Schmidt and Steve Carlton, heroes in my college years, have been inducted into baseball's Hall of Fame. I associate my Minnesota years with the resurgence of the Minnesota Twins and two exemplars of those Twins teams: Kirby Puckett and Kent Hrbek. Puckett is a very accomplished athlete whose splendid career is coming to a conclusion. Hrbek retired in 1994. I had the special opportunity, during the Phillies' 1994 Dream Week program, to play on a team coached by my two boyhood Phillies' heroes, Johnny Callison and Tony Taylor. I came away impressed with their warmth and their love of teaching baseball. I also came away reminding myself that Johnny and Tony were in their playing primes *exactly thirty years before,* when the 1964 Phillies "blew" the National League pennant and I was attending Nitschmann Junior High School in Bethlehem, Pannsylvania. I still root for those who wear the Phillies' and Twins' uniforms, but I cannot put my finger, as readily as I once could, on why I do. I am looking to find a new meaning for baseball in my life, while still believing in baseball.

In short, I am in the midst of an exercise in retrieval about baseball. I am not longing for the "good old days" as I try to retrieve the idea of baseball, nor does Charles Taylor in his project about authenticity. Such longing is tantamount to an act of reiteration. I do not want merely to repeat the kind of association that I have had with the sport. I want something that is more intellectually challenging than replication of a past meaning of baseball *and* something that still involves a game played on grass without a time limit.

5. See, for example, J. Lawlor, "Denny's Settles Bias Case," *USA Today*, 25 May 1994:2B, and S. Labaton, "Denny's Gets a Bill for the Side Orders of Bigotry," *New York Times*, 29 May 1994, Section 4:4.

6. A curious statement appeared not long ago in a Denny's coupon. The statement read: "Denny's is committed to providing the best possible service to all customers regardless of race, creed or national origin." On one hand, statements of this kind are no reason to sit up and take notice. Who would claim to provide something less than "the best possible service" at a restaurant? On the other hand, explicit reference to race sets this statement apart from other self-promotional claims about service. Perhaps retrieval of "service" is underway at Denny's.

7. Such opposition to the opening of Wal-Mart stores notwithstanding, there could be other reasons for Sam Walton's successors to engage in an exercise of retrieval of Walton's way of doing business. On more than one occasion, I have received the same kind of indifferent service near closing time on a weeknight in January and February at Wal-Mart as I can get at a half-dozen other discount retail establishments. On a general note regarding the importance of past corporate practices, see the thoughtful analysis in A. Kantrow, *The Constraints of Corporate Tradition: Doing the Correct Thing, Not Just What the Past Dictates* (New York: Harper & Row, 1987).

8. If you have been busily seeking those Wal-Mart specials and somehow missed the ruckus about Wal-Mart store openings, see this sampler of journalism: K. Blumenthal, "Arrival of Discounter Tears the Civic Fabric of Small-Town Life," *Wall Street Journal*, 14 April 1987:1, 25; H. Sidey, "The Two Sides of the Sam Walton Legacy," *Time*, 20 April 1992, 50–52; S. Rimer, "Across New England, Main Street's in Danger," *New York Times*, 28 February 1993:22; J. Eckhoff, "Residents Tell Wal-Mart to Take Its Business Someplace Else," *Philadelphia Inquirer*, 31 March 1994:B4; and J. Steinberg, "Fears and Fanfare for the New Store in Town," *New York Times*, 31 March 1994:B1, B5. See also Garry Trudeau's commentary in his "Doonesbury" comic strip during September 1994.

9. Richard Rorty has criticized members of the "cultural left" for what he sees as their distaste for critiquing worldly practices that they consider tawdry. See R. Rorty, "Two Cheers for the Cultural Left," in D. Gless and B. H. Smith, *The Politics of Liberal Education* (Durham, NC: Duke University Press, 1992), 233–240. To members of such a "cultural left," business and corporate strategy probably qualify as such tawdry subjects. I want us to follow Rorty's lead and talk openly about the worldly experiences that we share, such as the kind of com-

plicated, widespread institution of exchange that we commonly call business.

10. I have in mind as a primary audience those persons who have long been faithful to the idea of business policy. For them, two holy texts are A. Sloan, *My Years with General Motors* (New York: Doubleday, 1963), and A. Carnegie, *The Autobiography of Andrew Carnegie* (Boston: Houghton Mifflin, 1920).

11. So it is that pragmatist criticism is always a contest between two provisionally worthwhile ways of talking about the world. The pragmatist critic is an ironist, as Richard Rorty puts it. To practice pragmatist criticism in an ironic way, I must believe that the meaning of a particular idea—such as a Pragmatist Ethics of Differences, Centers, and Margins—is stable long enough for me to use it in a critique and to carry on subsequent discussions with others about the critique. On the other hand, I know that I could someday want to conduct a critique for which I have less use, or even none at all, for the idea of a Pragmatist Ethics of Differences, Centers, and Margins. In fact, the three building blocks for Strategy Through Convention are evidence of this irony in my projects. These three ideas bear some resemblance to the Projects, Contracts, and Responsibility Premises that I created for the critique that I conducted in D. Gilbert, Jr., *The Twilight of Corporate Strategy: A Comparative Ethical Critique* (New York: Oxford University Press, 1992). However, such premises, as Richard Rorty and Stanley Fish remind pragmatists, are not timeless truths. They were useful to me several years ago, but they are not as useful to me now. See R. Rorty, *Contingency, Irony, and Solidarity* (Cambridge: Cambridge University Press, 1989), 73–80. Fish warns pragmatists to resist the idea that, after conducting a comparative critique, "you cannot claim a new purity that has somehow arisen." S. Fish, *There's No Such Thing as Free Speech, and It's a Good Thing, Too* (New York: Oxford University Press, 1994), 20.

12. W. P. Kinsella, *Shoeless Joe* (New York: Ballantine, 1983). The film "Field of Dreams" is an adaptation of Kinsella's novel. © 1989 Universal City Studios, Inc.

13. S. Lewis, *Babbitt* (New York: New American Library, 1980; first published in 1922).

14. On this postmodern pragmatist reading of *Shoeless Joe* and *Babbitt*, these stories are "true" for our worldly conversations insofar as we can use the stories to do some things together—such as ask new questions about corporate strategy—that we could not do before. On this account, there is no ultimate truthful reading of either or any novel. Regarding this account of reading, see Rorty, *Contingency, Irony, and Solidarity;* A. Rosmarin, *The Power of Genre* (Minneapolis: University of Minnesota Press, 1985); and D. Gilbert, Jr., "A Critique and a Retrieval of Management and the Humanities," *Journal of Business Ethics* (1996), in press. For a view that I challenge regarding the truth in fiction, see J. Clancy, *The Invisible Powers: The Language of Business* (Lexington, MA: Lexington Books, 1989). By "inviting" the fictitious Kinsella and Babbitt into my account of Strategy Through Convention, I practice what Richard Rorty has called a "rational reconstruction" of hypothetical conversations with which we can better understand our worldly time and place. See R. Rorty, "The Historiography of Philosophy: Four Genres," in R. Rorty, J. Schneewind, and Q. Skinner, eds., *Philosophy in History* (Cambridge: Cambridge University Press, 1984), 49–56. It seems appropriate to arrange such conversations with the ficti-

tious Kinsella and Babbitt because imagination is such an important factor in the novels *Shoeless Joe* and *Babbitt*.

15. This discussion is an extension of the idea of Strategy as Purpose. See R. E. Freeman and D. Gilbert, Jr., *Corporate Strategy and the Search for Ethics* (Englewood Cliffs, NJ: Prentice-Hall, 1988), 13–20. In effect, I am working to retrieve the idea of autonomy. Autonomy has long been associated with the kind of psychological separation that many social critics are trying to replace. For an interesting struggle to reconcile autonomy and connections with others, see J. B. Miller, *Toward a New Psychology of Women*, 2nd ed. (Boston: Beacon Press, 1986). Arguing for a self-in-relation genre of feminism, Miller reminds us of the role that autonomy has played in male-dominated institutions. Ibid., 95.

16. If you are inclined, to any extent whatsoever, to read "isomorphism" into what I am saying about differences here, don't. Accomplishments, one's autonomy stakes, is one way to talk about differences. We could also talk about differences in terms of gender and educational experiences and favorite baseball teams. The truth of accomplishments, one's autonomy stakes, is in what we can do with the idea in critical arguments. If the previous sentence makes no sense to you, and you are still inclined to see isomorphism here, go to Rorty, *Contingency, Irony, and Solidarity;* Fish, *There's No Such Thing as Free Speech;* or Chapter 2 in Gilbert, *Twilight of Corporate Strategy.* The idea of isomorphism simply gets in the way of the argument that I create here.

17. I prefer accomplishment to aspiration, inspired by the distinction between doing and "show" that Ayn Rand/Howard Roark emphasized. Rand, *The Fountainhead*, 607. For a discussion about linking ethics and accomplishments, see B. J. Phillips, "It's a Question, Really, of Ethics," *Philadelphia Inquirer*, 16 June 1995:C1.

18. Lewis, *Babbitt*, 319.

19. Ibid., 191.

20. J. Cowan, *Small Decencies: Reflections and Meditations on Being Human at Work* (New York: HarperBusiness, 1993), 6. See also ibid., 112, regarding a person's search for a "bigger lake." I am grateful to Kate Rogers for introducing me to Cowan's writings.

21. D. Hall, *Life Work* (Boston: Beacon Press, 1993), 62.

22. J. Jordan, A. Kaplan, J. B. Miller, I. Stiver, and J. Surrey, *Women's Growth in Connection: Writings from the Stone Center* (New York: Guilford Press, 1991), 21.

23. N. Lyons, "Listening to Voices We Have Not Heard," in C. Gilligan, N. Lyons, and T. Hanmer, eds., *Making Connections: The Relational Worlds of Adolescent Girls at Emma Willard School* (Cambridge, MA: Harvard University Press, 1990), 49.

24. Rorty, *Contingency, Irony, and Solidarity*, 24–29. For a reflection on how contingent a self-creator's life can be, see the commentary about "how close everything is" in B. Meissner, *Hitting Into the Wind* (New York: Random House, 1994), 108.

25. Taylor, *Ethics of Authenticity*, 28–29. The "point of one's life" need not necessarily be synonymous with superstardom. In a published interview, professional baseball player Jim Eisenreich says as much. See B. Koenig, "The Ideal Role Player," *USA Today Baseball Weekly*, 21–27 June 1995:4.

26. C. West, *Race Matters* (Boston: Beacon Press, 1993), 12–15. See ibid., 104, for a discussion about "everyday people." It is rare when management re-

searchers pay any attention to the rhythms of everyday life, as sketched in A. Yarrow, "Resurgent Sing-Alongs Mix Banjos with Environmentalism," *New York Times*, 13 October 1992:B4. For a rare exception, see A. van Cauwenbergh and R. Martens, "Simplicity Behind Strategy: A Reflection on Strategic Management Theory Versus Its Practice," in R. Lamb and P. Shrivastava, eds., *Advances in Strategic Management*, Volume 4 (Greenwich, CT: JAI Press, 1986), 117–122.

27. E. Wolgast, *The Grammar of Justice* (Ithaca, NY: Cornell University Press, 1987), 179.

28. I can call on an eclectic genre of support for this idea about accomplishments-in-relation. One is self-in-relation feminism. A second is Ayn Rand's portrayal of Howard Roark as someone whose accomplishments are always made in ties to other, like-minded creators, such as Steven Mallory and Austen Heller. A third is the concept of "one to one marketing," about which Don Peppers and Martha Rogers write:

> But now technology is making it possible for the modern marketer—even the mass marketer—to assume the role of the small proprietor, doing business again with individuals, one at a time.

D. Peppers and M. Rogers, *The One to One Future: Building Relationships One Customer at a Time* (New York: Currency Doubleday, 1993), 22. I take a fourth source of support in the argument by Michael Piore and Charles Sabel about what they call "the second industrial divide." About the flourishing institution of craft production and the associated logic of "flexible specialization," Piore and Sabel write:

> Among the ironies of the resurgence of craft production is that its deployment of modern technology depends on its reinvigoration of affiliations that are associated with the preindustrial pact.

M. Piore and C. Sabel, *The Second Industrial Divide: Possibilities for Prosperity* (New York: Basic Books, 1984), 275. Piore and Sabel are talking about close human affiliations, much as Peppers and Rogers do. Piore and Sabel call attention to a "communitarian" aspect of flexible specialization that "violat[es] one of the assumptions of classical political economy: that the economy is separate from society." Ibid., 275. I take as a fifth source of support for the idea of accomplishment-in-relation the reinterpretation of individualism in the American West that Donald Worster creates. See Worster, *Under Western Skies*.

29. ". . . Trading promises like baseball cards," Kinsella and Shoeless Joe learn to trust each other. Kinsella, *Shoeless Joe*, 21. With each "trade" they revise their common ground, because each "trade" is marked by the appearance of another ballplayer who emerges from the cornfield to join in the game on Kinsella's ballfield.

30. Lewis, *Babbitt*, 80–81. See also ibid., 182, regarding Babbitt's joining the Presbyterian Church as a way to qualify for belonging to even more common grounds.

31. Cowan, *Small Decencies*, 15–18.

32. Lyons, "Listening to Voices We Have Not Heard," 42.

33. Hall, *Life Work*, 61–62. See also ibid., 117, where Hall discusses an Emersonian conception of a living on a few cherished common grounds, from which all others are asked to "keep out."

34. Rorty, *Contingency, Irony, and Solidarity*, 191.

35. J. Surrey, "The Self-in-Relation: A Theory of Women's Development," in J. Jordan, A. Kaplan, J. B. Miller, I. Stiver, and J. Surrey, *Women's Growth in Connection*, 57.

36. Taylor, *Ethics of Authenticity*, 9–10.

37. West, *Race Matters*, 105. See also ibid., 7, for a discussion of a "grass roots" context where this metaphor can be put into political practice.

38. Wolgast, *Grammar of Justice*, xii, 140.

39. Common grounds, contingent memberships turns on a strong prima facie presumption of the equal worth of the projects through which different persons seek to accomplish things in their lives. See C. Taylor, *Multiculturalism and The Politics of Recognition* (Princeton, NJ: Princeton University Press, 1992), 72. It could turn out that someone "unearns" equal worth, perhaps by acting as a bully. By Strategy Through Convention, as liberal a story as it is, that possibility is not sufficient reason a priori for designating someone's projects as unworthy. Of course, all of conventional management theory turns on just such an a priori assumption about the greater worth of managers' projects and the lesser worth of everyone else's projects!

40. Strategy Through Convention is populated by human beings, not corporate entities. Thus, the crucial margin here is one with human fingerprints all over it. By the popular models of strategic process and strategic planning, the margin is the strategy that executives attribute to the corporate entity. See Gilbert, *Twilight of Corporate Strategy*, with regard to Strategy Through Process. Still, Strategy Through Convention contains room for human beings to include, among their accomplishments, what they do as agents for some corporate principal. That accomplishment is simply one way to describe one's autonomy.

41. This is one way to fill a glaring hole in management theory regarding human beings' accountability for their actions. If we persist in talking about corporations as the agents "whose" actions make the difference in the business world, then, of course, it will be very difficult to talk about each person's responsibility to one another. That is the hole that many management theorists create and that some management theorists try to fill with ideas like an Ethics of Deadbeats, Dullards, and Derelicts' Disasters Driving the World Into Moral Decline. Strategy Through Convention is evidence that we need not talk that way anymore. One place where I began this project about responsibility is D. Gilbert, Jr., "Diane Vaughan, *Controlling Unlawful Organizational Behavior: Social Structure and Corporate Misconduct*," book review, *Journal of Business Ethics* 7, no. 10 (1988):800–802.

42. Strategy Through Convention is a story, as Geertzian anthropologists would say, that is "thick" with meaning about local conditions. See, in this vein, D. Berreby, "Clifford Geertz: Unabsolute Truths," *New York Times Magazine*, 9 April 1995, Section 6:44–47. The basic plot of common ground in Strategy Through Convention is the two-person common ground known as a game. We can complicate the story from there by linking one bilateral common ground to another and to still another. This web of common grounds, a web of games, is one of the primary concepts that I will introduce in Chapter 5. I call attention to this "thick" local story here, because many students of management will be lost at any level of analysis "lower" than the organizational entity. For a further discussion about local contexts, see Piore and Sabel, *Second Industrial Divide*, 306 regarding "the American tradition of localism."

43. Kinsella, *Shoeless Joe*, 28.

44. Lewis writes of George Babbitt:

He knew by the cheer that he was secure again and popular; he knew that he would no more endanger his security and popularity by straying from the Clan of Good Fellows.

Lewis, *Babbitt*, 316.

45. Cowan, *Small Decencies*, 12–14.

46. Hall, *Life Work*, 61.

47. J. Mendelsohn, "The View from Step Number 16," in C. Gilligan, N. Lyons, and T. Hanmer, eds., *Making Connections*, 243–244.

48. Rorty, *Contingency, Irony, and Solidarity*, 45. See also ibid., 84, regarding "social glue."

49. Surrey, "The Self-in-Relation: A Theory of Women's Development," 56.

50. Taylor, *Ethics of Authenticity*, 33, 48–49.

51. West, *Race Matters*, 19–20. See also ibid., 15, where West praises "the genius" of past leaders in black America for their efforts at sustaining certain institutions, particular understandings that made for conducive connections among members of local black communities.

52. Wolgast, *Grammar of Justice*, 183–186.

53. I designate these three ideas with complicated names because I want to talk about complicated lives led by complicated human beings. And, if you think that common grounds, contingent memberships, for example, is a complicated mouthful, wait until Chapter 5 when I add another layer of meaning to each of these building blocks. In this regard, I adapt what Stanley Fish says about pragmatism: "In a pragmatist world what you say is what you get." Fish, *There's No Such Thing as Free Speech*, 23. For many years, it has been common practice to describe corporate strategies with slogans. Differentiation, globalization, and niche are cases in point. There isn't much humanity evident in those slogans. What you say is what you get.

54. I conduct this retrieval under the influence of Cowan, Gilligan and colleagues, Hall, Jordan and colleagues, Rorty, Taylor, West, and Wolgast (listed alphabetically throughout), because they all give me confidence that I can say something about each person's distinctive worldly contribution. These works are thus eight inaugural texts for Strategy Through Convention.

I suspect that more than a few students of management have by now given up with my argument, muttering as they leave, "Whatever happened to simple business truths?" They have probably returned to the comforting words available in such sources as E. Archer, "Whatever Happened to the Principles of Management?," *Southern Business Review* 17, no. 1 (1991):1–11. If they have not given up by this point in the book, advocates of an ethics of prevention and an ethics of bullying might do their respective causes a big favor by coming forward with their respective canons. It is not clear what such lists of guiding texts might contain. It is particularly unclear what works these students of management would cite, if I added the stipulation that the texts must not be written about business and business truths, but rather about humanity.

55. K. Andrews, *The Concept of Corporate Strategy*, rev. ed. (Homewood, IL: Richard D. Irwin, 1980), 46.

56. Alfred Sloan's autobiography is a classic treatise on accomplishment. See Part One in A. Sloan, *My Years with General Motors*. That is why I have used

Sloan's book near the outset of a course about corporate strategy, as a way to trace a historical flow from business policy to strategic management. Thus, in the spirit of note 54 above, if I were to develop a set of inaugural business texts for Strategy Through Convention, Sloan's *My Years with General Motors* is a leading candidate.

57. This link between strategy formulation and accomplishment also is prominent in the "dominant logic," resource-based, strategy process, and Business and Society frameworks for corporate strategy. In those accounts, corporate strategists use their special methods—in effect, as strategic magicians—to conjure up a corporate strategy for what the corporation, as an actor, could accomplish.

58. One newcomer to strategy implementation is corporate reengineering. For an ethical critique of the corporate reengineering approach to strategy implementation, see D. Gilbert, Jr., "Management and Four Stakeholder Politics: Corporate Reengineering as a Crossroads Case," *Business & Society* 34, no. 1 (1995):90–97. I am grateful to Donna Wood for her encouragement with the ideas that became that paper.

59. The genre of game that I have in mind here is the coordination game that David Lewis and Andrew Schotter, among others, have developed. See D. Lewis, *Convention: A Philosophical Study* (Cambridge, MA: Harvard University Press, 1969), and A. Schotter, *The Economic Theory of Social Institutions* (Cambridge: Cambridge University Press, 1981). A coordination game is a context in which multiple equilibria are available for the two parties involved. These equilibria are common grounds, I propose in Chapter 5, on which conducive connections can be jointly shaped. It is this ethical possibility that leads me to seek a retrieval of the idea of game, a retrieval project for which Robert Solomon, I suspect, would have little use. Solomon interprets a game as something different from what I choose to interpret. See R. Solomon, *Ethics and Excellence: Cooperation and Integrity in Business* (New York: Oxford University Press, 1992).

60. A classic example of this approach to strategic fit can be read in Alfred Sloan's autobiography. Sloan argues that he and his colleagues had accomplished a "concept of the business" that was better suited to the times in America than did Henry Ford. Sloan, *My Years with General Motors*, 515.

61. Business and Society models of management are predicated on a twin accomplishment whereby executives simultaneously seek to accomplish "social good" and to accomplish sustained positive cash flows for the firm. This is commonly known as "enlightened self-interest." See Andrews, *Concept of Corporate Strategy*, 97. Many students of management believe that this is sufficient ethical obligation for executives. Strategy Through Convention is evidence that I do not share that belief.

62. With this interpretation, I retrieve convention from the collective level of analysis and make it something that each of us can see ourselves having a hand in sustaining. My students readily understand the point, as I take them on a pragmatist tour of language as a convention that they touch every time they speak. See Lewis, *Convention.* "Why is it," I ask my students, "that we call a table a table and not a baseball?"

63. I am indebted to Ed Freeman and John Rutland for their encouragement as I have endeavored to make convention a usable concept for each strategist's life.

64. So, to those who fret that postmodernism is tantamount to abandonment

of ethical principles, I say, "Watch me." Each person's distinctive worldly contribution is an ethical standard that I created through pragmatist, comparative argument and that I will apply in pragmatist, comparative argument. The pragmatist fact that there are many stories to tell about the world does not lead straightaway to the conclusion that we cannot choose among those stories. This book is one accomplishment that exposes that mistaken conclusion that is often directed at pragmatists.

65. For a forerunner to this statement, see Freeman and Gilbert, *Corporate Strategy and the Search for Ethics*, 158–175, regarding what we call personal projects. My thinking in this regard has been influenced by R. Derry, "Feminism: How Does It Play in the Corporate Theater?," paper presented at the Ruffin Lectures in Business Ethics, Charlottesville, Virginia, December 1990.

66. For a fascinating drama between the virtuous businessperson and the bully, see the two stories in H. Alger, *Ragged Dick and Struggling Upward* (New York: Penguin, 1985; first published in 1868). "Ragged Dick" Hunter, the shoeshine boy, outwits the bully who is intent on appropriating rents for himself. That bully is intent on physically intimidating his shoeshine competitors every chance he gets. The possibility that we can create this interpretation of a Horatio Alger novel—admittedly an alternative to the usual "rags to riches" reading—is one of several reasons why the first reading in my corporate strategy course is either *Ragged Dick* or *Struggling Upward*.

67. Both Charles Taylor and Richard Rorty provide a way to replace a story about the strong and the weak with a story about poets, who create new meanings, and those who could become poets. See Rorty, *Contingency, Irony, and Solidarity*, 28; and Taylor, *Ethics of Authenticity*, 61–63. Ray Kinsella ponders the poet's accomplishment as he thinks about his friend Eddie Scissons:

> I know that some of us, and for some reason I am one of them, get to reach out and touch our heart's desire. . . . And I know, too, that when most people reach for that heart's desire, it appears not as a horse but as a tiger, and they are rewarded with snarls, frustration, and disillusionment.

Kinsella, *Shoeless Joe*, 184. With the idea of person as poet, we can interpret corporate-strategy-through-convention as a life into which one can grow. Pushing this line of reasoning one step further, we might come to believe that a corporate strategist is not someone who occupies a particular position in a hierarchy. Rather, she is someone who has earned an honor called "corporate strategist," because that person accomplished something through self-restraint that strengthened connections among poets or poets-in-the-making on their common grounds.

68. Once the distinction between "inside" and "outside" becomes unnecessary, it is possible that anyone could act as a corporate strategist. One consequence of this is that we can free the idea of corporate strategy from the corporate strategic plan. Strategic plans are customarily the accomplishment of a business specialist who acts "outside" the world of business. One could read Strategy Through Convention as a vote for the so-called emergent view of corporate strategy formation. For instance, what I have to say about conventions seems related to the account of strategy emergence in F. Westley, "Vision Worlds: Strategic Vision as Social Interaction," in P. Shrivastava, A. Huff, and J. Dutton, eds., *Advances in Strategic Management*, Volume 8 (Greenwich, CT: JAI Press, 1992), 271–305. If

so, so be it. Still, I am interested in the meaning of strategic processes for the human beings involved, rather than in the process per se or in strategy typologies, a direction in which Westley eventually veers.

69. Ray Kinsella offers what we could take as an impassioned plea to keep merit in our vocabulary:

> He's young and rugged and unafraid and full of hope. It should be enough for me, to see him doing what he loves best.

Kinsella, *Shoeless Joe*, 195. The fictitious Kinsella is describing his father. The challenge in any retrieval of merit, it seems, is to give merit a meaning that does not undermine the idea of common grounds. Merit can all too easily be part of a vocabulary of separation, rather than contingent memberships.

70. See, for example, N. Lemann, "Taking Affirmative Action Apart," *New York Times Magazine*, 11 June 1995:36–43, 52, 54, 62, 66.

71. I take "nuisance" from Richard Rorty's vivid description of pragmatist criticism. See Rorty, *Contingency, Irony, and Solidarity*, 9. For a fascinating treatise about the clashing cultures of the bully and the contributor, see D. Quinn, *Ishmael* (New York: Bantam/Turner, 1992). In Quinn's clever narrative, Takers are bullies. Quinn names contributors as the Leavers who work through their common grounds, care deeply for their common grounds, and take great care to sustain longtime understandings about their care for common ground. I am indebted to Ed Freeman for introducing me to Quinn's novel.

CHAPTER 5.

1. To the pragmatist critic like me, a case is an example of human activity with which we can argue for the relative intellectual merits of a point. Case studies can thus be useful for purposes of replicating the usefulness of an idea. See R. Yin, *Case Study Research: Design and Method* (Newbury Park, CA: Sage Publications, 1984). This pragmatist conception of case study is compatible with the belief that a case study is a focal point for a rollicking discussion between a business school professor and his or her students. This pragmatist conception of case study is less likely to be compatible with the formalist belief that a case study is twenty to thirty pages in length, includes financial statements and organizational charts, and features a lone executive who is prone to looking out the office window at gathering storm clouds. For a parody of this latter belief about case studies, see D. Gilbert, Jr., *The Twilight of Corporate Strategy: A Comparative Ethical Critique* (New York: Oxford University Press, 1992), 75–80.

2. Interpretations of *Barbarians at the Gate* in this chapter are mine. My source of "data" is B. Burrough and J. Helyar, *Barbarians at the Gate: The Fall of RJR Nabisco* (New York: Harper & Row, 1990). As Edwin Hartman has reminded me, there is doing business, there is talking about doing business, and there is talking about talking about doing business. The participants in the RJR Nabisco buy-out were doing business. Burrough and Helyar are talking about doing business. In this chapter and across the entire book, I am talking about what those who talk about business have accomplished. For an explanation of the differences among these activities, see S. Fish, *Doing What Comes Naturally: Change, Rhetoric, and the*

Practice of Theory in Literary and Legal Studies (Durham, NC: Duke University Press, 1989), 372–398.

3. This entire discussion about my students and their educational experiences should not be read as a criticism of my students per se. I describe them as eager young adults who, probably unbeknownst to them, have been put in a position where they might miss a valuable educational opportunity.

4. My reference to businessmen is deliberate. There is only one businesswoman who plays any kind of important role in the story that Burrough and Helyar tell. One could conclude from *Barbarians at the Gate* that investment banking is a private men's club. If that is not the case with investment banking, then other stories must be told to defend that counterclaim.

5. The point is only that this is the account that Burrough and Helyar make available to us. Surely, other stories can be told from other angles on the RJR Nabisco buy-out.

6. Alfred Sloan's autobiography has been the best user's manual about the Story of Business Administration that I have used in my courses. See A. Sloan, *My Years with General Motors* (New York: Doubleday, 1963). A contender for that title is Brent Wade's novel *Company Man* (Chapel Hill, NC: Algonquin Books of Chapel Hill, 1992). It is possible that you might read *Company Man* as something other than an anthem to the Story of Business Administration. I thank Ed Freeman for encouraging for what turned out to be a two-year search for Wade's novel.

For a sampler of the Story of Business Administration, see J. Clancy, *The Invisible Powers: The Language of Business* (Lexington, MA: Lexington Books, 1989), 61, regarding "rules changes"; R. Bettis, "Strategic Management and the Straitjacket: An Editorial Essay," *Organization Science* 2, no. 3 (1991):315–319, and W. Kiechel III, "Corporate Strategy for the 1990s," *Fortune,* 29 February 1988, 34–38, 42.

7. On this pragmatist reading, whether or not *Barbarians at the Gate* is a "true" story depends on how well we can use it to make intellectual progress in our conversations. For an introduction to such a conception of truth, see R. Rorty, *Contingency, Irony, and Solidarity* (Cambridge: Cambridge University Press, 1989), 3–23. Consequently on this reading, the truth of *Barbarians at the Gate* is not a matter of whether Burrough and Helyar have discovered the "real" story of the RJR Nabisco buy-out. Burrough and Helyar appear to believe that their book must pass a "reality test." See their Introduction in Burrough and Helyar, *Barbarians at the Gate,* ix–xi. Helyar perpetuates this conception of truth in the subtitle of his subsequent work. See J. Helyar, *Lords of the Realm: The Real History of Baseball* (New York: Villard, 1994). Helyar puts "real" in italics.

8. I develop this idea on the premise that a life of enlistment is the exact opposite of a life of autonomous pursuit of truth. Of course, there are contexts in which we all must enlist, if we are to belong to any kind of civilized community. Paying our taxes is a case in point. Complying with airline security procedures is another. My first point is that a liberal education is not the place to be selling the seductive allure of a life of enlistment. Undergraduate business curricula at so-called liberal arts institutions deserve close scrutiny in this regard.

9. What I do here is make the political correctness of the Story of Business Administration an issue, in a sophisticated meaning of "political correctness." See S. Fish, *There's No Such Thing as Free Speech, and It's a Good Thing, Too* (New

York: Oxford University Press, 1994), 9–11. See also D. Gilbert, Jr., "*Multinational Corporations and the Impact of Public Advocacy on Corporate Strategy: Nestlé and the Infant Formula Controversy,* by S. Prakash Sethi," book review, *Academy of Management Review* 20, no. 1 (1995):225–229.

10. Rorty, *Contingency, Irony, and Solidarity,* 9.

11. For one application of this premise, see D. Gilbert, Jr., "A Critique and a Retrieval of Management and the Humanities," *Journal of Business Ethics* (1996), in press.

12. Ibid. I call this a fertilizer genre of Management and the Humanities. An important influence in my thinking on this point has been T. Mulligan, "The Two Cultures in Business Education," *Academy of Management Review* 12, no. 4 (1987):593–599.

13. H. Giroux, "Liberal Arts Education and the Struggle for Public Life: Dreaming About Democracy," in D. Gless and B. H. Smith, *The Politics of Liberal Education* (Durham, NC: Duke University Press, 1992), 127.

14. See ibid., 119–144. Having a story of one's own to tell is an accomplishment that sounds foreign to many of my students. If asked to tell a story, more often than not they recite the facts of a business case study prepared in the formal tradition. See note 1.

15. This means that liberal education is not a credential that automatically accompanies a bachelor's degree granted to someone who attended an institution called a liberal arts college. This means instead that one must earn a liberal education.

16. See W. P. Kinsella, *Shoeless Joe* (New York: Ballantine, 1983), and S. Lewis, *Babbitt* (New York: Harcourt Brace Jovanovich, 1922).

17. C. Taylor, *The Ethics of Authenticity* (Cambridge, MA: Harvard University Press, 1991), 2–4. See also Taylor's commentary about a "horizon of important questions." Ibid., 40–41.

18. Compare this statement of corporate strategy according to Strategy Through Convention with the model statement of corporate strategy in K. Andrews, *The Concept of Corporate Strategy,* rev. ed. (Homewood, IL: Richard D. Irwin, 1980), 22. The statement of corporate strategy that Andrews highlights is not about corporate strategists living inquisitively about their humanity. It is not a statement about anyone's humanity.

19. Organizations are not strategic actors in the Strategy Through Convention story. Organizations are nowhere to be found in the vocabulary of Strategy Through Convention.

20. I propose this as a minimum vocabulary for Strategy Through Convention. You can build from there by adding and connecting human beings who live by the concepts of stakes of distinction, stakes threshold, question of interdependence, "we game," local convention, shadow game, web of "we games," convention of local conventions, and member under a stakes threshold. Readers in my generation might recognize the influence of Tinkertoys here.

21. See D. Halberstam, *The Amateurs* (New York: Penguin, 1986). The Olympic rivals in this account are keen observers of each other's stakes of distinction and stakes threshold. According to Halberstam, rowing is a sport in which, sooner or later, each rower will face his own private threshold. See also Charles Taylor's discussion of "the slide to subjectivity" in Taylor, *Ethics of Authenticity,* 55–69.

22. As one consequence of linking the amateur with self-improvement, I make it possible to conclude that the opposite of "amateur" is not necessarily "professional." Rather, the opposite of amateur could be someone "whose fire had gone out," as Father Frank Healy sees his father in J. Hassler, *North of Hope* (New York: Ballantine, 1990), 17. Or, the opposite of amateur could be a bully, who is not interested in anyone's self-improvement but his own. See Chapter 3. Or, the opposite of amateur could be someone who styles himself as a finished product whom, he thinks, others would do well to emulate.

23. I am influenced here by Charles Taylor's concept of a "culture of authenticity." In that culture, persons do not confuse authenticity with narcissism. Taylor describes an authentic human being as someone who honors a duty to lead a public life as well as a life of self-improvement. In that spirit, the amateur corporate strategists in Strategy Through Convention begin to lead a public life by assuming that other corporate strategists are also amateurs. See Taylor, *Ethics of Authenticity*.

24. The condition that strategic alternatives must be mutually exclusive comes straight from conventional game theory.

25. It can be so easy and so self-congratulating simply to assume that others are less complicated and sophisticated than we are. A case in point was published on the front page of the *New York Times* in the aftermath of a round of U.S.—Japan trade negotiations. In a table summarizing the trade argeement, four goals are attributed to the American position. Only one goal is attributed to the Japanese. See D. Sanger, "U.S. Settles Trade Dispute, Averting Billions in Tariffs on Japanese Luxury Autos," *New York Times,* 29 June 1995:A1. That kind of narcissism is a hallmark of the Story of Business Administration. For a critique of one version of such narcissism that I call Strategy Through Process, see Gilbert, *Twilight of Corporate Strategy.* Thus, as both a reminder about this comfortable way of thinking and as a prod to take another person's life very seriously, I include what looks like an exaggerated range of actions available to another person.

26. The pragmatist reads a text with a curiosity about just how far and wide a particular intellectual framework can be useful as a way of talking. That is a logic of replication of the framework. See note 1.

27. See J. Smiley, *A Thousand Acres* (New York: Alfred A. Knopf, 1992).

28. This means that a person is not a neighbor simply because he or she lives on the same block, literally and figuratively. On this view, a person must earn recognition as a neighbor. A person earns that by honoring a duty, day in and day out, to take seriously common grounds and contingent memberships. The corporate strategists in Strategy Through Convention are not interested in posturing, either their own or by others.

29. With my concepts of question of interdependence and "we game," I distance myself from game theorists, even as I begin to retrieve game as a metaphor for human relationships. Game theorists are not interested, however, in memberships on those common grounds. Game theorists see no need for the interpretation of a question such as the one that I attribute here to pairs of investment bankers.

To the game theorist, games are situations that we will inevitably pass through throughout our adult lives. Hence, the reasoning goes, we should be prepared to use our involvement in games to our advantages. Thus, game players must think as pure egoists who reason with a logic that David Gauthier calls straightforward maximization. See D. Gauthier, *Morals by Agreement* (Oxford: Clarendon Press, 1986), 165–170.

The Prisoner's Dilemma game is a prime example of the game theorist's disinterest in something as potentially lasting as memberships on common grounds. The prisoners in the Prisoner's Dilemma are given options for how they can "save their own necks." They must worry about what each other might do. However, their skill at reading signals is a far cry from a concern with a sense of "we," or "us," on their common ground. For a further analysis of this and other aspects of the Prisoner's Dilemma that make it a relatively useless analytical device, see D. Gilbert, Jr., "The Prisoner's Dilemma and the Prisoners of the Prisoners Dilemma," *Business Ethics Quarterly* (1996), in press.

The Battle of the Sexes game, a favorite of game theorists, is also not about memberships on common grounds. It is instead a story about two persons who work through their own preference orderings. Look at the strategies specified for each player in J. K. Murnighan, *The Dynamics of Bargaining Games* (Englewood Cliffs, NJ: Prentice Hall, 1991), 44–61. Murnighan does not list a set of strategic actions that each player could take. Rather, he lists a set of preferred outcomes to the supposed "battle." All the Battle of Sexes involves is two persons reasoning in parallel on a plot of common ground. That has nothing to do with memberships.

Game theorists betray their disinterest in memberships when they refer to collective outcomes in a game. "Collective outcome" is a concept that game theorists like to invoke in their discussions of the Prisoner's Dilemma. Supposedly, the prisoners would do better collectively if they both kept quiet in the face of the district attorney's questioning. But, "collective" only refers to the payoff that one prisoner receives and the payoff that the other prisoner receives. There is nothing about a "we" in the concept of collective game outcome. For a general discussion about collective actions in game theory, see K. Weigelt, C. Camerer, and M. Hanna, "The Use of Experimental Economics in Strategy Research," in P. Shrivastava, A. Huff, and J. Dutton, eds., *Advances in Strategic Management*, Volume 8 (Greenwich, CT: JAI Press, 1992), 185.

30. All questions of interdependence are "How do we get along?" questions. In that genre, some questions of interdependence address the terms by which the parties play their "we game." This question about the public uproar is a case in point.

31. Some questions of interdependence address the consequences of a "we game." This question about the future of junk bonds is a case in point.

32. This statement is an indication that I am working to retrieve the concept of convention, as I work to retrieve the concept of corporate strategy, from a commonplace meaning whereby conventions are foreboding, mystical forces in people's lives. What I do is relocate convention to the daily experiences of "everyday" human beings. Conventions are ideas that we can "touch." Indeed, I argue that conventions are ideas that we must have a hand in shaping, as tied as we are to each other in this world. I am grateful to Doug Sturm for sharing his wisdom on this subject.

33. M. Beschloss and S. Talbott, *At the Highest Levels: The Inside Story of the End of the Cold War* (Boston: Little, Brown, 1993).

34. The interpretation is mine, drawing on the considerable attention that Beschloss and Talbott give to *perestroika*.

35. I draw inspiration here from the practice of constrained maximization that David Gauthier develops. See Gauthier *Morals by Agreement*, 165–184. My proposition is that no corporate strategist is ever "outside" some convention. As a consequence, a logic of "ethics from the outside" is that much more optional. See Chapter 1.

I propose here that a person is not a member simply because her name appears on an organization mailing list, literally and figuratively. On this view, one must earn a place as a member. She can do this by honoring a duty to restrain her behavior in such a way that she accomplishes something at the same time that she contributes to a convention through which she is able to accomplish something important to her.

36. The idea is that conventions can be "life-giving" ideas, tailored to specific circumstances, insofar as an amateur's pursuits are concerned. Here is where the concept of trust can enter Strategy Through Convention. Many students of management want to make trust an important ingredient in their stories about life at organizations, but they can only do so at some vague, transcendent level of discussion. After all, their stories are about organizations. Here in Strategy Through Convention, we can see two distinctive human beings living through a specific vehicle by which they can come to trust each other, or not. That is, Strategy Through Convention is a way to *see* the possibility of trust in each strategist's life. In short, a convention is a manifestation of trust between two human beings. In this regard, I write under the influence of Richard Rorty's proposition that the self can be a "nexus of relations rather than a substance." See R. Rorty, "Two Cheers for the Cultural Left," in Gless and Smith, eds., *Politics of Liberal Education*, 238.

37. On this view, a convention is a joint effort between two distinct persons. That is different from a collective effort and a collective entity. There is no place for "collective" in my vocabulary of Strategy Through Convention. My principal influence here is D. Lewis, *Convention: A Philosophical Study* (Cambridge, MA: Harvard University Press, 1969). Jill Graham and Dennis Organ propose a so-called covenantal organization as one of "three prototypical forms of agreement linking individual participants and their organizations." J. Graham and D. Organ, "Commitment and the Covenantal Organization," *Journal of Managerial Issues* 5, no. 4 (1993):497. Although covenant and convention are ideas that can serve a similar purpose, I assume that a member corporate strategist is *always* in at least one convention. There is no corporate strategy outside conventions, that is, by Strategy Through Convention.

38. Here is an example of a local convention in a context that many call "within an organization." Note that the organization per se is irrelevant in the concept of local convention. A local convention in Strategy Through Convention is what two human beings shape on their common ground. Period. Thus, there is no place in the vocabulary of Strategy Through Convention for "organization" and "within an organization."

39. This means that no matter how hard one tries, he cannot unilaterally create a convention. Colonial governors fool themselves into believing that they can. See Chapter 3 about the colonialism that I attribute to the idea of corporate strategy.

40. S. Tepper, *The Gate to Women's Country* (New York: Bantam, 1989), 40.

41. The women in Women's Country reaffirm their membership by commit-
ting themselves to study a science and a craft throughout their lives. In this way,
they maintain a heightened level of intellectual awareness that I take as a model
for student corporate strategists.

42. Robert Axelrod uses the idea of "shadow of the future." R. Axelrod, *The
Evolution of Cooperation* (New York: Basic Books, 1984), 126–132. A shadow
game is a "we game" that, in a particular historical time period and place, bears
some influence on at least one other we game in that same time and place.
Because members of a we game belong to a question of interdepencence of open-
ended duration, a concern for a future together is already built into a shadow
game.

43. A number of writers have found it useful to employ the web metaphor
when talking about management. These include T. Peters, *Liberation Management: Necessary Disorganization for the Nanosecond Nineties* (New York: Alfred A.
Knopf, 1992), 15; J. B. Quinn, *Intelligent Enterprise: A Knowledge and Service-
Based Paradigm for Industry* (New York: Free Press, 1992), 120–129; R. Mason
and I. Mitroff, "A Teleological Power-Oriented Theory of Strategy," in R. Lamb,
ed., *Advances in Strategic Management,* Volume 2 (Greenwich, CT: JAI Press,
1983), 37.

44. This means that a person is not a student merely because he attends school
and shows up for class session every time, literally and figuratively. On this view,
one must earn a place as a student. A student volunteers to take a complicated
view of the world. Not everyone who sits in class does that.

45. In standard game theory analyses, everything meaningful for two strategists presumably happens inside one game. That game, further, is always presented by the game theorist as an isolated episode. Against that rhetorical backdrop, I offer the idea of shadow game, and the associated concept of student
corporate strategist, as a new way to think and to act.

46. See J. B. Miller, *Toward a New Psychology of Women,* 2nd ed. (Boston:
Beacon Press, 1986), 3–12, regarding the difference between what she calls tem-
porary inequality and permanent inequality. A teacher knows the difference
between the two ideas. When someone who has earned a membership place is left
out of connections that could be conducive, the specter of permanent inequality
looms. A member under a stakes threshold faces a period of time on the short
end of permanent inequality. These are the kinds of challenges that a teacher
voluntarily undertakes, as an intellectual, as Henry Giroux proposes we think of
teachers. Giroux, "Liberal Arts Education and the Struggle for Public Life," in
Gless and Smith, *Politics of Liberal Education,* 139.

47. Hassler, *North of Hope.* I draw inspiration for the idea of convention of
local conventions from what Charles Taylor writes about multiculturalism:

> For real judgments of worth suppose a horizon of standards. . . . They suppose that
> we have been transformed by the study of the other, so that we are not simply judging by
> our original familiar standards.

C. Taylor, *Multiculturalism and The Politics of Recognition* (Princeton, NJ: Princeton University Press, 1992), 70. A convention of local conventions is one such
transformed judgment. It is a standard that corporate strategists can apply in
addition to their own stakes of distinction and stakes threshold. Without such a

convention of local conventions, there is nothing to prevent the members of common grounds to forget about one member under a stakes threshold, or several persons in such predicaments.

This interpretation of teacher is lost on those state legislators who want to mandate the number of hours that college professors spend in the classroom. These legislators are apparently stuck on the idea that teaching is nothing more than the transmission of settled facts about the world. However, we do not need common grounds to transmit facts. We can do that in isolation by turning on our computers and dialing into on-line databases. Teachers are persons who worry about the human neighborhoods in which learning could be accomplished, because they know from experience that learning is a contingent matter in each and every case. On this view, teaching is an accomplishment that can occupy a teacher around the clock, throughout the week, month by month, and year by year.

48. Father Healy is not necessarily the only teacher corporate strategist in the story. I discuss his pursuits solely for the purpose of explaining what I mean by teacher corporate strategist. One could make a strong case that Libby Pearsall, Father Healy's friend, also lives as a teacher corporate strategist.

49. This is my interpretation of what Burrough and Helyar tell us about the RJR Nabisco buy-out. There is no reason why someone could not have written a story about these events from the perspective of federal government officials watching the bidding process. If that story were told, this particular convention of local conventions would probably not apply.

50. Game theorists might recognize traces of the concept of Nash equilibrium in this discussion. My point is that *Barbarians at the Gate* lacks the evidence with which we could say very much about those Nash equilibria that some game players find unsatisfactory.

51. A critical reader might be moved to ask me, "Are not there certain persons, such as convicted criminals, for whom a convention of local conventions should not be a conducive connection?" I have this question in mind. Note that I refer to a member under stakes threshold, not an amateur under a stakes threshold. A member is already a contributor to a convention and hence to an instance of conducive connection between two human beings. That is necessarily the case with an amateur. A bully could be an amateur corporate strategist. That is why I create five new metaphors here, instead of being satisfied with amateur corporate strategist alone.

52. This means that a person is not a teacher simply because her name shows up on the roster of the instructional staff at an educational institution. On this view, a teacher earns her place. She does this by honoring a duty to accomplish what is important in ways that contribute to each convention to which she belongs with a student *and* to a convention of those local conventions. This does not mean that a teacher is necessarily a candidate for sainthood, at the top of a five-rung ladder of metaphors for corporate strategist. What it does mean is that teachers understand, among other things, what Giroux calls "the lived reality of difference." See Giroux, "Liberal Arts Education and the Struggle for Public Life," in Gless and Smith, eds., *Politics of Liberal Education*, 134. Teachers are human beings who choose to lead, and succeed at leading, complicated lives of self-restrained accomplishments. That is all. Still, that is saying a great deal about what a human being can accomplish in this world. See also R. Coles, *The Call of Stories: Teaching and the Moral Imagination* (Boston: Houghton Mifflin, 1989).

53. For an expression of this dogma, see K. Wing, "Two Cheers for the Academy," *Academy of Management Review* 19, no. 3 (1994):388–389. Business journalists can also adopt this imperative. A case in point is G. Belis, "Beware the Touchy-Feely Business Book," *Fortune*, 28 June 1993, 147–148. Belis concludes that the works of several authors are unpersuasive because those writers' ideas have not been incorporated into widespread use in large organizations. Apparently these authors take the dangerous step—about which we must "beware"—of proposing new ways to think about business. Thus, Bilis appears to apply a version of "Be practical; reduce uncertainty for business people" by which new vocabularies about business are sources of increased uncertainty. "Reduce uncertainty" apparently means that writers should tell business people what other business people have already done. Used in this way, "Be practical; reduce uncertainty for business people" probably makes perfect sense to Belis and his editors. On the other hand, if business people want to experience the uncertainty that goes with a distinctive approach to business, then the imperative that Belis appears to honor reads like a non sequitur.

54. For examples of this, see any paper that is written to perpetuate the resource-based view of the firm and the population ecology view. One of my nominees for a hall of fame in this regard is D. Datta, J. Grant, and N. Rajagopolan, "Management Incompatibility and Postacquisition Autonomy: Effects on Acquistion and Performance," in Shrivastava, Huff, and Dutton, eds., *Advances in Strategic Management*, Volume 7, 157–182.

55. For one expression of this position, see D. Schendel, "Notes from the Editor-in-Chief," *Strategic Management Journal* 16, no. 1 (1995):1–2.

56. Uncertainty is such a bane, in large part, because this dogma has no room for skepticism about the concept of bounded rationality. As long as bounded rationality is a condition used against the business person in management research, uncertainty and the reduction of uncertainty will be banes. For a discussion about Business Policy and uncertainty, see J. -C. Spender, "The Business Policy Problem and Industry Recipes," in Lamb, ed., *Advances in Strategic Management*, Volume 2, 211–229.

57. I take the phrase from Rorty, *Contingency, Irony, and Solidarity*, 9. Thus, I am giving the "Be practical; reduce uncertainty for business people" crowd a taste of their own medicine here. The astute reader will quickly realize that I am reducing one kind of uncertainty in each of these four instances and thereby adding the kind of greater uncertainty that pragmatists relish.

58. Ed Freeman will appreciate the irony here. He deserves the compliment.

59. See, for instance, P. Oresick and N. Coles, eds., *Working Classics: Poems on Industrial Life* (Urbana: University of Illinois Press, 1990).

60. A next destination along the road leading from this practical accomplishment is to critique the entire institution known as the undergraduate business curriculum.

61. I am influenced here by Charles Taylor's historical critique of the distinction between honor and dignity. See Taylor, *Multiculturalism and The Politics of Recognition*, 25–51.

62. By contrast, La Rue Hosmer appears to argue that a corporate strategy should be a business principle that is modified by certain ethical truths. See L. Hosmer, "Strategic Planning as if Ethics Mattered," *Strategic Management Journal* 15, Special Issue (1994):17–34.

63. Business school professors have debated for years whether ethics should be covered in a separate course or covered somewhere in each functional course. For one analysis, see J. Shea, "What's Good for Business," *The Pennsylvania Gazette,* November 1987, 17–23. It can follow from my practical accomplishment here that this debate can end.

64. See, for example, A. Wicks, D. Gilbert, Jr., and R. E. Freeman, "A Feminist Reinterpretation of the Stakeholder Concept," *Business Ethics Quarterly* 4, no. 4 (1994):475–497. Yes, I "force" solidarity into Strategy Through Convention just as, for instance, economists "force" equilibria and markets into their stories. On the latter point, see and enjoy D. McCloskey, *The Rhetoric of Economics* (Madison: University of Wisconsin Press, 1985).

65. See the argument in Rorty, *Contingency, Irony, and Solidarity,* 189–198.

66. Look at the verbs here. Every one of them is taken straight from the Story of Business Administration. I am grateful to Ed Freeman and Bill Evan for their curiosity and encouragement over the years that I have working out ideas about a grammar of business and ethics.

67. The challenge facing the corporate strategists in Strategy Through Convention is to contribute, common ground by common ground, to an "us." Situations of "us versus them" do not go away in Strategy Through Convention. These situations are part of the world in which corporate strategists live.

68. A business school is a human community in which the Story of Business Administration is the canon, scripture, and flag, all rolled into one. If the Story of Business Administration is ethically suspect, perhaps it is time to consider a retrieval of the idea of the business school.

69. The verb here is "argue." Argument is conversation. You might be tempted to take the arguments that I have made in this book as cues to carp, whine, complain, bluster, posture, wave the flag, and otherwise express exasperation about what I have said. However, those are actions that add nothing to conversation, because exasperation is a cover for having nothing to say. I believe that I have given readers cues to find something to say in response, if they choose.

In closing, I leave you, the reader, with this thought. It probably took you some time to read these five chapters. I hope so. I deliberately put together a complicated argument, because business as a way of talking about the world should be a complicated subject. Perhaps you are ready for a second reading. Perhaps you would make the argument differently. I encourage you, in either case. Either step brings us closer to some conversations about business and our humanity. Thank you for arriving at the brink of those conversations.

INDEX

1843